Bank Governance Structures and Risk Taking

AF841030

Corporate Finance and Governance

Edited by Dirk Schiereck

Volume 18

Zur Qualitätssicherung und Peer Review der vorliegenden Publikation

Die Qualität der in dieser Reihe erscheinenden Arbeiten wird vor der Publikation durch den Herausgeber der Reihe geprüft.

Notes on the quality assurance and peer review of this publication

Prior to publication, the quality of the work published in this series is reviewed by the editor of the series.

Dennis Froneberg

Bank Governance Structures and Risk Taking

PL ACADEMIC RESEARCH

Bibliographic Information published by the Deutsche Nationalbibliothek
The Deutsche Nationalbibliothek lists this publication in the Deutsche Nationalbibliografie; detailed bibliographic data is available in the internet at http://dnb.d-nb.de.

Zugl.: Darmstadt, Techn. Univ., Diss., 2015

Library of Congress Cataloging-in-Publication Data
Names: Froneberg, Dennis, 1981-
Title: Bank governance structures and risk taking / Dennis Froneberg.
Description: 1 Edition. | Frankfurt (Main) : Peter Lang, 2015. | Series: Corporate Finance and Governance ; Volume 18 | Includes bibliographical references.
Identifiers: LCCN 2015035555 | ISBN 9783631667132
Subjects: LCSH: Corporate governance. | Banks and banking. | Financial institutions—Law and legislation.
Classification: LCC HD2741 .F81476 2015 | DDC 332.1068/1—dc23 LC record available at http://lccn.loc.gov/2015035555

D 17
ISSN 1869-537X
ISBN 978-3-631-66713-2 (Print)
E-ISBN 978-3-653-06235-9 (E-Book)
DOI 10.3726/978-3-653-06235-9

© Peter Lang GmbH
Internationaler Verlag der Wissenschaften
Frankfurt am Main 2015
All rights reserved.
PL Academic Research is an Imprint of Peter Lang GmbH.

Peter Lang – Frankfurt am Main · Bern · Bruxelles · New York · Oxford · Warszawa · Wien

All parts of this publication are protected by copyright. Any utilisation outside the strict limits of the copyright law, without the permission of the publisher, is forbidden and liable to prosecution. This applies in particular to reproductions, translations, microfilming, and storage and processing in electronic retrieval systems.

This publication has been peer reviewed.

www.peterlang.com

Table of Contents

List of Tables 9

List of Abbreviations 11

List of Symbols 13

I Introduction 15

II The Manifest Financial Expertise of Supervisory Board Members of German Regional Banks 21

II.1 Introduction 21

II.2 Introduction to German Banking Sector and Legal Backdrop 25

II.3 Research Methodology 28

II.4 Data set 33

II.5 Empirical Analysis 34

II.6 Concluding Remarks 38

II.7 Appendix 41

III Impact of Supervisory Board Members' Professional Background on Regional Banks' Risk-Taking 61

III.1 Introduction 61

III.2 Related Literature 65

III.3 Data and Methodology 68

III.3.1 Sample and Data 68

III.3.2 Hypotheses and Model 69

III.3.3 Financial Expertise 69

III.3.4 Measurement of Performance and Risk 71
III.3.5 Control Variables 71
III.4 Results 72
III.4.1 Summary Statistics 72
III.4.2 Regression Results 77
III.4.3 Robustness Checks 82
III.5 Concluding Remarks 82
III.6 Appendix 84

IV Bank Governance Structures, Financial Expertise of Supervisory Board Members, Overconfidence, and Bank Risk Taking 103
IV.1 Introduction 103
IV.2 Literature Review 106
IV.3 Data set and Methodology 108
IV.3.1 Sample and Data set 108
IV.3.2 Hypotheses and Model 110
IV.3.3 Financial Expertise 111
IV.3.4 Measurement of Risk and Return 112
IV.3.5 Control Variables 112
IV.4 Results 114
IV.4.1 Summary Statistics 114
IV.4.2 Regression Results 121
IV.4.3 Robustness Checks 127
IV.5 Concluding Remarks 128
IV.6 Appendix 130

V CDS and Bank Ownership Structures: Does the Credit Side Show Who Advocates More Risk? 171
V.1 Introduction 171

V.2 Related Literature ... 174

V.3 Data and Methodology ... 176

V.3.1 Sample and Data ... 176

V.3.2 Ownership Concentration ... 177

V.3.3 Measurement of Credit Risk ... 177

V.3.4 Control Variables ... 178

V.3.5 Model ... 179

V.4 Results ... 180

V.4.1 Summary Statistics ... 180

V.4.2 Regression Results ... 187

V.5 Concluding Remarks ... 191

V.6 Appendix ... 192

VI Main Concluding Remarks ... 199

References ... 203

List of Tables

Table I.1: Structure and main focus of study....17
Table II.1: Classification of occupations....29
Table II.2: Assignment of financial expertise....32
Table II.3: Supervisory board composition regional banks (mean values 2004–2009)....34
Table II.4: Financial expertise regional banks (mean values 2004–2009)....36
Table II.5: Comparison of mean values of regional banks (mean values 2004–2009)....37
Table II.6: Financial expertise of regional banks clustered by bank and board size (largest banks in bank and board size in Cluster 1, smallest banks in Cluster 4)....38
Table II.7: Distribution of regional banks across expertise clusters (based on mean values 2004–2009)....38
Table III.1: Professional backgrounds with assumed financial expertise....70
Table III.2: Definition of control variables and sources....72
Table III.3: Supervisory board composition, Top 200 cooperative banks....73
Table III.4: Summary statistics, Top 200 cooperative banks....75
Table III.5: Bank level variables, clustered by financial expertise, Top 200 cooperative banks....76
Table III.6: Pairwise test of the significance between expertise clusters, Top 200 cooperative banks....77
Table III.7: Random-effect regressions with dependent variables RORWA and ROE, Top 200 cooperative banks....79
Table III.8: Random-effect regressions with dependent variables z-score and NPL ratio, Top 200 cooperative banks....81
Table IV.1: Professional backgrounds with assumed financial expertise....111
Table IV.2: Definition of control variables and sources....114
Table IV.3: Supervisory board composition, Top 200....115
Table IV.4: Summary statistics, Top 200....117
Table IV.5: Summary statistics, clustered by financial expertise, Top 200....119
Table IV.6: Pairwise test of significance between expertise clusters, Top 200....120

Table IV.7:	Random-effect regressions with dependent variables z-score and NPL ratio, Top 200	123
Table IV.8:	Coefficient comparison, random-effect regressions with dependent variables z-score and NPL ratio, Top 200	124
Table IV.9:	Random-effect regressions with dependent variables RORWA and ROE, Top 200	126
Table IV.10:	Coefficient comparison, random-effect regressions with dependent variables RORWA and ROE, Top 200	127
Table V.1:	Definition sources of control variables	179
Table V.2:	Summary statistics	181
Table V.3:	Development over time from 2005–2008	182
Table V.4:	Bank cluster by size	183
Table V.5:	Pairwise test of significance between clusters by bank size	184
Table V.6:	Banks clustered by regulation	185
Table V.7:	Pairwise test of significance between clusters by level of regulation	186
Table V.8:	Regression results with iTraxx financial spread as dependent variable	188
Table V.9:	Regression results with iTraxx non-financial spread as dependent variable	189
Table V.10:	Regression results with country spread as dependent variable	190

List of Abbreviations

AktG	Aktiengesetz
AO	Abgabenordnung
BaFin	Bundesanstalt für Finanzdienstleistungsaufsicht
Bn	Billion
CAR	Capital Assets Ratio
CEO	Chief Executive Officer
Cf.	Compare
CIR	Cost-Income Ratio
CDS	Credit Default Swap
Coeff.	Coefficient
Df	Degrees of freedom
E.g.	For example (exempli gratia)
EAEG	Einlagensicherungs- und Anlegerentschädigungsgesetz
EUR	Euro
FE	Fixed-Effect Regression
GDP	Gross Domestic Product
GenG	Genossenschaftsgesetz
GwG	Geldwäschegesetz
HASPA	Hamburger Sparkasse
HGB	Handelsgesetzbuch
KWG	Kreditwesengesetz
Ln	Logarithm
Market Cap	Market Capitalization
MFI	Monetary Financial Institution
No	Number
Non-MFI	Non-Monetary Financial Institution
NPL	Non-Performing Loan
Prob.	Probability
RE	Random-Effect Regression
ROA	Return on Assets
ROE	Return on Equity
RORWA	Return on risk-weighted Assets
R-sq	R squared
SOX	Sarbanes-Oxley Act

Std. dev.	Standard deviation
SE	Standard error
SpG	Sparkassengesetz
t	Test statistic
USD	US-Dollar
Vol.	Volume
Vs.	Versus
WpHG	Wertpapierhandelsgesetz

List of Symbols

α	Regression intercept Alpha
β	Regression coefficient Beta
γ	Regression coefficient Gamma
δ	Regression coefficient Delta
ε	Error term of the regression
θ	Regression coefficient Theta
Σ	Sum
σ	Standard deviation
τ	Regression coefficient Tau
§	Paragraph
%	Percent
B	Bank level variables
C	Country level variables
Cov	Covariance
$CR\ 3$	Concentration ratio 3
c	Subscript denoting cooperative banks
DV	Dependent variable
FE	Financial expertise
H_0	Null hypothesis
i	Subscript denoting individual banks
j	Subscript denoting individual shareholders
M	Macroeconomic variables
m	Subscript denoting market portfolio
OC	Ownership concentration
OS	Ownership share
R	Return
S	Sector level variables
s	Subscript denoting savings banks
SD	Savings banks dummy variable
t	Subscript denoting time (year)
v	Subscript denoting variable
z	constant for time fixed effects

I Introduction

The importance of banks for business activity and developing economic activity is thought be central and formed the initiative trigger in the context of financial distress for the provision of various forms of rescue actions during the financial crisis. Notable amount of research has debated the role of corporate governance mechanisms within that framework given corporate governance represents a key element for the understanding of economic stability and growth in general and the role of financial factors in particular. A growing strand of literature discusses which significant impact financial institutions exercise on the economic development (Beck and Levine, 2003; Levine and Zervos, 1998) on the basis of provision of external funding, capital accumulation and productivity improvements. The fact that the level of economic activity as well as development of a certain jurisdiction is closely linked to the performance of the stock market and banking system underlines this relevance (Demirguc-Kunt and Maksimovic, 2000). Simultaneously, there is some meaningful empirical support outlining that the most recent financial crises over the last 20 years have been caused through the globalisation and liberalisation of the financial system (Kose, Prasad, Rogoff, and Wei, 2006). In addition to that, banks are intrinsically weak having a high financial fragility given their lending and deposit activities creating a mismatch of liquidity and fundamental incompatibility between the two activities (Diamond and Rajan, 2001; R. Rajan, 2006). In that regard, complexity and bank size are not the only consideration. Worst economic downturns are almost constantly related to bank panics caused by a large enough number of banks failing at the same time ('too many to fail') and financial crisis triggered by a failing bank which plays an important role in the financial system ('too big to fail') (Mishkin, Stern, and Ron, 2006; Stern and Feldman, 2004).

Further, bank governance has certain unique features compared to other industries. In particular the traditional principal agency theory displaying the manager-owner antagonism with diverging interests of the two parties as the core of the problem and the mere alignment of the owners' and managers' interests, suggested as the traditional solution, is not transferable to the banking sector given the divergent interest of the risk takers and required government interventions in order to stabilise the financial system (Jensen and Meckling, 1976; Mullineux, 2006, 2013). Furthermore, the goals of the bank's stakeholders are quite conflicting and even mutually exclusive. Issues arise mainly by the mismatch of interests between shareholders and bank's depositors – also considered as the non-mutually owners – since shareholder maximisation has to be paid at the expesene of depositors's safety (Myers and Majluf, 1984). This will be further reinfornced in the case when banks are facing bankrupcty since other stakeholders such as regulatory bodies, deposit insurance agencies, and taxpayers are also affected.

One of the central open points is reviewing the theme: "What did cause the financial crisis and why did banks fail?" This question has been addressed after every crisis by a diverse set of groups such as regulators, politicians, bank managers, customers, investors, and academics, with the desire to investigate the root of the problem in order to improve the stability of the financial system and/or prevent future crises. One of the key identified elements are failures in effective corporate governance mechanisms which are promoting risk-taking and instabilities in financial institutions (Ard and Berg, 2010; Choundhry, 2011; International Monetary Fund, 2010; Kirkpatrick, 2009). Consequently, new regulations have been released and institutions have been created to improve bank monitoring and foster governance structures (Moshirian, 2011). Despite of having implemented new regulations and fostering governance structures there is still the demand for more expertise in internal bank governance (Ard and Berg, 2010; Walker, 2009).

Given the complexity of the business model and the continuous regulatory changes bank supervision has become more complex calling for superior expertise (Mehran, Morrison, and Shapiro, 2011a). This leads to the key governance issue and question whether a board of a bank have been composited in such a manner that it has adequate expertise assessing management's efforts in measuring and managing risks. It is difficult to conclude and rather complex to analyse whether a firm takes the right risks. Coherently it remains open who or what drives risk-taking of a bank. This leads to the dilemma that bank shareholders have an interest in high returns on the one side but at the same time are also very keen on stability as well as on safeguarding the successful development and persistence of the institution. The theoretical literature has not finally concluded whether large shareholders advocate more risk or whether they exert a risk-decreasing effect since they can influence bank's business operations and decisions (e.g., Berle and Means, 1933; Galai and Masulis, 1976). In line with diverging theoretical evidence, empirical studies are not clear as well (e.g., Aebi, Sabato, and Schmid, 2012; Brandao-Marques, Correa, and Sapriza, 2013; Laeven and Levine, 2009; Magalhaes, Gutiérrez, and Tribó, 2008; Shehzad, de Haan, and Scholtens, 2010). Although the existing strand of literature has clearly shown a connection between governance and bank risk taking behaviour they have still left room for further research in three specific areas: the risk adjustment of banks' performance based on its risk profile, the role of debtholders as stakeholder group and its impact on risk, and the analysis over time.

Table I.1: Structure and main focus of study

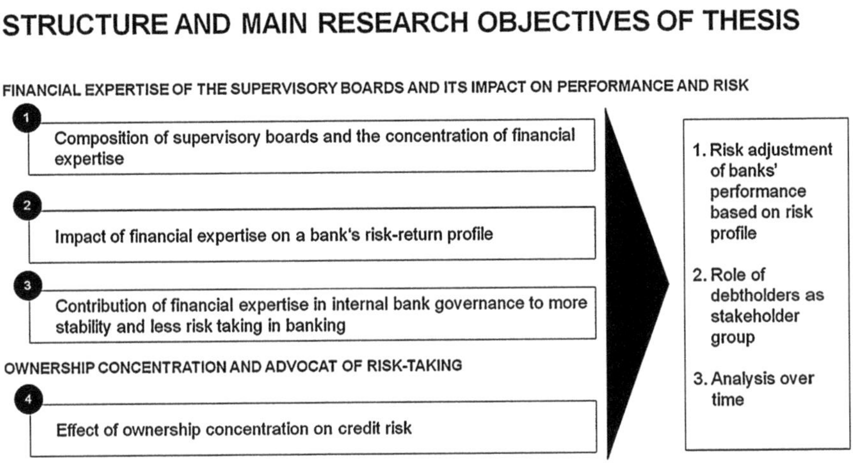

The first three studies of this thesis focus on financial expertise of the supervisory boards and its impact on performance and risk. In this context three specific objectives are central for the analysis: first, how the supervisory boards are composed and how much financial expertise their members have; second, impact of financial expertise on a banks' risk-return profiles; third, does financial expertise in internal bank governance contribute to more stability and less risk taking in banking.

The German banking system with its three pillars and its magnitude of banks provides an ideal field for research as displayed by the literature. Out of the three pillars the regional banking sector, consisting of cooperative and savings banks, allows for comparative analyses given a similar business model and focus as well as organizational structures despite of having different legal characteristics and ownership types. The first three analyses in this thesis are based on the data of supervisory board members of 257 cooperative and 209 savings banks with 39,365 data points at the individual level. The underlying analysis follows recent developments of German bank regulators who asked for more expertise in the context of the issue of adequate qualification of board members and released in this context new legal requirements concerning the financial competence of bank supervisory board members (BaFin and Deutsche Bundesbank, 2010).

The governance structure at regional banks have a peculiarity since both subgroups (cooperative and savings banks) within this sector are not attached to capital markets for equity funding and therefore do not have the same "market for corporate control" as exchange-listed banks do (Manne, 1965). This leads to the consequence that supervisory boards take over a significant and decision-making role in the governance system of regional banks given the lack of equity investors who are controlling exchange-listed commercial banks with a limited investment horizon. This element provides additional support and relevance for our analysis.

The results of the main questions of these analyses are of high importance for various groups. First, the answers are of significant relevance to regulatory bodies of financial institutions. The analyses display evidence on the impact of some regulatory measures and are able to extract the fact that some regulations miss their target. The findings deliver facts in respect to the composition of banks' supervisory boards and provide transparency how members' assumed expertise is associated with risk and return. In that regard, the results shed light on the research question whether the demand for more competence in internal bank governance is legitimated. Second, the through the underlying analysis gained knowledge delivers useful facts as well as ideas for public discussions. The recent banking crisis from 2007–2010 has shown that the banking system is to some extent fragile. It demonstrates that many aspects have not been identified and not analysed in the broad universe of variables which could help improving the robustness of the financial system. In particular, there is only scarce empirical evidence in relation to the influence of governance mechanisms. Therefore, the underlying analyses are valuable input for the development of further public and political discussions. In addition to that, the findings deliver evidence for the assessment of the regulatory framework and potential improvements. Lastly, the two principal stakeholders, management and owners, shall also have a genuine interest in that context. Notably, it is of high relevance to them how the expertise of supervisory board members' is related to performance, bank stability, and risk.

In that context the analyses have been performed as follows: The first study focuses on the evaluation of the board composition. The classification of the supervisory board members leads to three main categories: self-employed, employed, and retired. Following that, within each category, individuals are subdivided according to their explicit profession. Lastly, individuals are assigned financial expertise based on their profession.

Based on that examination of the supervisory board composition, the second study evaluates further the impact of financial expertise on risk and performance of regional banks, being the 200 largest German cooperative banks. The key element of this analysis is the impact of the financial expertise of the total supervisory board and of board outsiders – people who are not employed at the respective regional banks – on the bank's risk-return profile.

The research strand is completed by the third study which investigates to which extent financial expertise contributes to bank stability. In order to address this question the underlying dataset has been expanded into the complete regional banking sector, e.g. cooperative and savings banks, comprising in total 400 banks. Given their similar characteristics, savings banks are an ideal addition to the cooperative bank data points and can serve as control group confirming the robustness of the results. Regional banks have similar business models, comparable regional reach, strategies, and organizational structures by concentrating on the typical lending and deposit taking activities. The client base is primarily composed of small and midsized companies as well as private households (Hakenes, Hasan, Molyneux, and Xie, 2014).

Results show that, on average, the supervisory board members of both regional bank subgroups have a similar level of financial expertise, being 65% for German savings banks' and 48% for German cooperative banks'. This finding is in line with a sample of the largest 100 banks which have been analysed by Johansen, Laser, Neuberger and Andreani (2013). However, they show that bank managers comprise the largest group since their share has even been increased over time. This development reflects the share blocks held by banks, the same applies to the other board members which are closely linked to the shareholder structure. Further investigations provide evidence that financial expertise of the supervisory board members exercises impact on the risk-return profile of German regional banks. It is evident that financial expertise influences the risk-return profile, but does not suspend the trade-off. In the case of cooperative banks the findings induce concerns that mandating financial expertise on boards is not beneficial for the risk-return profile. This is based on the fact that the data indicate that with more financial expertise bank performance declines and risk goes up. However, on a total basis they seem to benefit from financial expertise and the positive influence on performance emerges to be dominant. The trade-off displays that superior returns are associated with higher risk. The pattern of higher risk and less stability is consistent across the regional banking sector. Consequently the third study delivers no support to the hypothesis that financial expertise in supervisory boards increases the stability of the banking system.

Beside from the research questions how the risk-return profile of banks can be better supervised and managed, the focus is also on the open point which party advocates risk in banks. In that respect another strand of investigation can be provided by the banks' ownership structure. The fourth study examines the effects of ownership concentration on credit risk for the years from 2005 to 2008.

The findings of this evaluation are of significant relevance for the respective national regulative environment as well as for the respective financial institutions themselves.

Regulatory bodies have to be aware of whether certain ownership compositions lead to a significant risk factor and which risk indicators exhibit the risk more precisely and in timely fashion. Further, it remains open whether regulatory instruments accomplish their targets within the framework of different ownership compositions and deliver beneficial results. For the financial institutions themselves, it is of high relevance acquainting knowledge in relation to the question how their own credit risk profile is impacted by different ownership compositions. The question is addressed in detail how more powerful owners of a bank in the context of a concentrated ownership are impacting the credit risk profile.

Based on 86 international banks, the results show that ownership concentration tends to be correlated with higher credit risk. Furthermore, the analysis demonstrates that the regulative environment has a negative impact on bank's credit risk. Banks in heavily regulated countries display higher CDS spreads. The question on whether regulation achieves its goals is unresolved, at least from a credit risk perspective. Lastly, the analysis confirms that larger banks tend to take greater risk compared to smaller institutions

The evaluation of the research questions within this thesis has been structured as follows: The main chapters are II to IV and are accompanied by the main introduction at the very beginning and the main conclusion at the end which summarizes the key findings. All four chapters show the interrelation and relevance of the central theme bank governance.

II The Manifest Financial Expertise of Supervisory Board Members of German Regional Banks[1]

Abstract New requirements on the expertise of the supervisory board members of German Banks were released in 2009. Following the existing requirement of the Stock Corporation Act (AktG), prospective members have to prove relevant expertise. This leads to a har-monization of requirements independent of the legal status of the bank. Regional banks in the form of cooperative banks and savings banks play a significant role in the three-sector structure of the German banking system, in particular for the local and regional small- and medium-sized companies as well as for private households. However, due to their legal status, specific ownership structure, and business models, well-known control mechanisms such as the capital markets or control by family owners do not have an effect. Accordingly, the supervisory boards of both banking groups take on much of the responsibility of controlling, in particular with respect to management monitoring. The present analysis - examining supervisory board members' assumed financial expertise of regional banks - shows that savings banks have, on average, a significantly higher share of financial expertise than do cooperative banks. Bank size has only a positive impact on the financial expertise of cooperative banks; board size does not materially influence the financial expertise of either group.

II.1 Introduction

In September 2010, the German finance newspaper "Financial Times Deutschland" published headlines that the German Federal Financial Supervisory Authority (BaFin) had demonstrated its authority by rejecting supervisory board members of German banks (Luttmer, 2010). The article outlined the first analysis and review by BaFin of the supervisory boards of German banks in regard to expertise and competence. The review is based on recent legislations which have been implemented in order to strengthen financial and insurance supervision. They came into force on July 29, 2009, and were codified in the Banking Act (KWG). The new amendment prescribes the demonstration of financial expertise of the members of the supervisory boards of German banks, which is considered indispensable for exercising bank management supervision as well as for assessing and monitoring bank operations. BaFin's first review resulted in ten complaints with three different backgrounds: in one case about the lack of competence, in six cases about dubious

1 This chapter is based on a joint paper (Böhm, Froneberg, and Schiereck, 2012b).

reliability, and in three cases about too many supervisory board mandates being held by individuals (Luttmer, 2010).

Issues of banking supervision, control, and governance came to the fore with the 2008 banking crisis since established supervisory mechanisms were not able to limit the magnitude of the financial crisis. The issues of understanding bank risks, management monitoring, and implementation of risk-minimizing compensation structures were frequently discussed (Ard and Berg, 2010; Erkens, Hung, and Matos, 2009; Kirkpatrick, 2009). Management monitoring and control is of particular importance for German banks due to the prevailing two-tier system which separates management and supervision (Köhler, 2010). This system is unique and completely different from the Anglo-Saxon one-tier board system. The management of banks is overseen by the Board of Directors whereas the supervisory board is responsible for management supervision. The success of this structure requires the staffing of governing in such a manner that their assigned tasks and duties are sufficiently met.

The German banking industry is divided into three sectors, private banks, public banks (which include savings banks), and cooperative banks. The latter two sectors are also commonly called regional banks. The legal characteristics and the internal structure of the associations in each sector differentiates the sectors (Köhler, 2010). Public-law savings banks are owned by the public authorities, mostly the municipality or the county in which the bank operates and is located. Further, there are some savings banks which are owned by an association of local authorities and/or counties. In addition to public-sector savings banks, there are so-called free savings banks, which usually operate as legal entities under private law, foundations, or associations (Büschgen, 1998). Savings banks in public-law sponsorship are characterized by public mandate, common public interest, regional principle, and a high degree of affiliation (Börner and Büschgen, 2003; Brämer, Gischer, Pfingsten, and Richter, 2010). The business policies of savings banks are specifically derived from the public mandate. The achievement of tasks such as ensuring regionwide access to banking services, in opposition to strict profit maximization, prevails the business strategy (Geiger, 1992)., Through the guarantee system of public guarantee obligation and maintenance obligation, these targets were easily achievable up to 2005. Savings banks were able to operate without creditors fearing default of obligations (guarantee obligation) or the risk of filing for insolvency as a final consequence (maintenance obligation) (Engerer and Schrooten, 2004). The business area is geographically defined by the area of the owning municipality and/or counties. Accordingly, there is a horizontal division of work between savings banks, at the customer level, in the savings banks sector (Geiger, 1992). Affiliation is reflected in the vertical division of work between the hierarchy levels. In addition to locally operating primary savings banks, there are the Landesbanken at the federal state level and savings banks associations (Breuer and Mark, 2005).

The other group of regional banks, the cooperative banks, is owned by their members and operates as registered cooperatives (Becker and Peppmeier, 2006). These banks are characterized by the mandate to support their clients and the principles of self-aid, self-government, and affiliation (Hackethal, 2004). Cooperative banks perform their financial services activities in order to promote regional and local enterprises as well as to support their members' social or cultural needs. Cooperative banks are obligated to offer the service to their members that would be priced higher at other, strictly profit-oriented banks (Kammlott and Schiereck, 2000). Similar to savings banks, in most cases, they limit their business activities to particular regions. This regional orientation is derived from its corporate purpose of member support, which is codified in § 1 of the Cooperative Act (GenG). Since this is not statutory, there are also cooperative institutions with nationwide operations, such as the Deutsche Apotheker- und Ärztebank eG. Similar to savings banks, there is a horizontal distribution of work in the cooperative banking sector at the primary level, resulting in limited competition between cooperative banks.

Beyond business focus and corporate strategy, the different ownership structures result in peculiarities with respect to the control mechanisms (corporate governance) at regional banks. Savings banks cannot be acquired by other banks or companies outside the savings bank sector, as they are owned by the respective local or regional public authority. However, the ownership of a savings bank is not a fungible asset like tradable shares (Pfingsten, 2010). Mergers within the savings bank sector are possible only through explicit approval from the owning municipality or county. Consequently, a partial sale of shares similar to a joint-stock corporation is not possible. Hence, although savings banks are either merged or are incorporated by another savings bank, political aspects play a dominant role in the decision-making process (Drees, Keisers, and Schiereck, 2006). Public ownership leads to another special feature: savings banks are publicly owned and are consequently not directly owned by individuals or enterprises, but only indirectly by citizens. However, these citizens do not enjoy any control rights (Böhm-Dries, Eggers, and Hortmann, 2010).

The shareholder structure of cooperative banks – characterized by its members – leads to a widely dispersed ownership. There is no option to acquire all the shares of the institution. Company shares generally cannot be acquired by a third party (D. Schiereck and Timmreck, 2001). Additionally, the value of the company shares is not based on the current value of the company, so these company shares cannot be compared to the shares of listed companies (Theurl, 2002). Therefore, the consolidation process takes place only within the sector, similar to savings banks. Each member has one vote that is independent of factual ownership (one member, one vote). In terms of the supervision of business activities, this leads to critical issues. The ultimate owners have the opportunity to exercise control via their vote at the general annual assembly. However, the increasing size and complexity of business activities, on the one hand, and the free-rider problem arising from the "one member, one vote" principle, on the other hand, can impact corporate control negatively (Kammlott and Schiereck, 2000).

Given the ownership structures of regional banks, based on the underlying legal characteristics, there is no corporate control via the capital markets. However, capital markets are effective control instruments that immediately indicate shortcomings in profitability and efficiency (Manne, 1965). Consequently, there is no so-called "market for corporate control" in this way. Additionally, the governance structures of regional banks are not driven towards value maximization to solve the problem between management and owners in terms of value maximization (Jensen and Ruback, 1983). Family-owned companies solve the agency problem through the identities of owner and manager. This second option is not applicable to regional banks, too. As a result, the supervisory boards of regional banks play an important role in the supervision of management. Additionally, the new requirements on expertise shed light on the question of manifest and assumable financial expertise and the qualifications of supervisory board members. This raises the question of whether the supervisory boards of German regional banks are staffed such that there is manifest financial expertise on the supervisory board.

Despite the importance of supervisory board members in German regional banks, no detailed examination has yet been performed, although research has alluded to such analysis in specific corporate governance papers (Cihák and Hesse, 2007). This study targets systematically analyzing the manifest financial expertise of supervisory board members who exercise management supervision in German regional banks for the first time. This study is based on more than 400 institutions for the period from 2004 to 2009.

The analysis shows that there are some differences within the regional banks. Savings banks have a higher share of supervisory board members with assumable financial expertise than do cooperative banks. This is partially driven by the savings banks laws, which ensure employee representation of one-third on the supervisory board in nearly all federal states.[2] Both banking groups have a relatively

2 Notice has been taken of potential conflicts of interests arising from working and exercising supervisory mandates at the same bank. This applies to executive employees in particular. However, this is not further discussed and analyzed in the present study.

high proportion of supervisory board members whose bank-related economic expertise is not immediately obvious. Regarding outsiders – supervisory board members who are not employed at the respective bank – the results on financial expertise converge between savings and cooperative banks. However, savings banks still have a higher share. There are also differences in the compositions of the boards. The supervisory boards of cooperative banks show a significantly higher share of self-employed individuals than do the supervisory boards of savings banks. This can be traced back to the statuary employee representation of savings banks, on the one hand, and the observable high presence of local and regional politicians on the supervisory boards, on the other hand. Cooperative banks, conversely, have a high number of entrepreneurs, which is in line with the goal of member sponsorship. This result is further supported by the fact that more executive employees, (managing) partners, and owners are members of the supervisory boards of cooperative banks than of the supervisory boards of savings banks.

The study is structured as follows: Chapter II.2 briefly introduces the German banking sector, the background of the legislative regulations in each sector, and the revision of the requirements of supervisory board members. Chapter II.3 outlines the methodology for the assessment of professional background. Chapter II.4 includes the database, Chapter II.5 presents the results of the analysis, and Chapter II.6 concludes the study and provides an outlook for the future.

II.2 Introduction to German Banking Sector and Legal Backdrop

The total assets of the German banking sector were EUR 7.5 trillion at the end of 2009. These assets are allocated to 1,939 banks, of which 1,157 belong to the cooperative banks sector and 431 to the savings banks sector.[3] The regional banks that are considered in the present study account for approximately 16% of the total assets of the German banking sector. The regional focus and characteristics of regional banks indicate a focus on traditional credit and deposit taking activities. This is documented by the relatively high share of regional banks in the overall credit volume to domestic enterprises and private households. In this category, they account for 42%. Their share of savings deposits of domestic individuals is 77% (Deutsche Bundesbank, 2011).

---

3 A further 351 banks comprise commercial banks, state banks, cooperative central banks, mortgage banks, building associations, and banks with specific functions (Deutsche Bundesbank, 2011).

There is no law that encompasses all legal requirements regarding German banking institutions. The KWG represents the central German banking law and is effective for individual institutions as well as for banking groups of all three sectors (Koetter, Nestmann, Stolz, and Wedow, 2004). Further relevant acts can be divided into institutional and business oriented laws. The savings banks laws (SpG) of the federal states and the GenG are institutional laws. Examples of business-orientated laws are the Securities Trading Act (WpHG), the Act for the Prevention of Money Laundering (GwG), and the Act for Deposit Insurance and Investors' Compensation (EAEG).

Savings banks are governed by the savings banks laws of the federal states (Claussen, 2003). However, these laws are applicable to the so-called free savings banks. For instance, there is no savings banks law in Hamburg, since the free Hamburger Sparkasse (HASPA) is incorporated in the legal form of a stock corporation (Hackethal, 2004). By and large, the key elements of savings banks laws do not diverge materially. In general, the laws govern legal status, ownership, objectives of the bank, and organizational structure. Concerning the supervisory board, the laws regulate the following key elements: term, chair, appointment of remaining members, employee representatives, limitations to appointments, duties of the board, and competence requirements for individual members.[4] Additionally, there are further detailed regulations for the individual savings bank in its respective charter (Hartmann-Wendels, Pfingsten, and Weber, 2007). The savings bank laws require that a third of the supervisory members be elected by the employees, with the exception of the Bavarian Savings Banks Law. In the Bavarian state, the chief executive officer (CEO) has a seat and voting rights on the supervisory board.[5] In Lower Saxony, the Personnel Representation Act regulates employee representation on the supervisory board.[6]

Remarkably, there are significant regional differences in the requirements of individuals' expertise, which are stated in each savings banks law in addition to the KWG.[7] While 10 out of 15 laws prescribe expertise as a target requirement, only in five states is individual expertise compulsory. A review of members' expertise by local and/or regional governing bodies is currently compulsory only

4 E.g. cf §§ 11ff. Savings Banks Law of Baden-Wuerttemberg.

5 Cf. § 6, para. 1, Savings Banks Law of Bavaria.

6 Cf. § 11, para. 1, no. 3, Savings Banks Law of Lower Saxony.

7 According to the version of the savings banks laws of February 2011.

in the Savings Banks Law of the federal state North Rhine-Westphalia.[8] Four savings banks laws hold that at least one member has to have the required expertise in accounting and audit of financial statements if the respective savings bank participates in the organized market.

Cooperative banks are governed by the GenG in addition to the KWG. The Act refers to cooperatives in general and not to credit cooperatives in particular. In comparison to the savings banks laws, the GenG has only general requirements for the determination of the supervisory board. The only requirement that is specific to individuals states that in capital market-oriented cooperatives, in the sense of § 264d, Commercial Code (HGB), at least one member of the supervisory board needs to have expertise in accounting or auditing.

The modification of the KWG leads to a homogenization of the requirements of supervisory board members across the three sectors. In accordance with § 24, para. 1, no. 15, KWG, newly elected supervisory board members have to provide documents for the assessment of their expertise and reliability. The required expertise depends on the size, complexity, and systematic relevance of the institution (BaFin and Deutsche Bundesbank, 2010). This implies that the supervisory boards of larger institutions should have a higher degree of financial expertise. In accordance with § 36, para. 3, sentence 4 KWG, controlling bodies have to exercise their duties in such a manner that potential misconduct of the management board can be discovered. The mere presence of supervisory board members on the supervisory board is insufficient (Böhm-Dries, et al., 2010).

The joint bulletin by BaFin and Deutsche Bundesbank (2010) does not specifically prescribe the requirements that have to be satisfied by members and how the monitoring abilities of these members should be assessed. However, the bulletin outlines that, for individuals who are members of the supervisory board because of mandates, expertise is assumed. Among these members are mayors and district administrators who head the governing bodies of the supporting organization. The same applies for employee representatives in codetermined controlling and administration bodies. For merchants, in terms of §§ 1ff., HGB, and foresters, farmers (who are obliged to keep books of accounts), and other entrepreneurs, in terms of § 141 German fiscal code (AO), expertise can also be assumed. However, this depends on the size and business model of the company. The bulletin also states that expertise can be acquired through several activities, such as experience in other sectors, public authority, or through political

8 Cf. § 12, para. 1, Savings Banks Law North Rhine-Westphalia.

mandate. If a member lacks expertise, this expertise can be acquired through additional educational training (BaFin and Deutsche Bundesbank, 2010).

II.3 Research Methodology

The present study focuses on regional banks with the legal status of registered cooperative and public law savings banks, respectively. Hence, regional banks with the legal status of stock corporations and private limited companies are excluded. At the moment, there is no public commercial database that provides historical data on the individual members of the supervisory boards of German banks. For this reason, the analysis is based on a unique, manually collected dataset derived from publicly available annual reports. The main criterion for the assumption of financial expertise is the stated professional background of the member. This approach follows other studies that were conducted in relation to the US-American Sarbanes-Oxley Act (SOX), which was released in 2002. SOX comprises requirements for the Audit Committees of companies whose securities are traded in the United States. Related studies analyze the impact of financial expertise in general and knowledge in accounting and auditing in particular on the risk and performance of companies (e.g., Carcello, Hollingsworth, Klein, and Neal, 2008; Dhaliwal, Naiker, and Navissi, 2006; Güner, Malmendier, and Tate, 2008; Hau and Thum, 2008; Hermalin and Weisbach, 2003). These studies mainly used individuals' professional backgrounds as indications of qualifications. Only Hau and Thum (2008) and the recent study of Körner, Müller, Paul, and Schmidt (2014) considered additionally the educational background.

First, supervisory board members are grouped into self-employed, employed, retired persons, and others (Level 1). The category "others" comprises individuals who cannot be assigned to an occupation due to the lack of available information or insufficient data granularity. Second, these categories are further detailed as follows (Level 2). The category "self-employed persons" comprises owners, partners, managing partners, entrepreneurs, merchants, and self-employed persons with freelance professions, e.g., architects. The category "employed persons" includes all employees, public officers, and politicians.

Table II.1: Classification of occupations

Level 1: Employment	Self-employed persons	Employed persons	Retirees	Others
Level 2: Occupation	Partner	Member of management boards	Retired self-employed person	
	Managing Partner	Bank employee	Retired employed person	
	Merchant, Owner, Entrepreneur	Other employee or public officer with explicit financial focus		
	Freelance professional	Other employee or public officer without explicit financial focus		
		Politician		
Level 3: Occupation groups	Executive management (CEO, partner, managing partner, owner, entrepreneur, merchant)			
	Chartered accountant, registered auditors, tax consultant			

In order to assess the supervisory board composition, certain groups of job descriptions are examined, independent of the differentiation between self-employed and employed persons (Level 3). The first group includes executives such as chief executives, partners, managing partners, entrepreneurs, and merchants. The second group comprises chartered accountants, registered auditors, and tax consultant. Additionally, politicians are categorized into federal, federal state, regional, and local to increase granularity. Based on their legal status and public ownership, savings banks have close ties to regional and local politics.

The classification of politicians with regard to their assumable financial expertise is rather complex. In the present dataset, ministers, state secretaries, and members of parliament at the federal and federal state level are federal politicians or federal state politicians, respectively. The number of members of the European parliament is not material to the dataset, and these members are classified as federal politicians. At the regional and local level, the identification of politicians is even much more complex. Due to the multitude of administrative bodies at the regional and local levels, a multi-level approach is applied to categorize regional and local politicians. The objective of this is differentiating between politicians in the strict sense and holders of political electoral office.

Individuals who are potential mandatory members of the supervisory boards due to their mandates are identifiable straight away. The joint bulletin by BaFin and Deutsche Bundesbank (2010) states that, for example, mayors and district administrators are potential mandatory members. However, cross-federal state analysis requires a methodology for the classification of electoral office at the regional and local levels. There are remarkable differences between the federal states and subsequent differences in public authorities and their organizational structures. For example, this is evident in the formerly effective divergent Northern and Southern council regulations. The differences can be delineated by three essential characteristics: split of competencies, management structure, and management of public authorities. In the past, a trend towards the Southern council regulation has been observed (Gabriel and Holtmann, 2005; Naßmacher and Naßmacher, 2007). The Southern council regulation is characterized by the division of responsibilities of the public administrative authority and the governing body, identity of chairs of the administrative authority and the respective legislative body, as well as the sole management of the public authority with the right to give directives to the respective authority. After changes to the charters of local authorities, the head of the administration is the supreme representative of the municipality in most states (Gabriel and Holtmann, 2005; Naßmacher and Naßmacher, 2007).

First, a differentiation between full-time and voluntary electoral offices is made. Individuals officiating in political electoral offices voluntarily are not considered as politicians in this study. For instance, these include honorary county councils, city councils, and municipal councils. This criterion can be applied consistently nationwide. For the further differentiation of full-time professionals, the hierarchical level of the function is considered. In our analysis, we classify the concerned person as a politician if he is the head of the administration. This selection step assures that politicians in the present dataset are directly elected. In this context, the county administrators in Baden-Wuerttemberg are an exception as they are indirectly elected through the county council.

In the second step, persons who are subject to directives and who have to report to the head of the administration do not count as politicians in the present analysis. Therefore, district administrators, lord mayors, and mayors are consistently counted nationwide as politicians. Furthermore, there are few federal states in which city directors, presidents of regional committees, presidents of local committees, and presidents of regional committees are also counted as politicians if all the criteria outlined above are satisfied. Corresponding to the outlined approach, other holders of state-specific functions are not counted as politicians even though they are indirectly or directly elected and represent a political position and/or party, such as full-time city councilors in Bavaria, magistrates in Hessen, and (county) deputies in several federal states. All of these persons violate the criterion regarding heading the administration. If the function is exercised full-time, the office holders are typically responsible for particular divisions or departments, respectively. At the same time, they are subject to the directives of the head of the administration (Gabriel and Holtmann, 2005).

The quality of data on individual supervisory board members provided in the annual reports has not been consistent. For this reason, the following assumptions have to be made and applied consistently for the present analysis:

- For the information merchant, we assume a merchant in terms of § 1, HGB.
- For information entrepreneurs, we assume that the person is a managing partner/owner of a company.
- A farmer is treated as self-employed, if not otherwise explicitly stated.
- In cases of jobs based on apprenticeships, which could suggest both self-employed and employed occupations, an employed occupation has been assumed if no further information is available.
- If the academic title is the only available information, no classification is attributed (others).

For the determination of board size, as well as for further analysis, we do not consider the following board members:

- Advisory members,
- Honorary members,
- Members with tenures of less than half a year.

For analysis of board competence, based on the methodology outlined above, assumable financial expertise is assigned to certain job descriptions and professional backgrounds. The main idea behind this is the obvious relation to financial issues. For instance, financial expertise is expected in the case of managing directors of companies. For the assigning of financial expertise, we generally considered the information available over the time frame 2004–2009. For this study, professional backgrounds are assigned financial expertise as follows:

Table II.2: Assignment of financial expertise

Level 1: Employment	Self-employed persons with assumed financial expertise	Employed persons with assumed financial expertise	Retired persons with assumed financial expertise
Level 2: Occupation	Entrepreneur, Merchant, Owner	Non-bank employee with assumed financial focus (e.g. member of management board)	Retired self-employed person with assumed financial expertise
	Managing Partner	Bank employee	Retired employed person with assumed financial expertise
	Partner	Public officer with assumed financial focus (e.g. treasurer) Federal and State Minister, State Secretary	
		Local and regional politician	

With regard to the holders of electoral office, who are not counted as politicians, an individual evaluation is conducted in order to determine how close their activities are related to financial and business issues. Financial expertise is attributed based on this evaluation. Due to the legislative requirements outlined in Chapter II.2, there is a significantly higher expected share of employee representatives on the boards of savings banks than on those of cooperative banks. For this reason, the analysis is conducted twice. First, the overall financial expertise of the board is analyzed. Second, the focus shifts to so-called outside financial expertise. This refers to the financial expertise of board members who are not employees of the respective supervised bank. The composition of the boards, which is not regulated by legal requirements, will be compared. Retired persons are categorized on the basis of their last available professional occupation. For instance, a retired person is assigned financial expertise when he or she is a former managing director of company. The classification of financial expertise for professional occupation is geared to the outline of BaFin and Deutsche Bundesbank (2010). Only farmers are treated differently, as their job description significantly differs from the occupational focus of managers. For consistency reasons, publicly irreproducible information cannot be considered in this study.

II.4 Data set

Our analysis is based on a unique, manually collected dataset derived from publicly available annual reports. The financial statements are either provided by the individual bank or by the Bundesanzeiger via the Unternehmensregister or LexisNexis databases. In total, our dataset comprises the characteristics of supervisory board members of 257 cooperative banks and 209 savings banks. A total of 39,365 data points at the individual level were collected. In order to secure the highest possible degree of data quality, the regional banks included satisfy the following criteria. The analysis is based on a balanced panel. For this reason, the data on the considered regional banks must be available through the years 2004–2009. Furthermore, only a maximum of 10% of the board members can belong to the "other" category. Due to the relative difficulty of applying this to small boards, a maximum of one person in absolute terms can belong to this category, even if the ratio rises to above 10%. This refers in particular to boards with a size of up to nine persons, as one person in the "other" category makes up more than 10% of the board. If a financial institution has been eliminated due to lack of data or too high a representation of the category "other", the succeeding institution in the size ranking is included.

First, the largest 200 banks (Top 200) in each sector are analyzed over the period 2004–2009. For banks that are listed in the 2009 ranking under a different name due to merger(s) that have taken place in the interim, the name of the acquiring entity was applied for the former years. In order to account for potential distortions due to mergers in the regional banking sector, the analysis is repeated for a merger-controlled panel over the same time horizon. For the merger adjustments, a black-out period of three years is introduced for the respective institution (merger year plus the two previous years). This eliminates banks that were involved in merger activities in the period between 2002 and 2009. The merger-controlled sample includes 150 institutions in each sector (Top 150). Data on the merger history of each bank was accessed via the Hoppenstedt Banken database. The largest 200 cooperative banks and 200 savings banks of 2009 account for 57% and 71% of total assets of all banks in their sectors, respectively. The 150 merger-controlled institutions account for 35% and 45% of total assets of their respective sectors. In the Top 200, the average total assets of the cooperative banks amounted to EUR 1.9 billion, and the average total assets of the savings banks amounted to EUR 3.8 billion (Top 150: EUR 1.6 billion and EUR 3.2 billion, respectively). We refer constantly to the results of the Top 200 institutions if the merger-controlled panel (Top 150) does not show any different qualitative results.

II.5 Empirical Analysis

Board size analysis reveals that supervisory boards of savings banks are on average 35% larger than those of cooperative banks. The average size of savings banks' supervisory boards is 17 board members, compared with 12 board members at cooperative banks. Basically, these results represent the expected variance due to bank size differences between cooperative and savings banks. The differences in board size are also driven by mandatory employee representation in savings banks. Apart from actual bank size, the savings bank laws lead to one-third of the board members being employee representatives – except in the case of the Bavarian savings banks. When considering the size of boards without employee representatives, the average numbers of board members in both sectors converge.

Table II.3: Supervisory board composition regional banks (mean values 2004–2009)

Variable	Cooperative banks		Savings banks	
	Top 200	Top 150	Top 200	Top 150
Board size	12	11	17	16
Insider	1	1	4	4
Outsider	11	10	13	12
Self-employed individuals	39.6%	39.7%	12.6%	13.5%
Employed individuals	50.2%	49.6%	73.3%	72.5%
Retirees	9.2%	9.7%	12.7%	12.6%
Others	1.0%	0.9%	1.4%	1.3%
Politicians (officiating)	2.2%	2.3%	24.4%	24.7%
Federal politicians	0.1%	0.3%	0.8%	0.7%
State politicians	0.2%	0.2%	2.6%	2.6%
Regional politicians	0.0%	0.0%	5.9%	5.5%
Local politicians	1.8%	1.9%	15.2%	15.8%
Executive employees / Owners / Partners	33.3%	34.7%	11.8%	12.2%
Accountants / Auditors / Tax consultants	7.2%	7.3%	1.2%	1.3%

The composition of the supervisory boards, based on the employment of members, reveals significant differences within the regional banking groups. Self-employed persons roughly account for three times as many members of the supervisory boards of cooperative banks than of savings banks. This observation matches the fundamental expectation that cooperative banks are motivated to promote their members and regional and local enterprises. Conversely, savings banks have a significantly higher share of employed persons than cooperative banks (73% vs. 50%). This is due to the fact that savings banks have a comparatively high share of employee representatives and politicians. The results remain robust when excluding insiders from the analysis. The share of retired persons is only slightly higher at savings banks. However, it is remarkable that there are some institutions in either the savings or the cooperative banking sector that have a share of more than 50% retired persons on the board.

Public ownership and the consequent legal requirements regarding the representation of public office holders lead to the high presence and importance of politicians on the supervisory boards of savings banks. This assumption is confirmed by this analysis (see Appendix II.7.4). At savings banks, politicians account for approximately a quarter of the board, on average. The representation of the owning governing body is shown by the fact that local and regional politicians are primarily on these boards. When retired politicians are included in the analysis, the share of politicians on the supervisory board increases to 28%, on average (see Appendix II.7.5). In contrast, at cooperative banks, politicians hardly play a role, with a share of 2% on average. Only the cooperative bank with the highest politician share (25%) is in line with the average share of the savings banks.

A differentiation within the cooperative banking group between employed and self-employed persons shows that financial expertise is distributed over both categories almost equally. For approximately 50% of the persons in each category, financial expertise can be assumed. The same share applies for savings banks with regard to self-employed persons. In regard to employed persons, employee representatives and the high share of politicians indicate that financial expertise can be assumed for the majority of these employed persons (see Appendix II.7.6). Apart from the attribution to employed or self-employed persons, two groups are of high relevance because for both groups, financial expertise can be assumed with high certainty: persons in executive positions and auditors, tax consultants, and accountants. Comparing the two regional banking groups it is evident that savings banks have a subordinated role in contrast to cooperative banks (see Appendix II.7.7). Directors, managing directors, and entrepreneurs/owners represent, on average, 33% of the supervisory boards of cooperative banks, but only 12% in savings banks; auditors, tax consultants, and accountants account for 7% of cooperative banks' supervisory boards and 1% in savings banks, on average.

Overall, the analysis of assumed financial expertise indicates a higher share of expertise on the supervisory boards of savings banks than on those of cooperative banks. For around two-thirds of the board, financial expertise can be assumed. Therefore, the supervisory boards of savings banks significantly outperform the average of approximately 48% at cooperative banks (see Table II.4). The results remain robust considering the merger-controlled panel. However, the results converge only when considering outsiders. The financial expertise of outsiders accounts for approximately 53% at savings banks and approximately 45% at cooperative banks. When considering the merger-controlled panel, there is no significant difference to the base analysis (54% vs. 46%).

Hau and Thum (2008) analyze the financial expertise of 29 large German banks on the basis of 14 characteristics which are used to gauge financial expertise. For this reason both studies' results are only partially comparable. The criteria financial market experience, banking experience, top-level financial management experience, and multiple board memberships are closest to our methodology. But contrary to our results, they provide competence values between 31% and 40% for private banks and only between 10% and 30% for public banks. A rececent study by Körner, Müller, Paul and Schmidt (2014) undermines that the general expertise level of supervisory board members is relatively high; however, they also demonstrate that the assumed expertise is derived mainly from employee representatives who have assumed bank expertise. Further, the study observes that the chairman of the supervisory board is the main source of the lack of expertise.

Table II.4: Financial expertise regional banks (mean values 2004–2009)

Variable	**Cooperative banks**		**Savings banks**	
	Top 200	**Top 150**	**Top 200**	**Top 150**
Financial expertise	47.8%	47.5%	65.0%	65.5%
Outside financial expertise	45.2%	45.8%	53.2%	53.8%

Based on the characteristics of the regional banks, the following hypotheses have been developed for comparing the two sectors:

H1: *The statuary employee representation and the assumed financial literacy of potential mandatory members, lead to significantly more financial expertise at savings banks.*

H2: *Since regional banks have a similar business model, the outside financial expertise of both groups does not differ significantly.*

H3: *Cooperative banks are explicitly dedicated to local and regional enterprises and merchants and have therefore a significantly higher share of self-employed individuals on their supervisory boards.*

H4: *The statuary employee representation leads to a significantly higher share of employed individuals on savings banks' supervisory boards.*

H5: *Since regional banks operate locally and foster local and regional enterprises and local public investments, there is no significant difference in the share of executive employees on regional banks' supervisory boards.*

The following Table II.5 presents significance of the mean comparison tests between the both groups of the regional banking sector and provides evidence on the hypotheses.

Table II.5: Comparison of mean values of regional banks (mean values 2004–2009)

Variable		Mean	Std. error	t	df	p-value
Top 200						
Financial expertise	Cooperative banks	47.7642	0.6602	-20.8182	2229.7100	0.0000
	Savings banks	64.9789	0.4980			
Outside financial expertise	Cooperative banks	45.2461	0.6705	-8.4056	2397.3900	0.0000
	Savings banks	53.1539	0.6599			
Self-employed individuals	Cooperative banks	39.5510	0.6782	36.7786	1585.8700	0.0000
	Savings banks	12.6191	0.2761			
Employed individuals	Cooperative banks	50.2240	0.6623	-30.7596	1830.7500	0.0000
	Savings banks	73.3169	0.3535			
Executive employees	Cooperative banks	33.3130	0.6059	32.8389	1586.4700	0.0000
	Savings banks	11.8263	0.2469			
Top 150						
Financial expertise	Cooperative banks	47.5350	0.7581	-18.8507	1674.5600	0.0000
	Savings banks	65.4584	0.5738			
Outside financial expertise	Cooperative banks	45.8105	0.7883	-7.3056	1796.4100	0.0000
	Savings banks	53.8369	0.7652			
Self-employed individuals	Cooperative banks	39.7042	0.8478	28.7784	1166.0000	0.0000
	Savings banks	13.5196	0.3304			
Employed individuals	Cooperative banks	49.6071	0.7964	-25.5930	1338.5800	0.0000
	Savings banks	72.4959	0.4070			
Executive employees	Cooperative banks	34.7240	0.7561	27.6554	1177.2900	0.0000
	Savings banks	12.2170	0.3012			

Confidence level: 95%

The following Table II.6 shows expertise levels of banks clustered by bank and board size. The differentiation by bank size – by creating groups of 50 financial institutions each – shows that savings banks with more total assets do not have a higher share of financial expertise than do smaller banks (for the development over time, see Appendices II.7.9, II.7.10). On the other hand, larger cooperative banks show higher average financial expertise than do smaller banks. However, this is only significant for overall board expertise but not for outside expertise (for significance levels, see Appendix II.7.14). The similar analysis of board size also shows no consistent evidence that the assumed financial expertise is determined by the number of board members (see Appendices II.7.11, II.7.12, II.7.15).

Table II.6: Financial expertise of regional banks clustered by bank and board size (largest banks in bank and board size in Cluster 1, smallest banks in Cluster 4)

Variable	**Cooperative banks**				**Savings banks**			
Clustered by bank size	1	2	3	4	1	2	3	4
Top 200								
Financial expertise	54.5%	49.6%	45.8%	41.3%	64.4%	65.0%	64.9%	65.6%
Outside financial expertise	46.7%	47.9%	45.1%	41.3%	48.5%	55.9%	53.2%	55.1%
Top 150								
Financial expertise	51.5%	47.4%	43.7%	-	66.3%	65.1%	64.9%	-
Outside financial expertise	46.9%	47.1%	43.4%	-	54.5%	54.0%	53.0%	-
Clustered by board size	1	2	3	4	1	2	3	4
Top 200								
Financial expertise	49.9%	45.8%	50.9%	44.5%	64.5%	65.4%	64.2%	65.8%
Outside financial expertise	43.5%	44.5%	49.7%	43.3%	50.2%	52.4%	49.0%	61.0%
Top 150								
Financial expertise	45.4%	47.7%	49.5%	-	67.6%	61.2%	67.5%	-
Outside financial expertise	42.3%	46.5%	48.6%	-	56.5%	44.2%	60.7%	-

The following table shows the distribution of both groups within the regional banking sector across four expertise clusters.

Table II.7: Distribution of regional banks across expertise clusters (based on mean values 2004–2009)

Variable	**Cooperative banks**				**Savings banks**			
	0%–25%	26%–50%	51%–75%	76%–100%	0%–25%	26%–50%	51%–75%	76%–100%
Top 200								
Financial expertise	29	76	69	26	1	44	97	38
Outside financial expertise	36	76	69	19	23	72	67	
Top 150								
Financial expertise	19	62	48	21	1	30	77	42
Outside financial expertise	23	62	47	18	18	48	56	28

II.6 Concluding Remarks

The financial crisis has once more illustrated the relevance of effective supervision of financial institutions. For effective supervision, a comprehensive understanding of financial issues (financial expertise) is unconditionally necessary. For smaller institutions, in particular, some doubts arise. In fact, the analysis of the professional background of the supervisory board of savings banks and cooperative banks shows a relatively high degree of assumable financial expertise, though this is not entirely consistent. The comparison between cooperative banks and savings banks shows that a higher share of financial expertise can be assumed for savings banks. Comparing our results with the study of Hau and Thum (2008) underlines the relatively high levels of financial expertise of the more than 400 cooperative and savings banks in our sample. The values of their criteria which come closest to our methodology provide expertise ratios of 31%–40% for private banks and 10%–30% for public banks based on a sample of 29 large German banks.

Savings banks benefit from the legal requirements of employee representation and the fact that employees of banks are assigned financial expertise by the regulatory bodies. Adjusted for insiders, the quotients of cooperative and savings banks converge. However, the boards of savings banks still have a higher share of financial expertise. It is remarkable that there is no significant difference between the values with or without the adjustment for mergers. Contrary to initial expectations, neither bank size nor board size increases financial expertise consistently across both sectors. Financial expertise in only cooperative banks increases with an increase in bank size. This is of high relevance as the requirements of board members also depend on the size of the institution. In summary, around 50% or more in both banking groups have financial expertise. As the requirements on financial expertise of supervisory board members refer to the whole board, and not to a certain quota, a question remains: What are the consequences that would be applied by the regulatory authorities for the remainder of the board?

A detailed view on the composition of the boards shows significant differences in terms of the share of self-employed persons versus that of employed persons, politicians, and the volatility of the composition. Cooperative banks have on average three times as many self-employed persons than do savings banks. Conversely, savings banks have a much higher share of employed persons. This can be traced back to the employees of savings banks as employee representatives who make up, on average, 26% of the board. Considering financial expertise, the source of financial expertise in savings banks is mainly employed persons. Although cooperative banks have a relevant share of financial expertise through self-employed persons, financial expertise is mainly represented by employed persons. Apart from the differentiation between employed and self-employed people, it is noticeable that board members at cooperative banks have more executive positions than do those at savings banks.

The comparatively higher share of politicians at savings banks is in line with expectations based on the legal characteristics of savings banks. Notwithstanding this, the share exceeds the magnitude expected through the savings banks laws, which list mandatory members. In particular, the maximum values of up to two-thirds of politicians on the board are a remarkable factor. Current office holders, retired regional and local politicians, and banking employees account, on average, for around 50% of the supervisory board financial expertise. In the light of the assumed expert knowledge of both groups, by BaFin and Deutsche Bundesbank, a relatively high degree of financial expertise can be consequently assumed for boards of savings banks by definition. In regard to outside financial expertise, it can be stated that cooperative banks and savings banks converge. The reason behind is a higher number of self-employed persons and executives in the supervisory boards of cooperative banks.

With regard to the volatility of financial expertise, bank employees are stabilizing members. Financial expertise in individual cooperative banks ranges from 0% to 100%. On the other hand, savings banks have a minimum level that is required by savings banks laws. Excluding insiders, the results converge in terms of distribution and range. This leads to the conclusion that, in general, the focus on the election process of "freely eligible" members of the controlling body is comparable between both banking sectors.

The methodology of the classification is an approximation of evident banking expertise. It is therefore left to subsequent studies, which will have a broader basis, to evaluate specific individual personal data to refine the findings. The quality of supervision is another area of investigation. From our point of view, it cannot be concluded that persons who do not have financial expertise according to the underlying classifications of this study do not have financial expertise at all.

On the basis of this investigation, on the one hand, corporate governance discussions of the three sector structure of the German banking system can be extended to a broader basis. On the other hand, the heterogeneity of the shown data allows further investigation. For instance, the relationship of controlling quality and risk-adjusted performance are further avenues of research.

II.7 Appendix

Appendix II.7.1: No. of institutions and supervisory board size regional banks (absolute numbers)

	Cooperative banks						Savings banks					
Top 200	**2009**	**2008**	**2007**	**2006**	**2005**	**2004**	**2009**	**2008**	**2007**	**2006**	**2005**	**2004**
No. of banks	200	200	200	200	200	200	200	200	200	200	200	200
Board size												
Mean	12	12	12	12	13	13	17	17	17	17	17	17
Median	12	12	12	12	12	12	15	15	15	15	15	15
Std. Dev.	4.9	4.4	4.1	4.3	4.4	4.6	4.8	5.0	4.9	5.1	5.3	6.5
Min	6	5	5	5	5	5	8	8	8	8	7	7
Max	37	33	30	33	32	32	38	39	39	36	38	48
Insider												
Mean	1	1	1	1	1	1	5	4	4	4	4	5
Median	0	0	0	0	0	0	5	5	5	5	5	5
Std. Dev.	2.0	2.1	1.9	2.0	2.0	1.9	2.5	2.7	2.7	2.7	2.7	3.1
Min	0	0	0	0	0	0	0	0	0	0	0	0
Max	9	10	9	10	10	10	12	12	12	11	12	16
Outside												
Mean	12	11	11	12	12	12	12	12	12	12	12	13
Median	11	10,5	11	11	12	12	11	12	12	12	11	12
Std. Dev.	4.4	3.9	3.6	3.8	4.1	4.5	3.5	3.6	3.5	3.6	3.7	4.4
Min	5	5	5	5	5	5	6	6	6	6	6	6
Max	37	33	30	33	32	32	27	27	27	27	27	32

Top 150	**2009**	**2008**	**2007**	**2006**	**2005**	**2004**	**2009**	**2008**	**2007**	**2006**	**2005**	**2004**
No. of banks	150	150	150	150	150	150	150	150	150	150	150	150
Board size												
Mean	10	10	11	11	11	11	16	16	16	16	16	16
Median	9	9	10	10	10	11	15	15	15	15	15	15
Std. Dev.	3.4	3.4	3.6	3.8	3.8	4.0	4.0	4.0	3.9	4.2	4.3	4.5
Min	5	4	4	4	4	5	8	8	8	8	7	7
Max	26	27	30	33	32	32	31	33	32	33	32	31
Insider												
Mean	0	0	0	0	0	0	4	4	4	4	4	4
Median	0	0	0	0	0	0	5	5	5	5	5	5
Std. Dev.	1.4	1.5	1.3	1.4	1.4	1.4	2.2	2.4	2.3	2.4	2.4	2.5
Min	0	0	0	0	0	0	0	0	0	0	0	0
Max	9	10	9	10	10	10	11	12	11	11	11	11
Outside												
Mean	10	10	10	11	11	11	12	12	12	12	12	12
Median	9	9	10	10	10	10	11	11	11	11	11	11
Std. Dev.	3.1	3.2	3.4	3.7	3.6	3.8	3.1	3.2	3.2	3.3	3.3	3.3
Min	5	4	4	4	4	5	7	7	7	7	6	6
Max	26	27	30	33	32	32	27	27	27	27	27	27

Appendix II.7.2: Total supervisory board composition, self-employed, employees, retirees, other (in % of total supervisory board size)

	Cooperative banks						Savings banks					
Top 200	**2009**	**2008**	**2007**	**2006**	**2005**	**2004**	**2009**	**2008**	**2007**	**2006**	**2005**	**2004**
Self-employed individuals												
Mean	40.1%	39.6%	39.4%	39.4%	39.2%	39.5%	12.5%	12.6%	13.0%	12.7%	12.5%	12.4%
Median	44.1%	44.4%	41.7%	41.7%	40.0%	42.9%	11.1%	12.3%	12.0%	12.5%	11.1%	11.1%
Std. Dev.	23.7%	24.1%	23.6%	23.2%	23.3%	23.4%	9.5%	9.4%	9.9%	9.6%	9.7%	9.5%
Min	0.0%	0.0%	0.0%	0.0%	0.0%	0.0%	0.0%	0.0%	0.0%	0.0%	0.0%	0.0%
Max	91.7%	91.7%	88.9%	83.3%	83.3%	83.3%	41.7%	38.9%	41.7%	41.7%	47.1%	47.4%
Employed individuals												
Mean	50.9%	51.6%	50.6%	49.8%	49.7%	48.7%	73.8%	73.4%	73.1%	72.7%	74.4%	72.5%
Median	50.0%	50.0%	50.0%	44.9%	45.2%	44.7%	73.9%	73.2%	73.3%	72.7%	73.3%	73.3%
Std. Dev.	22.4%	23.4%	23.2%	22.8%	23.2%	22.7%	11.9%	12.3%	12.9%	12.2%	11.9%	12.3%
Min	0.0%	0.0%	0.0%	0.0%	0.0%	0.0%	41.7%	36.4%	36.4%	36.4%	36.4%	41.7%
Max	100.0%	100.0%	100.0%	100.0%	100.0%	100.0%	100.0%	100.0%	100.0%	100.0%	100.0%	100.0%
Retirees												
Mean	7.9%	7.7%	8.9%	9.6%	10.2%	10.7%	12.5%	12.7%	12.6%	13.3%	11.7%	13.5%
Median	6.3%	5.9%	6.1%	7.1%	7.1%	7.1%	11.1%	11.1%	11.1%	11.1%	10.0%	12.9%
Std. Dev.	10.6%	10.5%	11.9%	12.1%	12.8%	12.8%	10.0%	10.3%	10.1%	10.1%	9.4%	9.7%
Min	0.0%	0.0%	0.0%	0.0%	0.0%	0.0%	0.0%	0.0%	0.0%	0.0%	0.0%	0.0%
Max	63.6%	77.8%	77.8%	66.7%	66.7%	66.7%	55.6%	47.4%	46.7%	46.7%	40.0%	40.0%
Other												
Mean	1.0%	1.0%	1.0%	1.1%	1.0%	1.1%	1.2%	1.2%	1.3%	1.4%	1.4%	1.7%
Median	0.0%	0.0%	0.0%	0.0%	0.0%	0.0%	0.0%	0.0%	0.0%	0.0%	0.0%	0.0%
Std. Dev.	2.6%	2.7%	2.8%	2.8%	2.7%	2.9%	2.6%	2.7%	2.7%	2.8%	2.8%	2.9%
Min	0.0%	0.0%	0.0%	0.0%	0.0%	0.0%	0.0%	0.0%	0.0%	0.0%	0.0%	0.0%
Max	10.0%	14.3%	14.3%	14.3%	14.3%	14.3%	11.1%	12.5%	12.5%	12.5%	12.5%	12.5%

Top 150	**2009**	**2008**	**2007**	**2006**	**2005**	**2004**	**2009**	**2008**	**2007**	**2006**	**2005**	**2004**
Self-employed individuals												
Mean	40.5%	40.1%	40.1%	39.4%	39.0%	39.2%	13.8%	13.8%	13.9%	13.4%	13.4%	12.9%
Median	43.8%	43.7%	40.8%	39.2%	40.0%	40.0%	13.3%	13.3%	13.3%	13.3%	13.3%	11.8%
Std. Dev.	26.1%	26.0%	25.7%	25.1%	24.8%	25.3%	10.0%	9.8%	10.2%	9.8%	9.9%	9.9%
Min	0.0%	0.0%	0.0%	0.0%	0.0%	0.0%	0.0%	0.0%	0.0%	0.0%	0.0%	0.0%
Max	88.9%	90.9%	88.9%	88.9%	90.0%	87.5%	41.7%	38.9%	41.7%	41.7%	47.1%	47.4%
Employed individuals												
Mean	51.2%	51.3%	49.5%	48.7%	48.8%	48.2%	72.4%	72.1%	72.0%	71.9%	73.8%	72.8%
Median	50.0%	50.0%	46.4%	45.5%	45.8%	48.3%	73.3%	72.7%	73.3%	72.5%	73.3%	73.3%
Std. Dev.	24.0%	24.3%	24.2%	23.9%	23.8%	23.4%	12.1%	12.3%	12.6%	12.1%	11.7%	12.5%
Min	9.1%	9.1%	0.0%	0.0%	0.0%	0.0%	41.7%	36.4%	36.4%	36.4%	36.4%	41.7%
Max	100.0%	100.0%	100.0%	100.0%	100.0%	100.0%	100.0%	100.0%	100.0%	100.0%	100.0%	100.0%
Retirees												
Mean	7.4%	7.6%	9.4%	10.9%	11.3%	11.7%	12.7%	12.9%	12.8%	13.3%	11.4%	12.8%
Median	0.0%	0.0%	7.7%	8.3%	9.1%	8.7%	12.5%	12.5%	11.1%	12.5%	9.3%	11.1%
Std. Dev.	10.5%	10.6%	11.9%	12.3%	13.2%	13.0%	10.3%	10.6%	10.3%	10.5%	9.8%	10.1%
Min	0.0%	0.0%	0.0%	0.0%	0.0%	0.0%	0.0%	0.0%	0.0%	0.0%	0.0%	0.0%
Max	63.6%	77.8%	77.8%	66.7%	66.7%	66.7%	55.6%	47.4%	46.7%	46.7%	38.9%	38.9%

	Cooperative banks						Savings banks					
Top 150	**2009**	**2008**	**2007**	**2006**	**2005**	**2004**	**2009**	**2008**	**2007**	**2006**	**2005**	**2004**
Other												
Mean	1.0%	1.0%	1.0%	1.0%	0.9%	0.9%	1.1%	1.2%	1.3%	1.4%	1.5%	1.6%
Median	0.0%	0.0%	0.0%	0.0%	0.0%	0.0%	0.0%	0.0%	0.0%	0.0%	0.0%	0.0%
Std. Dev.	2.9%	3.0%	2.9%	2.9%	2.8%	2.8%	2.6%	2.8%	2.8%	2.9%	2.9%	2.9%
Min	0.0%	0.0%	0.0%	0.0%	0.0%	0.0%	0.0%	0.0%	0.0%	0.0%	0.0%	0.0%
Max	16.7%	16.7%	16.7%	16.7%	16.7%	16.7%	11.1%	12.5%	12.5%	12.5%	12.5%	12.5%

Appendix II.7.3: Outside supervisory board composition, self-employed, employees, retirees, other (in % of outside supervisory board members)

	Cooperative banks						Savings banks					
Top 200	**2009**	**2008**	**2007**	**2006**	**2005**	**2004**	**2009**	**2008**	**2007**	**2006**	**2005**	**2004**
Self-employed individuals												
Mean	42.4%	42.1%	41.6%	41.7%	41.2%	41.5%	12.5%	12.6%	13.0%	12.7%	12.5%	12.4%
Median	45.7%	44.4%	44.4%	46.6%	44.1%	44.4%	11.1%	12.3%	12.0%	12.5%	11.1%	11.1%
Std. Dev.	25.3%	25.8%	25.3%	24.8%	24.7%	24.7%	9.5%	9.4%	9.9%	9.6%	9.7%	9.5%
Min	0.0%	0.0%	0.0%	0.0%	0.0%	0.0%	0.0%	0.0%	0.0%	0.0%	0.0%	0.0%
Max	91.7%	100.0%	100.0%	100.0%	100.0%	100.0%	41.7%	38.9%	41.7%	41.7%	47.1%	47.4%
Employed individuals												
Mean	48.1%	48.7%	47.9%	47.0%	47.0%	46.0%	73.8%	73.4%	73.1%	72.7%	74.4%	72.5%
Median	46.0%	46.0%	45.8%	42.9%	42.9%	41.7%	73.9%	73.2%	73.3%	72.7%	73.3%	73.3%
Std. Dev.	23.7%	24.7%	24.4%	24.0%	24.0%	23.5%	11.9%	12.3%	12.9%	12.2%	11.9%	12.3%
Min	0.0%	0.0%	0.0%	0.0%	0.0%	0.0%	41.7%	36.4%	36.4%	36.4%	36.4%	41.7%
Max	100.0%	100.0%	100.0%	100.0%	100.0%	100.0%	100.0%	100.0%	100.0%	100.0%	100.0%	100.0%
Retirees												
Mean	8.4%	8.2%	9.4%	10.2%	10.8%	11.4%	12.5%	12.7%	12.6%	13.3%	11.7%	13.5%
Median	6.5%	6.1%	6.5%	7.4%	7.4%	8.0%	11.1%	11.1%	11.1%	11.1%	10.0%	12.9%
Std. Dev.	11.7%	11.1%	12.5%	12.8%	13.7%	13.9%	10.0%	10.3%	10.1%	10.1%	9.4%	9.7%
Min	0.0%	0.0%	0.0%	0.0%	0.0%	0.0%	0.0%	0.0%	0.0%	0.0%	0.0%	0.0%
Max	70.0%	77.8%	77.8%	66.7%	66.7%	70.0%	55.6%	47.4%	46.7%	46.7%	40.0%	40.0%
Other												
Mean	1.1%	1.1%	1.1%	1.2%	1.0%	1.1%	1.2%	1.2%	1.3%	1.4%	1.4%	1.7%
Median	0.0%	0.0%	0.0%	0.0%	0.0%	0.0%	0.0%	0.0%	0.0%	0.0%	0.0%	0.0%
Std. Dev.	2.8%	2.9%	3.0%	3.0%	2.8%	3.1%	2.6%	2.7%	2.7%	2.8%	2.8%	2.9%
Min	0.0%	0.0%	0.0%	0.0%	0.0%	0.0%	0.0%	0.0%	0.0%	0.0%	0.0%	0.0%
Max	11.1%	14.3%	14.3%	14.3%	14.3%	14.3%	11.1%	12.5%	12.5%	12.5%	12.5%	12.5%

Top 150	**2009**	**2008**	**2007**	**2006**	**2005**	**2004**	**2009**	**2008**	**2007**	**2006**	**2005**	**2004**
Self-employed individuals												
Mean	41.6%	41.3%	41.2%	40.5%	40.0%	40.2%	18.5%	18.1%	18.1%	17.4%	17.4%	16.5%
Median	44.1%	43.7%	41.7%	40.0%	40.0%	40.8%	18.2%	18.2%	18.2%	17.9%	18.2%	16.7%
Std. Dev.	27.0%	27.0%	26.6%	26.0%	25.6%	26.1%	13.1%	12.3%	12.7%	11.9%	12.0%	11.7%
Min	0.0%	0.0%	0.0%	0.0%	0.0%	0.0%	0.0%	0.0%	0.0%	0.0%	0.0%	0.0%
Max	90.9%	100.0%	100.0%	100.0%	100.0%	100.0%	62.5%	50.0%	50.0%	50.0%	50.0%	50.0%

	Cooperative banks						Savings banks					
Top 150	**2009**	**2008**	**2007**	**2006**	**2005**	**2004**	**2009**	**2008**	**2007**	**2006**	**2005**	**2004**
Employed individuals												
Mean	49.7%	49.9%	48.2%	47.3%	47.3%	46.8%	62.4%	63.1%	63.1%	62.8%	65.3%	64.0%
Median	50.0%	49.1%	46.2%	44.4%	44.9%	44.9%	63.6%	63.6%	63.1%	62.5%	66.7%	64.7%
Std. Dev.	24.7%	25.2%	24.9%	24.7%	24.4%	23.7%	16.3%	15.3%	15.5%	15.2%	14.4%	16.2%
Min	9.1%	0.0%	0.0%	0.0%	0.0%	0.0%	16.7%	30.0%	30.0%	30.0%	30.0%	20.0%
Max	100.0%	100.0%	100.0%	100.0%	100.0%	100.0%	100.0%	100.0%	100.0%	100.0%	100.0%	100.0%
Retirees												
Mean	7.8%	7.9%	9.7%	11.3%	11.8%	12.1%	17.6%	17.3%	17.0%	17.9%	15.3%	17.3%
Median	0.0%	0.0%	7.7%	9.1%	9.5%	10.0%	16.0%	15.4%	14.3%	14.3%	11.1%	13.3%
Std. Dev.	11.3%	10.8%	12.2%	12.7%	13.9%	13.7%	14.7%	14.0%	13.8%	14.6%	13.5%	14.3%
Min	0.0%	0.0%	0.0%	0.0%	0.0%	0.0%	0.0%	0.0%	0.0%	0.0%	0.0%	0.0%
Max	70.0%	77.8%	77.8%	66.7%	66.7%	66.7%	83.3%	70.0%	70.0%	70.0%	58.3%	58.3%
Other												
Mean	1.0%	1.0%	1.0%	1.0%	0.9%	0.9%	1.5%	1.6%	1.7%	1.9%	2.0%	2.2%
Median	0.0%	0.0%	0.0%	0.0%	0.0%	0.0%	0.0%	0.0%	0.0%	0.0%	0.0%	0.0%
Std. Dev.	2.9%	3.0%	2.9%	3.0%	2.8%	2.8%	3.5%	3.6%	3.7%	3.8%	3.9%	4.1%
Min	0.0%	0.0%	0.0%	0.0%	0.0%	0.0%	0.0%	0.0%	0.0%	0.0%	0.0%	0.0%
Max	16.7%	16.7%	16.7%	16.7%	16.7%	16.7%	12.5%	14.3%	14.3%	14.3%	14.3%	15.4%

Appendix II.7.4: Differentiation between politicians (in % of total supervisory board size)

	Cooperative banks						Savings banks					
Top 200	**2009**	**2008**	**2007**	**2006**	**2005**	**2004**	**2009**	**2008**	**2007**	**2006**	**2005**	**2004**
Politicians (total)												
Mean	2.3%	2.2%	2.2%	2.2%	2.1%	2.1%	23.8%	24.8%	24.7%	24.1%	24.7%	24.1%
Median	0.0%	0.0%	0.0%	0.0%	0.0%	0.0%	25.5%	26.5%	25.0%	22.2%	25.0%	22.6%
Std. Dev.	4.6%	4.6%	4.7%	4.5%	4.5%	4.6%	13.8%	14.5%	14.0%	14.3%	14.6%	14.4%
Min	0.0%	0.0%	0.0%	0.0%	0.0%	0.0%	0.0%	0.0%	0.0%	0.0%	0.0%	0.0%
Max	25.0%	25.0%	25.0%	25.0%	25.0%	23.5%	61.5%	75.0%	60.0%	62.5%	62.5%	62.5%
Federal politicians												
Mean	0.1%	0.1%	0.1%	0.1%	0.0%	0.0%	0.8%	0.7%	0.8%	0.7%	0.8%	0.8%
Median	0.0%	0.0%	0.0%	0.0%	0.0%	0.0%	0.0%	0.0%	0.0%	0.0%	0.0%	0.0%
Std. Dev.	1.1%	1.1%	1.0%	1.0%	0.5%	0.5%	2.3%	2.3%	2.3%	2.2%	2.3%	2.4%
Min	0.0%	0.0%	0.0%	0.0%	0.0%	0.0%	0.0%	0.0%	0.0%	0.0%	0.0%	0.0%
Max	11.1%	11.1%	11.1%	11.1%	7.7%	7.7%	14.3%	14.3%	14.3%	14.3%	15.4%	15.4%
State politicians												
Mean	0.2%	0.2%	0.2%	0.2%	0.2%	0.4%	2.6%	2.7%	2.7%	2.6%	2.5%	2.3%
Median	0.0%	0.0%	0.0%	0.0%	0.0%	0.0%	0.0%	0.0%	0.0%	0.0%	0.0%	0.0%
Std. Dev.	1.3%	1.3%	1.4%	1.4%	1.5%	2.1%	4.3%	4.3%	4.3%	4.2%	4.3%	3.9%
Min	0.0%	0.0%	0.0%	0.0%	0.0%	0.0%	0.0%	0.0%	0.0%	0.0%	0.0%	0.0%
Max	11.1%	11.1%	12.5%	12.5%	12.5%	20.0%	21.4%	21.4%	21.4%	21.4%	23.1%	20.0%

	Cooperative banks						Savings banks					
Top 200	**2009**	**2008**	**2007**	**2006**	**2005**	**2004**	**2009**	**2008**	**2007**	**2006**	**2005**	**2004**
Regional politicians												
Mean	0.0%	0.0%	0.0%	0.0%	0.0%	0.0%	5.8%	6.0%	6.1%	5.9%	5.9%	5.5%
Median	0.0%	0.0%	0.0%	0.0%	0.0%	0.0%	6.3%	6.5%	6.7%	6.5%	6.3%	5.9%
Std. Dev.	0.0%	0.0%	0.0%	0.0%	0.0%	0.0%	4.6%	4.8%	4.9%	4.7%	4.7%	4.5%
Min	0.0%	0.0%	0.0%	0.0%	0.0%	0.0%	0.0%	0.0%	0.0%	0.0%	0.0%	0.0%
Max	0.0%	0.0%	0.0%	0.0%	0.0%	0.0%	22.2%	22.2%	23.8%	23.8%	23.8%	28.6%
Local politicians												
Mean	1.9%	1.8%	1.9%	1.8%	1.8%	1.7%	14.6%	15.4%	15.1%	15.0%	15.5%	15.4%
Median	0.0%	0.0%	0.0%	0.0%	0.0%	0.0%	11.1%	11.1%	11.1%	11.8%	13.3%	13.3%
Std. Dev.	4.3%	4.3%	4.4%	4.2%	4.3%	4.0%	12.6%	12.7%	12.5%	12.7%	12.7%	12.4%
Min	0.0%	0.0%	0.0%	0.0%	0.0%	0.0%	0.0%	0.0%	0.0%	0.0%	0.0%	0.0%
Max	25.0%	25.0%	25.0%	25.0%	25.0%	23.5%	50.0%	54.5%	50.0%	53.3%	53.3%	53.3%

Top 150	**2009**	**2008**	**2007**	**2006**	**2005**	**2004**	**2009**	**2008**	**2007**	**2006**	**2005**	**2004**
Politicians (total)												
Mean	2.3%	2.2%	2.2%	2.2%	2.4%	2.2%	23.9%	25.0%	24.8%	24.4%	24.9%	25.0%
Median	0.0%	0.0%	0.0%	0.0%	0.0%	0.0%	26.5%	26.7%	25.0%	21.4%	24.6%	25.0%
Std. Dev.	5.2%	4.8%	4.8%	4.7%	4.9%	4.8%	14.1%	14.7%	14.4%	14.7%	15.1%	14.7%
Min	0.0%	0.0%	0.0%	0.0%	0.0%	0.0%	0.0%	0.0%	0.0%	0.0%	0.0%	0.0%
Max	25.0%	25.0%	25.0%	25.0%	25.0%	23.5%	61.5%	75.0%	61.5%	62.5%	75.0%	69.2%
Federal politicians												
Mean	0.3%	0.3%	0.3%	0.3%	0.2%	0.2%	0.8%	0.8%	0.8%	0.7%	0.6%	0.7%
Median	0.0%	0.0%	0.0%	0.0%	0.0%	0.0%	0.0%	0.0%	0.0%	0.0%	0.0%	0.0%
Std. Dev.	1.6%	1.7%	1.7%	1.6%	1.3%	1.2%	2.5%	2.5%	2.5%	2.3%	2.3%	2.3%
Min	0.0%	0.0%	0.0%	0.0%	0.0%	0.0%	0.0%	0.0%	0.0%	0.0%	0.0%	0.0%
Max	11.1%	11.1%	11.1%	11.1%	11.1%	9.1%	14.3%	14.3%	14.3%	14.3%	15.4%	15.4%
State politicians												
Mean	0.1%	0.1%	0.1%	0.1%	0.2%	0.3%	2.5%	2.7%	2.8%	2.7%	2.7%	2.5%
Median	0.0%	0.0%	0.0%	0.0%	0.0%	0.0%	0.0%	0.0%	0.0%	0.0%	0.0%	0.0%
Std. Dev.	1.1%	1.1%	1.1%	1.0%	1.1%	1.6%	4.3%	4.5%	4.5%	4.5%	4.4%	4.0%
Min	0.0%	0.0%	0.0%	0.0%	0.0%	0.0%	0.0%	0.0%	0.0%	0.0%	0.0%	0.0%
Max	11.1%	11.1%	11.1%	11.1%	11.1%	11.1%	21.4%	21.4%	21.4%	21.4%	23.1%	15.4%
Regional politicians												
Mean	0.0%	0.0%	0.0%	0.0%	0.0%	0.0%	5.4%	5.6%	5.5%	5.4%	5.5%	5.6%
Median	0.0%	0.0%	0.0%	0.0%	0.0%	0.0%	6.3%	6.3%	6.3%	6.1%	6.3%	6.3%
Std. Dev.	0.0%	0.0%	0.0%	0.0%	0.0%	0.0%	4.1%	4.1%	4.1%	4.0%	4.2%	4.1%
Min	0.0%	0.0%	0.0%	0.0%	0.0%	0.0%	0.0%	0.0%	0.0%	0.0%	0.0%	0.0%
Max	0.0%	0.0%	0.0%	0.0%	0.0%	0.0%	20.0%	20.0%	20.0%	20.0%	20.0%	20.0%

	Cooperative banks						Savings banks					
Top 150	**2009**	**2008**	**2007**	**2006**	**2005**	**2004**	**2009**	**2008**	**2007**	**2006**	**2005**	**2004**
Local politicians												
Mean	1.9%	1.8%	1.8%	1.8%	2.0%	1.8%	15.2%	15.9%	15.7%	15.6%	16.1%	16.3%
Median	0.0%	0.0%	0.0%	0.0%	0.0%	0.0%	11.8%	13.3%	13.2%	13.3%	13.3%	13.5%
Std. Dev.	4.8%	4.4%	4.4%	4.3%	4.5%	4.3%	12.7%	12.8%	12.8%	13.0%	13.3%	12.7%
Min	0.0%	0.0%	0.0%	0.0%	0.0%	0.0%	0.0%	0.0%	0.0%	0.0%	0.0%	0.0%
Max	25.0%	25.0%	25.0%	25.0%	25.0%	23.5%	50.0%	54.5%	53.8%	53.8%	66.7%	61.5%

Appendix II.7.5: Officiating and retired politicians (in % of total supervisory board size)

	Cooperative banks						Savings banks					
Top 200	**2009**	**2008**	**2007**	**2006**	**2005**	**2004**	**2009**	**2008**	**2007**	**2006**	**2005**	**2004**
Politicians (total)												
Mean	2.8%	2.7%	2.7%	2.8%	2.8%	3.0%	27.6%	28.6%	28.4%	28.1%	28.3%	27.8%
Median	0.0%	0.0%	0.0%	0.0%	0.0%	0.0%	27.8%	27.8%	27.8%	27.4%	28.6%	26.7%
Std. Dev.	5.5%	5.6%	5.5%	5.3%	5.5%	5.9%	14.9%	15.3%	14.8%	15.3%	15.3%	15.7%
Min	0.0%	0.0%	0.0%	0.0%	0.0%	0.0%	0.0%	0.0%	0.0%	0.0%	0.0%	0.0%
Max	31.3%	31.3%	31.3%	31.3%	33.3%	35.3%	61.5%	75.0%	64.3%	64.3%	62.5%	62.5%

Top 150	**2009**	**2008**	**2007**	**2006**	**2005**	**2004**	**2009**	**2008**	**2007**	**2006**	**2005**	**2004**
Politicians (total)												
Mean	3.0%	3.2%	3.1%	3.3%	3.4%	3.3%	27.8%	29.0%	28.8%	28.8%	28.8%	28.8%
Median	0.0%	0.0%	0.0%	0.0%	0.0%	0.0%	27.8%	27.8%	27.8%	27.8%	29.8%	28.8%
Std. Dev.	6.5%	6.3%	6.2%	6.1%	6.3%	6.6%	15.1%	15.7%	15.2%	15.4%	15.6%	15.5%
Min	0.0%	0.0%	0.0%	0.0%	0.0%	0.0%	0.0%	0.0%	0.0%	0.0%	0.0%	0.0%
Max	33.3%	31.3%	31.3%	31.3%	33.3%	35.3%	69.2%	75.0%	69.2%	69.2%	75.0%	69.2%

Appendix II.7.6: Self-employed and employees with assumed financial expertise (in % of total supervisory board size)

	Cooperative banks						Savings banks					
Top 200	**2009**	**2008**	**2007**	**2006**	**2005**	**2004**	**2009**	**2008**	**2007**	**2006**	**2005**	**2004**
Self-employed individuals with financial expertise												
Mean	19.1%	19.0%	18.4%	18.0%	18.3%	18.8%	6.6%	6.5%	6.7%	6.4%	6.3%	6.2%
Median	15.7%	15.4%	16.7%	16.0%	15.4%	16.7%	5.6%	5.6%	5.6%	5.6%	5.6%	5.6%
Std. Dev.	17.6%	17.7%	17.5%	17.0%	17.2%	17.6%	7.7%	7.3%	7.3%	6.9%	7.2%	7.1%
Min	0.0%	0.0%	0.0%	0.0%	0.0%	0.0%	0.0%	0.0%	0.0%	0.0%	0.0%	0.0%
Max	75.0%	75.0%	71.4%	69.2%	73.3%	83.3%	37.5%	37.5%	33.3%	33.3%	33.3%	33.3%
Employed individuals with financial expertise												
Mean	27.3%	27.5%	26.9%	25.7%	25.0%	24.1%	54.6%	53.1%	52.6%	52.5%	53.1%	52.3%
Median	25.0%	23.9%	23.9%	25.0%	22.2%	21.4%	52.6%	52.4%	50.0%	52.4%	53.3%	52.6%
Std. Dev.	19.6%	20.1%	19.6%	19.3%	19.2%	18.9%	15.8%	16.2%	16.0%	15.9%	15.8%	15.6%
Min	0.0%	0.0%	0.0%	0.0%	0.0%	0.0%	10.0%	9.1%	9.1%	9.1%	9.1%	14.3%
Max	91.7%	100.0%	100.0%	100.0%	100.0%	90.9%	93.8%	93.3%	93.3%	95.8%	93.3%	93.3%
Top 150	**2009**	**2008**	**2007**	**2006**	**2005**	**2004**	**2009**	**2008**	**2007**	**2006**	**2005**	**2004**
Self-employed individuals with financial expertise												
Mean	18.8%	19.1%	18.8%	18.2%	18.3%	18.0%	7.2%	7.1%	7.1%	6.7%	6.6%	6.5%
Median	16.0%	16.7%	16.7%	16.7%	16.0%	16.7%	5.9%	5.9%	5.9%	5.9%	5.6%	5.6%
Std. Dev.	17.5%	17.6%	17.5%	17.2%	17.1%	16.6%	8.3%	7.8%	7.7%	7.3%	7.4%	7.5%
Min	0.0%	0.0%	0.0%	0.0%	0.0%	0.0%	0.0%	0.0%	0.0%	0.0%	0.0%	0.0%
Max	75.0%	75.0%	71.4%	69.2%	77.8%	71.4%	37.5%	37.5%	33.3%	33.3%	33.3%	33.3%
Employed individuals with financial expertise												
Mean	28.7%	27.0%	25.9%	25.0%	24.4%	23.9%	54.3%	52.9%	52.3%	52.4%	53.2%	53.1%
Median	25.0%	22.5%	22.2%	22.2%	21.1%	19.1%	52.9%	51.2%	50.0%	50.0%	53.3%	53.3%
Std. Dev.	21.0%	21.4%	20.6%	20.7%	20.3%	20.1%	15.6%	15.7%	15.6%	15.5%	15.4%	15.6%
Min	0.0%	0.0%	0.0%	0.0%	0.0%	0.0%	10.0%	9.1%	9.1%	9.1%	9.1%	14.3%
Max	87.5%	85.7%	85.7%	85.7%	75.0%	75.0%	93.8%	93.3%	93.3%	95.8%	93.3%	93.3%

Appendix II.7.7: Cross-category groups with assumed financial expertise (in % of total supervisory board size)

	Cooperative banks						Savings banks					
Top 200	**2009**	**2008**	**2007**	**2006**	**2005**	**2004**	**2009**	**2008**	**2007**	**2006**	**2005**	**2004**
Executives / Managing Partners / Partners, Owners												
Mean	34.9%	34.7%	33.8%	32.5%	32.0%	31.9%	12.6%	11.9%	11.6%	11.6%	11.6%	11.6%
Median	33.3%	33.3%	33.3%	30.4%	33.3%	33.3%	11.1%	11.1%	11.1%	11.1%	11.1%	10.6%
Std. Dev.	20.7%	20.9%	21.1%	21.2%	21.0%	21.0%	9.6%	8.7%	8.3%	8.1%	8.3%	8.4%
Min	0.0%	0.0%	0.0%	0.0%	0.0%	0.0%	0.0%	0.0%	0.0%	0.0%	0.0%	0.0%
Max	91.7%	90.9%	92.3%	100.0%	92.3%	92.3%	37.5%	37.5%	35.7%	35.7%	38.5%	38.5%
Accountants / Auditors / Tax consultant												
Mean	7.6%	7.6%	7.3%	6.9%	6.9%	6.8%	1.3%	1.3%	1.3%	1.1%	1.1%	1.1%
Median	6.7%	7.1%	7.1%	6.5%	6.7%	6.9%	0.0%	0.0%	0.0%	0.0%	0.0%	0.0%
Std. Dev.	7.9%	8.0%	7.4%	7.5%	7.4%	7.0%	2.8%	2.7%	2.6%	2.6%	2.6%	2.4%
Min	0.0%	0.0%	0.0%	0.0%	0.0%	0.0%	0.0%	0.0%	0.0%	0.0%	0.0%	0.0%
Max	33.3%	33.3%	33.3%	37.5%	37.5%	40.0%	12.5%	11.1%	11.1%	14.3%	13.3%	11.1%

Top 150	**2009**	**2008**	**2007**	**2006**	**2005**	**2004**	**2009**	**2008**	**2007**	**2006**	**2005**	**2004**
Executives / Managing Partners / Partners, Owners												
Mean	37.5%	36.3%	35.2%	33.9%	33.0%	32.4%	13.1%	12.2%	12.0%	11.9%	11.9%	12.1%
Median	37.5%	33.3%	33.3%	33.3%	33.3%	31.0%	12.5%	12.5%	12.1%	12.5%	11.4%	11.1%
Std. Dev.	23.2%	23.4%	23.1%	23.0%	22.0%	21.3%	10.1%	9.1%	8.8%	8.5%	8.8%	8.8%
Min	0.0%	0.0%	0.0%	0.0%	0.0%	0.0%	0.0%	0.0%	0.0%	0.0%	0.0%	0.0%
Max	100.0%	88.9%	88.9%	90.0%	85.7%	90.0%	37.5%	37.5%	35.7%	35.7%	38.5%	38.5%
Accountants / Auditors / Tax consultant												
Mean	7.8%	7.5%	7.4%	6.9%	7.1%	7.0%	1.5%	1.5%	1.4%	1.3%	1.3%	1.1%
Median	7.7%	7.4%	8.0%	7.1%	7.1%	7.1%	0.0%	0.0%	0.0%	0.0%	0.0%	0.0%
Std. Dev.	8.2%	8.0%	7.6%	7.4%	7.7%	7.3%	3.0%	2.9%	2.8%	2.8%	2.8%	2.5%
Min	0.0%	0.0%	0.0%	0.0%	0.0%	0.0%	0.0%	0.0%	0.0%	0.0%	0.0%	0.0%
Max	33.3%	33.3%	33.3%	33.3%	33.3%	33.3%	12.5%	11.1%	11.1%	14.3%	13.3%	11.1%

Appendix II.7.8: Financial expertise (in % of total supervisory board size) and outside financial expertise (in % of outside supervisory board members)

	Cooperative banks						Savings banks					
Top 200	**2009**	**2008**	**2007**	**2006**	**2005**	**2004**	**2009**	**2008**	**2007**	**2006**	**2005**	**2004**
Financial expertise												
Mean	49.1%	48.9%	48.3%	47.2%	46.8%	46.2%	66.4%	65.4%	64.8%	64.7%	64.7%	63.9%
Median	50.0%	50.0%	50.0%	46.9%	46.7%	46.4%	66.7%	64.2%	63.6%	66.7%	66.7%	66.7%
Std. Dev.	22.3%	23.1%	23.0%	23.4%	22.7%	22.9%	17.4%	17.6%	16.9%	17.4%	17.3%	17.0%
Min	0.0%	0.0%	0.0%	0.0%	0.0%	0.0%	20.0%	20.0%	20.0%	20.0%	23.1%	21.4%
Max	100.0%	100.0%	100.0%	100.0%	100.0%	100.0%	100.0%	100.0%	100.0%	100.0%	100.0%	100.0%
Outside financial expertise												
Mean	46.6%	46.4%	45.9%	44.7%	44.2%	43.6%	54.0%	53.9%	53.2%	52.9%	52.9%	51.9%
Median	48.3%	45.8%	46.2%	44.4%	44.4%	42.9%	55.1%	53.8%	53.8%	51.7%	50.0%	50.0%
Std. Dev.	22.9%	23.5%	23.5%	23.6%	23.0%	23.0%	24.0%	23.2%	22.3%	22.8%	22.8%	22.3%
Min	0.0%	0.0%	0.0%	0.0%	0.0%	0.0%	0.0%	4.8%	4.8%	4.8%	7.1%	0.0%
Max	100.0%	100.0%	100.0%	100.0%	100.0%	100.0%	100.0%	100.0%	100.0%	100.0%	100.0%	100.0%
Top 150	**2009**	**2008**	**2007**	**2006**	**2005**	**2004**	**2009**	**2008**	**2007**	**2006**	**2005**	**2004**
Financial expertise												
Mean	50.1%	48.7%	48.0%	46.9%	46.2%	45.3%	67.0%	65.9%	65.2%	65.1%	64.9%	64.6%
Median	50.0%	50.0%	48.7%	45.3%	45.8%	45.5%	66.7%	66.7%	66.7%	66.7%	66.7%	66.7%
Std. Dev.	22.3%	23.3%	22.9%	23.4%	22.1%	22.4%	17.3%	17.5%	17.0%	17.2%	17.0%	17.4%
Min	0.0%	0.0%	0.0%	0.0%	0.0%	0.0%	20.0%	20.0%	20.0%	20.0%	23.1%	21.4%
Max	100.0%	100.0%	100.0%	100.0%	100.0%	100.0%	100.0%	100.0%	100.0%	100.0%	100.0%	100.0%
Outside financial expertise												
Mean	48.2%	47.0%	46.3%	45.2%	44.5%	43.6%	54.9%	54.7%	53.8%	53.4%	53.2%	53.1%
Median	50.0%	46.2%	45.3%	43.7%	44.4%	44.4%	57.1%	56.3%	54.5%	54.8%	51.9%	53.6%
Std. Dev.	23.6%	24.3%	23.8%	24.2%	22.9%	23.1%	23.9%	23.2%	22.4%	22.9%	22.8%	22.9%
Min	0.0%	0.0%	0.0%	0.0%	0.0%	0.0%	0.0%	0.0%	0.0%	0.0%	0.0%	0.0%
Max	100.0%	100.0%	100.0%	100.0%	100.0%	100.0%	100.0%	100.0%	100.0%	100.0%	100.0%	100.0%

Appendix II.7.9: Financial expertise clustered by bank size (in % of total supervisory board size)

	Cooperative banks						Savings banks					
Top 200	**2009**	**2008**	**2007**	**2006**	**2005**	**2004**	**2009**	**2008**	**2007**	**2006**	**2005**	**2004**
Financial expertise Group 1	n=50; average total assets: EUR 4.55 bn						n=50; average total assets 2009: EUR 7.76 bn					
Mean	55.1%	54.8%	55.5%	55.1%	53.6%	52.6%	64.0%	64.5%	64.6%	64.4%	64.8%	64.1%
Median	55.8%	53.6%	58.3%	55.9%	55.1%	56.3%	65.3%	66.0%	66.7%	66.7%	66.7%	66.7%
Std. Dev.	26.0%	26.3%	25.9%	25.8%	25.1%	25.2%	15.7%	15.1%	15.1%	15.1%	14.5%	14.5%
Min	0.0%	0.0%	0.0%	0.0%	0.0%	0.0%	27.8%	38.1%	38.1%	37.5%	37.0%	38.1%
Max	100.0%	100.0%	100.0%	100.0%	100.0%	100.0%	93.3%	93.3%	93.3%	93.3%	88.2%	93.8%

	Cooperative banks						Savings banks					
Financial expertise Group 2	n=50; average total assets 2009: EUR 1.46 bn						n=50; average total assets 2009: EUR 3.38 bn					
Mean	49.7%	51.2%	50.1%	48.7%	48.9%	48.8%	67.5%	65.3%	64.8%	64.8%	64.3%	63.1%
Median	53.6%	54.2%	50.0%	46.6%	46.6%	48.7%	66.7%	66.7%	66.7%	66.7%	66.7%	65.8%
Std. Dev.	22.9%	23.4%	23.2%	23.1%	22.0%	22.6%	18.5%	19.5%	18.8%	18.9%	18.4%	17.6%
Min	0.0%	0.0%	0.0%	0.0%	0.0%	0.0%	20.0%	20.0%	20.0%	20.0%	27.3%	30.8%
Max	100.0%	100.0%	100.0%	100.0%	100.0%	100.0%	100.0%	100.0%	100.0%	100.0%	96.7%	93.3%
Financial expertise Group 3	n=50; average total assets 2009: EUR 0.99 bn						n=50; average total assets 2009: EUR 2.33 bn					
Mean	48.3%	47.9%	46.4%	43.7%	44.5%	43.6%	66.2%	65.7%	64.8%	64.5%	64.9%	63.4%
Median	50.0%	44.9%	44.4%	44.4%	44.9%	44.9%	61.5%	62.8%	61.8%	64.9%	66.7%	66.7%
Std. Dev.	19.5%	20.5%	20.1%	21.0%	20.6%	19.9%	17.7%	18.2%	16.9%	18.6%	19.1%	19.2%
Min	11.1%	11.1%	0.0%	0.0%	0.0%	0.0%	38.1%	35.7%	35.7%	35.7%	35.7%	21.4%
Max	83.3%	100.0%	88.9%	88.9%	83.3%	83.3%	100.0%	100.0%	96.2%	100.0%	100.0%	100.0%
Financial expertise Group 4	n=50; average total assets 2009: EUR 0.76 bn						n=50; average total assets 2009: EUR 1.70 bn					
Mean	43.4%	41.9%	41.3%	41.1%	40.1%	39.8%	68.0%	66.0%	65.0%	65.1%	64.8%	64.9%
Median	43.3%	40.0%	39.3%	38.0%	38.7%	40.0%	65.7%	62.5%	62.0%	62.5%	62.5%	66.7%
Std. Dev.	19.3%	20.4%	20.5%	21.7%	21.3%	21.9%	17.7%	17.9%	17.1%	17.2%	17.3%	16.8%
Min	12.5%	0.0%	0.0%	0.0%	0.0%	0.0%	23.1%	23.1%	23.1%	23.1%	23.1%	26.7%
Max	90.0%	90.9%	92.3%	92.3%	92.3%	92.3%	100.0%	100.0%	100.0%	94.4%	94.4%	94.4%
Top 150	**2009**	**2008**	**2007**	**2006**	**2005**	**2004**	**2009**	**2008**	**2007**	**2006**	**2005**	**2004**
Financial expertise Group 1	n=50; average total assets 2009: EUR 3.36 bn						n=50; average total assets 2009: EUR 5.53 bn					
Mean	52.0%	52.1%	52.6%	50.7%	50.7%	51.1%	67.4%	66.5%	65.9%	65.9%	66.4%	65.7%
Median	55.1%	55.1%	55.6%	54.5%	54.2%	55.6%	71.8%	70.2%	69.9%	67.5%	66.7%	66.7%
Std. Dev.	25.5%	26.3%	25.7%	25.4%	25.2%	26.2%	16.0%	16.6%	16.5%	15.9%	15.4%	15.6%
Min	0.0%	0.0%	0.0%	0.0%	0.0%	0.0%	28.6%	28.6%	28.6%	28.6%	28.6%	30.8%
Max	100.0%	100.0%	100.0%	100.0%	100.0%	100.0%	100.0%	100.0%	100.0%	100.0%	93.3%	93.8%
Financial expertise Group 2	n=50; average total assets 2009: EUR 0.80 bn						n=50; average total assets 2009: EUR 2.54 bn					
Mean	49.6%	48.6%	46.8%	46.8%	47.1%	45.5%	66.5%	65.6%	65.2%	64.6%	64.3%	64.6%
Median	50.0%	46.2%	43.7%	43.7%	48.3%	45.6%	64.8%	61.7%	62.1%	64.9%	62.4%	66.7%
Std. Dev.	18.6%	20.4%	20.0%	21.3%	20.0%	19.5%	18.0%	18.2%	17.3%	18.7%	18.6%	18.9%
Min	16.7%	0.0%	0.0%	0.0%	0.0%	0.0%	20.0%	20.0%	20.0%	20.0%	30.0%	21.4%
Max	85.7%	100.0%	88.9%	88.9%	85.7%	85.7%	100.0%	100.0%	96.2%	100.0%	100.0%	100.0%
Financial expertise Group 3	n=50; average total assets 2009: EUR 0.57 bn						n=50; average total assets 2009: EUR 1.62 bn					
Mean	48.7%	45.5%	44.6%	43.1%	40.8%	39.4%	67.0%	65.7%	64.5%	64.6%	64.1%	63.6%
Median	48.3%	44.4%	40.0%	40.0%	37.2%	36.0%	66.7%	65.7%	62.5%	62.5%	62.5%	65.7%
Std. Dev.	22.5%	22.9%	22.3%	23.2%	20.1%	19.8%	18.2%	18.0%	17.4%	17.3%	17.3%	17.7%
Min	0.0%	0.0%	0.0%	0.0%	0.0%	0.0%	23.1%	23.1%	23.1%	23.1%	23.1%	26.7%
Max	100.0%	88.9%	88.9%	90.0%	83.3%	88.9%	100.0%	100.0%	100.0%	94.4%	94.4%	94.4%

Appendix II.7.10: Outside financial expertise clustered by bank size (in % of outside supervisory board members)

	Cooperative banks						Savings banks					
Top 200	**2009**	**2008**	**2007**	**2006**	**2005**	**2004**	**2009**	**2008**	**2007**	**2006**	**2005**	**2004**
Out. financial expertise Group 1	n=50; average total assets: EUR 4.55 bn						n=50; average total assets 2009: EUR 7.76 bn					
Mean	47.3%	47.0%	48.2%	47.5%	45.8%	44.6%	48.1%	48.5%	48.7%	48.5%	49.0%	48.4%
Median	50.0%	50.0%	51.7%	52.3%	47.2%	44.2%	53.6%	50.9%	51.3%	50.0%	50.0%	50.0%
Std. Dev.	28.2%	27.8%	28.2%	27.5%	26.8%	25.8%	23.0%	22.3%	22.6%	22.2%	21.4%	20.5%
Min	0.0%	0.0%	0.0%	0.0%	0.0%	0.0%	0.0%	4.8%	4.8%	4.8%	7.1%	11.1%
Max	100.0%	100.0%	100.0%	100.0%	100.0%	100.0%	90.0%	90.0%	90.0%	90.0%	81.8%	90.0%
Out. financial expertise Group 2	n=50; average total assets 2009: EUR 1.46 bn						n=50; average total assets 2009: EUR 3.38 bn					
Mean	48.1%	49.5%	48.3%	47.0%	47.2%	47.1%	57.5%	56.8%	56.1%	56.0%	55.3%	53.5%
Median	50.0%	51.9%	50.0%	46.6%	46.6%	45.9%	60.0%	58.3%	58.7%	56.9%	56.7%	50.0%
Std. Dev.	22.8%	23.4%	23.0%	22.9%	21.8%	23.1%	23.0%	22.5%	21.7%	21.8%	21.7%	21.4%
Min	0.0%	0.0%	0.0%	0.0%	0.0%	0.0%	13.3%	12.5%	12.5%	12.5%	12.5%	4.2%
Max	100.0%	100.0%	100.0%	100.0%	100.0%	100.0%	100.0%	100.0%	100.0%	100.0%	95.0%	90.0%
Out. financial expertise Group 3	n=50; average total assets 2009: EUR 0.99 bn						n=50; average total assets 2009: EUR 2.33 bn					
Mean	47.7%	47.3%	45.8%	43.1%	43.8%	42.9%	53.6%	54.5%	53.5%	52.8%	53.3%	51.3%
Median	50.0%	44.9%	44.4%	44.4%	44.9%	44.9%	52.3%	56.4%	56.1%	50.0%	57.7%	50.0%
Std. Dev.	20.5%	21.7%	21.3%	22.1%	21.7%	21.0%	25.5%	24.5%	22.9%	25.1%	25.7%	25.6%
Min	0.0%	0.0%	0.0%	0.0%	0.0%	0.0%	7.1%	7.1%	7.1%	7.7%	7.1%	7.1%
Max	83.3%	100.0%	88.9%	88.9%	83.3%	83.3%	100.0%	100.0%	94.1%	100.0%	100.0%	100.0%
Out. financial expertise Group 4	n=50; average total assets 2009: EUR 0.76 bn						n=50; average total assets 2009: EUR 1.70 bn					
Mean	43.4%	41.9%	41.3%	41.1%	40.1%	39.8%	56.8%	55.7%	54.7%	54.5%	54.2%	54.5%
Median	43.3%	40.0%	39.3%	38.0%	38.7%	40.0%	51.9%	51.5%	50.0%	50.0%	50.0%	54.5%
Std. Dev.	19.3%	20.4%	20.5%	21.7%	21.3%	21.9%	24.1%	23.0%	21.7%	22.0%	22.2%	21.5%
Min	12.5%	0.0%	0.0%	0.0%	0.0%	0.0%	8.3%	8.3%	8.3%	8.3%	8.3%	0.0%
Max	90.0%	90.9%	92.3%	92.3%	92.3%	92.3%	100.0%	100.0%	100.0%	91.7%	91.7%	91.7%
Top 150	**2009**	**2008**	**2007**	**2006**	**2005**	**2004**	**2009**	**2008**	**2007**	**2006**	**2005**	**2004**
Out. financial expertise Group 1	n=50; average total assets 2009: EUR 3.36 bn						n=50; average total assets 2009: EUR 5.53 bn					
Mean	47.6%	47.5%	48.0%	46.0%	45.9%	46.4%	55.3%	54.9%	54.1%	54.1%	54.6%	54.0%
Median	53.6%	53.8%	54.7%	54.5%	51.9%	54.2%	60.0%	59.4%	59.4%	59.2%	59.2%	58.3%
Std. Dev.	27.8%	28.7%	28.1%	27.5%	27.4%	28.3%	22.0%	22.1%	22.0%	21.3%	20.2%	20.2%
Min	0.0%	0.0%	0.0%	0.0%	0.0%	0.0%	10.0%	10.0%	10.0%	10.0%	18.8%	11.1%
Max	100.0%	100.0%	100.0%	100.0%	100.0%	100.0%	100.0%	100.0%	100.0%	100.0%	90.0%	90.0%

	Cooperative banks						Savings banks					
Top 150	**2009**	**2008**	**2007**	**2006**	**2005**	**2004**	**2009**	**2008**	**2007**	**2006**	**2005**	**2004**
Out. financial expertise Group 2	n=50; average total assets 2009: EUR 0.80 bn						n=50; average total assets 2009: EUR 2.54 bn					
Mean	49.3%	48.2%	46.5%	46.5%	46.8%	45.2%	55.0%	54.8%	54.2%	53.5%	52.9%	53.6%
Median	50.0%	46.2%	43.7%	43.7%	48.3%	45.6%	54.2%	53.8%	53.8%	53.8%	51.9%	50.0%
Std. Dev.	19.4%	21.1%	20.7%	21.9%	20.6%	20.1%	24.5%	24.0%	23.0%	24.7%	25.0%	24.8%
Min	0.0%	0.0%	0.0%	0.0%	0.0%	0.0%	7.1%	7.1%	7.1%	7.7%	7.1%	7.1%
Max	85.7%	100.0%	88.9%	88.9%	85.7%	85.7%	100.0%	100.0%	94.1%	100.0%	100.0%	100.0%
Out. financial expertise Group 3	n=50; average total assets 2009: EUR 0.57 bn						n=50; average total assets 2009: EUR 1.62 bn					
Mean	47.8%	45.4%	44.5%	43.0%	40.7%	39.3%	54.4%	54.3%	53.0%	52.7%	52.0%	51.7%
Median	45.3%	44.4%	40.0%	40.0%	37.2%	36.0%	50.0%	51.5%	50.0%	50.0%	50.0%	52.3%
Std. Dev.	23.3%	22.8%	22.3%	23.2%	20.0%	19.7%	25.5%	23.8%	22.8%	23.0%	23.2%	23.9%
Min	0.0%	0.0%	0.0%	0.0%	0.0%	0.0%	0.0%	0.0%	0.0%	0.0%	0.0%	0.0%
Max	100.0%	88.9%	88.9%	90.0%	83.3%	88.9%	100.0%	100.0%	100.0%	91.7%	91.7%	91.7%

Appendix II.7.11: Financial expertise clustered by supervisory board size (in % of total supervisory board size)

	Cooperative banks						Savings banks					
Top 200	**2009**	**2008**	**2007**	**2006**	**2005**	**2004**	**2009**	**2008**	**2007**	**2006**	**2005**	**2004**
Financial expertise Group 1	n=50; average board size: 18 members						n=50; average board size: 23 members					
Mean	50.9%	51.0%	50.7%	49.9%	48.8%	48.0%	63.9%	64.9%	65.4%	64.9%	64.5%	63.5%
Median	53.3%	51.7%	50.0%	50.0%	50.0%	48.7%	61.9%	64.2%	63.6%	64.3%	66.7%	65.0%
Std. Dev.	22.7%	22.9%	21.9%	22.3%	21.5%	21.4%	17.9%	17.4%	17.3%	17.1%	17.0%	16.4%
Min	5.3%	5.3%	4.5%	0.0%	0.0%	0.0%	27.8%	38.1%	38.1%	37.5%	37.0%	36.1%
Max	93.8%	94.1%	92.6%	92.6%	86.7%	86.7%	100.0%	100.0%	100.0%	100.0%	96.7%	93.3%
Financial expertise Group 2	n=50; average board size: 13 members						n=50; average board size: 17 members					
Mean	48.5%	47.1%	46.1%	44.6%	44.4%	43.8%	67.0%	66.0%	66.3%	65.3%	65.0%	62.9%
Median	45.5%	45.5%	41.7%	40.1%	35.7%	40.0%	63.9%	61.8%	62.5%	62.5%	61.8%	63.4%
Std. Dev.	22.6%	23.7%	23.8%	24.0%	23.8%	24.3%	14.9%	15.3%	15.1%	15.8%	16.1%	16.6%
Min	16.7%	0.0%	0.0%	0.0%	0.0%	0.0%	46.7%	31.3%	33.3%	38.1%	37.5%	35.0%
Max	100.0%	100.0%	100.0%	100.0%	100.0%	100.0%	100.0%	100.0%	100.0%	94.4%	94.4%	94.4%
Financial expertise Group 3	n=50; average board size: 11 members						n=50; average board size: 15 members					
Mean	50.3%	51.6%	51.8%	50.8%	49.8%	51.2%	65.6%	64.6%	63.6%	63.7%	63.8%	63.8%
Median	50.0%	52.3%	55.6%	50.0%	50.0%	50.0%	64.3%	63.3%	66.7%	66.7%	66.7%	66.7%
Std. Dev.	18.5%	20.4%	20.0%	21.0%	18.6%	18.9%	16.8%	17.9%	17.2%	17.8%	17.7%	17.9%
Min	11.1%	10.0%	11.1%	11.1%	11.1%	20.0%	40.0%	35.7%	28.6%	28.6%	28.6%	21.4%
Max	100.0%	100.0%	100.0%	100.0%	100.0%	91.7%	100.0%	100.0%	93.3%	100.0%	93.3%	93.8%

	Cooperative banks						Savings banks					
Top 200	**2009**	**2008**	**2007**	**2006**	**2005**	**2004**	**2009**	**2008**	**2007**	**2006**	**2005**	**2004**
Financial expertise Group 4	n=50; average board size: 8 members						n=50; average board size: 12 members					
Mean	46.7%	46.1%	44.8%	43.3%	44.1%	41.9%	69.1%	65.9%	64.0%	64.9%	65.5%	65.3%
Median	50.0%	47.2%	44.4%	43.7%	44.4%	44.4%	71.4%	66.7%	66.7%	66.7%	66.7%	66.7%
Std. Dev.	25.4%	25.3%	25.7%	25.9%	26.2%	25.7%	19.8%	20.1%	18.3%	19.1%	18.8%	17.5%
Min	0.0%	0.0%	0.0%	0.0%	0.0%	0.0%	20.0%	20.0%	20.0%	20.0%	23.1%	30.8%
Max	100.0%	100.0%	100.0%	100.0%	100.0%	100.0%	100.0%	100.0%	92.9%	93.3%	100.0%	100.0%

Top 150	2009	2008	2007	2006	2005	2004	2009	2008	2007	2006	2005	2004
Financial expertise Group 1	n=50; average board size: 15 members						n=50; average board size: 20 members					
Mean	48.5%	46.3%	45.6%	44.4%	44.1%	43.6%	68.2%	68.2%	68.7%	67.8%	67.1%	65.6%
Median	46.2%	46.2%	46.2%	44.5%	44.5%	45.6%	66.0%	65.0%	69.9%	68.7%	68.4%	67.4%
Std. Dev.	22.1%	23.5%	22.9%	23.2%	22.6%	22.7%	16.0%	16.3%	16.2%	16.3%	16.3%	16.6%
Min	11.8%	0.0%	0.0%	0.0%	0.0%	0.0%	38.1%	38.1%	38.1%	38.1%	38.1%	38.1%
Max	100.0%	100.0%	100.0%	100.0%	100.0%	100.0%	100.0%	100.0%	100.0%	100.0%	94.4%	94.4%
Financial expertise Group 2	n=50; average board size: 10 members						n=50; average board size: 15 members					
Mean	48.4%	49.0%	48.1%	48.1%	46.7%	45.9%	62.6%	61.6%	60.7%	60.6%	61.0%	60.9%
Median	50.0%	49.7%	47.2%	44.4%	44.9%	45.5%	60.0%	60.0%	60.0%	60.0%	60.0%	60.0%
Std. Dev.	18.4%	20.1%	18.9%	19.1%	18.5%	20.3%	15.7%	16.4%	16.1%	15.8%	15.7%	17.4%
Min	0.0%	0.0%	0.0%	0.0%	0.0%	0.0%	33.3%	33.3%	28.6%	28.6%	28.6%	21.4%
Max	88.9%	100.0%	88.9%	90.0%	83.3%	91.7%	100.0%	100.0%	93.3%	93.3%	93.8%	93.8%
Financial expertise Group 3	n=50; average board size: 8 members						n=50; average board size: 12 members					
Mean	53.4%	50.8%	50.3%	48.1%	47.8%	46.5%	70.2%	67.9%	66.2%	66.7%	66.7%	67.5%
Median	52.8%	50.0%	50.0%	50.0%	50.0%	47.7%	74.2%	73.0%	67.9%	69.2%	67.9%	69.6%
Std. Dev.	25.8%	26.2%	26.5%	27.4%	25.1%	24.4%	19.4%	19.2%	18.0%	18.9%	18.6%	17.7%
Min	0.0%	0.0%	0.0%	0.0%	0.0%	0.0%	20.0%	20.0%	20.0%	20.0%	23.1%	30.8%
Max	100.0%	100.0%	100.0%	100.0%	100.0%	100.0%	100.0%	100.0%	92.9%	100.0%	100.0%	100.0%

Appendix II.7.12: Outside financial expertise clustered by supervisory board size (in % of outside supervisory board members)

	Cooperative banks						Savings banks					
Top 200	**2009**	**2008**	**2007**	**2006**	**2005**	**2004**	**2009**	**2008**	**2007**	**2006**	**2005**	**2004**
Out. financial expertise Group 1	n=50; average board size: 18 members						n=50; average board size: 23 members					
Mean	44.3%	44.4%	44.6%	43.7%	42.4%	41.6%	49.7%	50.7%	51.3%	50.5%	50.2%	48.8%
Median	46.4%	46.1%	48.3%	48.3%	43.7%	39.6%	52.8%	50.0%	51.3%	52.5%	50.0%	46.9%
Std. Dev.	23.4%	23.0%	22.3%	22.1%	21.9%	21.3%	25.9%	25.7%	25.6%	25.1%	24.7%	23.4%
Min	0.0%	0.0%	0.0%	0.0%	0.0%	0.0%	0.0%	4.8%	4.8%	4.8%	7.1%	4.2%
Max	87.5%	88.9%	88.9%	88.9%	80.0%	85.7%	100.0%	100.0%	100.0%	100.0%	95.0%	90.0%
Out. financial expertise Group 2	n=50; average board size: 13 members						n=50; average board size: 17 members					
Mean	47.3%	46.0%	44.9%	43.4%	43.2%	42.2%	53.4%	53.5%	53.8%	52.2%	51.9%	49.4%
Median	45.5%	45.5%	41.7%	40.1%	35.7%	40.0%	50.0%	50.0%	50.0%	50.0%	50.0%	50.0%
Std. Dev.	22.0%	23.0%	23.3%	23.1%	22.8%	23.6%	20.9%	20.1%	20.3%	21.3%	21.4%	21.5%
Min	9.1%	0.0%	0.0%	0.0%	0.0%	0.0%	20.0%	20.0%	20.0%	18.8%	18.2%	11.1%
Max	100.0%	100.0%	100.0%	100.0%	100.0%	100.0%	100.0%	100.0%	100.0%	91.7%	91.7%	91.7%
Out. financial expertise Group 3	n=50; average board size: 11 members						n=50; average board size: 15 members					
Mean	49.3%	50.4%	50.5%	49.5%	48.4%	50.1%	49.5%	49.8%	48.4%	48.6%	48.7%	49.1%
Median	50.0%	50.0%	55.6%	50.0%	50.0%	50.0%	50.0%	50.0%	50.0%	50.0%	50.0%	50.0%
Std. Dev.	19.4%	21.1%	20.8%	21.8%	19.2%	18.8%	25.0%	24.6%	23.5%	24.3%	24.3%	24.1%
Min	0.0%	0.0%	0.0%	0.0%	11.1%	20.0%	10.0%	10.0%	10.0%	10.0%	10.0%	0.0%
Max	100.0%	100.0%	100.0%	100.0%	100.0%	90.0%	100.0%	100.0%	90.0%	100.0%	90.0%	90.0%
Out. financial expertise Group 4	n=50; average board size: 8 members						n=50; average board size: 12 members					
Mean	45.6%	44.9%	43.6%	42.1%	42.9%	40.7%	63.3%	61.5%	59.3%	60.5%	61.0%	60.5%
Median	50.0%	47.2%	44.4%	42.9%	44.4%	44.4%	64.6%	62.5%	61.3%	62.5%	62.5%	61.3%
Std. Dev.	26.5%	26.8%	27.0%	27.2%	27.6%	27.1%	22.0%	20.5%	18.0%	18.8%	18.9%	18.0%
Min	0.0%	0.0%	0.0%	0.0%	0.0%	0.0%	20.0%	20.0%	20.0%	20.0%	23.1%	30.8%
Max	100.0%	100.0%	100.0%	100.0%	100.0%	100.0%	100.0%	100.0%	90.0%	90.0%	100.0%	100.0%

Top 150	**2009**	**2008**	**2007**	**2006**	**2005**	**2004**	**2009**	**2008**	**2007**	**2006**	**2005**	**2004**
Out. financial expertise Group 1	n=50; average board size: 15 members						n=50; average board size: 20 members					
Mean	45.0%	43.2%	42.7%	41.5%	41.0%	40.3%	57.1%	57.7%	58.3%	56.7%	55.7%	53.7%
Median	45.3%	43.7%	40.8%	37.1%	36.3%	37.9%	58.3%	58.6%	59.0%	59.2%	58.3%	56.9%
Std. Dev.	24.0%	24.4%	23.5%	23.5%	23.0%	23.1%	21.7%	21.9%	22.0%	22.3%	22.0%	22.4%
Min	0.0%	0.0%	0.0%	0.0%	0.0%	0.0%	7.1%	7.1%	7.1%	7.7%	7.1%	7.1%
Max	100.0%	100.0%	100.0%	100.0%	100.0%	100.0%	100.0%	100.0%	100.0%	100.0%	91.7%	91.7%

Top 150	Cooperative banks 2009	2008	2007	2006	2005	2004	Savings banks 2009	2008	2007	2006	2005	2004
Out. financial expertise Group 2	n=50; average board size: 10 members						n=50; average board size: 15 members					
Mean	47.3%	47.8%	46.8%	46.9%	45.4%	45.0%	45.0%	44.8%	43.6%	43.5%	43.7%	44.6%
Median	50.0%	45.5%	44.4%	43.1%	44.4%	44.9%	41.4%	40.0%	40.0%	40.0%	40.0%	40.0%
Std. Dev.	19.1%	20.6%	19.6%	19.9%	19.1%	20.5%	23.7%	23.4%	22.6%	22.4%	22.5%	23.4%
Min	0.0%	0.0%	0.0%	0.0%	0.0%	0.0%	0.0%	0.0%	0.0%	0.0%	0.0%	0.0%
Max	88.9%	100.0%	88.9%	90.0%	83.3%	90.0%	100.0%	100.0%	90.0%	90.0%	90.9%	90.9%
Out. financial expertise Group 3	n=50; average board size: 8 members						n=50; average board size: 12 members					
Mean	52.4%	50.0%	49.5%	47.2%	47.0%	45.6%	62.6%	61.4%	59.3%	60.1%	60.0%	60.9%
Median	52.8%	50.0%	50.0%	50.0%	50.0%	47.7%	66.7%	62.5%	62.5%	62.5%	61.3%	62.5%
Std. Dev.	26.8%	27.4%	27.7%	28.5%	26.2%	25.5%	23.3%	21.2%	19.4%	20.8%	21.0%	20.2%
Min	0.0%	0.0%	0.0%	0.0%	0.0%	0.0%	12.5%	18.2%	18.2%	18.2%	10.0%	10.0%
Max	100.0%	100.0%	100.0%	100.0%	100.0%	100.0%	100.0%	100.0%	90.0%	100.0%	100.0%	100.0%

Appendix II.7.13: T-Test, comparison of mean values financial expertise and outside financial expertise between cooperative and savings banks over time

	Top 200						Top 150					
Financial expertise	**2009**	**2008**	**2007**	**2006**	**2005**	**2004**	**2009**	**2008**	**2007**	**2006**	**2005**	**2004**
Levene Test												
F	10.779	11.403	16.480	15.184	11.478	13.314	6.098	10.275	12.447	12.129	8.568	7.211
Significance	0.001	0.001	0.000	0.000	0.001	0.000	0.014	0.001	0.000	0.001	0.004	0.008
T Test												
T	−8.647	−7.994	−8.172	−8.511	−8.878	−8.756	−7.333	−7.213	−7.379	−7.671	−8.218	−8.350
df (equal variances)	398.000	398.000	398.000	398.000	398.000	398.000	298.000	298.000	298.000	298.000	298.000	298.000
Significance (two-sided)	0.000	0.000	0.000	0.000	0.000	0.000	0.000	0.000	0.000	0.000	0.000	0.000
df (different variances)	375.457	372.071	365.902	367.051	372.019	367.706	280.996	276.454	274.737	273.989	279.669	280.460
Significance (two-sided)	0.000	0.000	0.000	0.000	0.000	0.000	0.000	0.000	0.000	0.000	0.000	0.000

Outside financial expertise	**2009**	**2008**	**2007**	**2006**	**2005**	**2004**	**2009**	**2008**	**2007**	**2006**	**2005**	**2004**
Levene Test												
F	2.411	0.431	0.031	0.012	0.296	0.003	0.674	0.011	0.153	0.068	0.147	0.121
Significance	0.121	0.512	0.860	0.912	0.587	0.954	0.412	0.916	0.696	0.794	0.701	0.728
T Test							−2.434	−2.784				
T	−3.141	−3.201	−3.208	−3.559	−3.797	−3.670	298.000	298.000	−2.786	−3.035	−3.301	−3.555
df (equal variances)	398.000	398.000	398.000	398.000	398.000	398.000	0.016	0.006	298.000	298.000	298.000	298.000
Significance (two-sided)	0.002	0.001	0.001	0.000	0.000	0.000	297.948	297.315	0.006	0.003	0.001	0.000
df (different variances)	397.051	397.925	396.910	397.500	397.960	397.603	0.016	0.006	296.938	297.062	297.981	297.977
Significance (two-sided)	0.002	0.001	0.001	0.000	0.000	0.000			0.006	0.003	0.001	0.000

Confidence level: 95%

Appendix II.7.14: T-Test, comparison of mean values of financial expertise and outside financial expertise of banks clustered by bank size

		Cluster 1 vs. 2	Cluster 1 vs. 3	Cluster 1 vs. 4	Cluster 2 vs. 3	Cluster 2 vs. 4	Cluster 3 vs. 4
		t *(p-value)*	t *(p-value)*	t *(p-value)*	t *(p-value)*	t *(p-value)*	t *(p-value)*
Top 200							
Financial expertise	Cooperative banks	2.9376*** *0.0036*	4.4992*** *0.0000*	7.2798*** *0.0000*	2.0716** *0.0392*	4.3519*** *0.0000*	2.8218*** *0.0051*
	Savings banks	−0.3936 *0.6942*	−0.3804 *0.7039*	−0.8960 *0.3710*	0.0368 *0.9707*	−0.4398 *0.6604*	−0.5178 *0.6050*
Outside financial expertise	Cooperative banks	−0.6284 *0.5302*	0.8173 *0.4144*	2.8828*** *0.0042*	1.4697 *0.1427*	3.4688*** *0.0006*	2.2880** *0.0228*
	Savings banks	-3.9633*** *0.0001*	-2.5484** *0.0113*	-3.6695*** *0.0003*	1.2928 *0.1971*	0.4462 *0.6558*	-1.0215 *0.3078*
Top 150							
Financial expertise	Cooperative banks	−0.4722 *0.6371*	0.6365 *0.5249*	n/a	1.1141 *0.2662*	n/a	n/a
	Savings banks	4.8476*** *0.0000*	0.0543 *0.9568*	n/a	-4.4112*** *0.0000*	n/a	n/a
Outside financial expertise	Cooperative banks	-1.4641 *0.1442*	−0.3112 *0.7558*	n/a	0.8978 *0.3700*	n/a	n/a
	Savings banks	6.6849*** *0.0000*	-2.4480** *0.0149*	n/a	-8.8421*** *0.0000*	n/a	n/a

Confidence level: 95%
* indicates significance at the 10% level, ** at the 5% level, and *** at the 1% level, respectively.

Appendix II.7.15: T-Test, comparison of mean values of financial expertise and outside financial expertise of of banks clustered by board size

		Cluster 1 vs. 2	Cluster 1 vs. 3	Cluster 1 vs. 4	Cluster 2 vs. 3	Cluster 2 vs. 4	Cluster 3 vs. 4
		t *(p-value)*	t *(p-value)*	t *(p-value)*	t *(p-value)*	t *(p-value)*	t *(p-value)*
Top 200							
Financial expertise	Cooperative banks	1.2460 *0.2137*	0.6197 *0.5359*	2.7528*** *0.0063*	-0.6146 *0.5393*	1.6805* *0.0939*	2.6308*** *0.0090*
	Savings banks	-0.7156 *0.4748*	0.2279 *0.8199*	-0.8805 *0.3793*	0.9676 *0.3340*	-0.2703 *0.7871*	-1.1494 *0.2513*
Outside financial expertise	Cooperative banks	-1.8542* *0.0647*	-2.4440** *0.0151*	0.1402 *0.8886*	-0.4633 *0.6435*	1.6973* *0.0907*	2.3797** *0.0180*
	Savings banks	-1.2232 *0.2222*	0.6015 *0.5479*	-6.1808*** *0.0000*	2.0529** *0.0410*	-4.9134*** *0.0000*	-7.0605*** *0.0000*
Top 150							
Financial expertise	Cooperative banks	-0.4722 *0.6371*	0.6365 *0.5249*	n/a	1.1141 *0.2662*	n/a	n/a
	Savings banks	4.8476*** *0.0000*	0.0543 *0.9568*	n/a	-4.4112*** *0.0000*	n/a	n/a
Outside financial expertise	Cooperative banks	-1.4641 *0.1442*	-0.3112 *0.7558*	n/a	0.8978 *0.3700*	n/a	n/a
	Savings banks	6.6849*** *0.0000*	-2.4480** *0.0149*	n/a	-8.8421*** *0.0000*	n/a	n/a

Confidence level: 95%
* indicates significance at the 10% level, ** at the 5% level, and *** at the 1% level, respectively.

Appendix II.7.16: Distribution average (outside) financial expertise per sector, Top 200 banks

Financial expertise	**Cooperative banks (Top 200)**	**Savings banks (Top 200)**

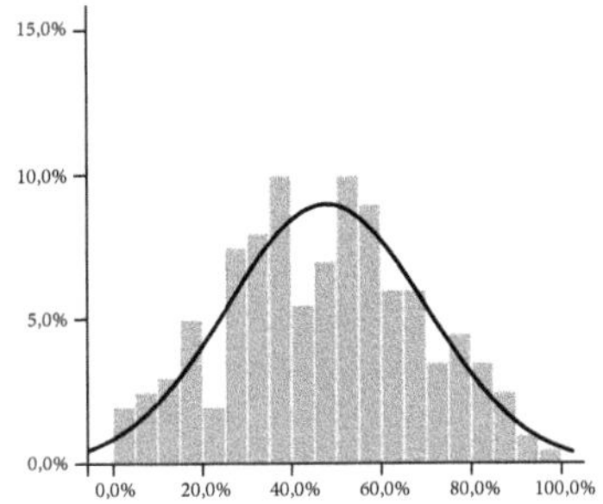

Skewness	0.0744
Stand error Skewness	0.1719
Kurtosis	–0.4595
Standard error Kurtosis	0.3422

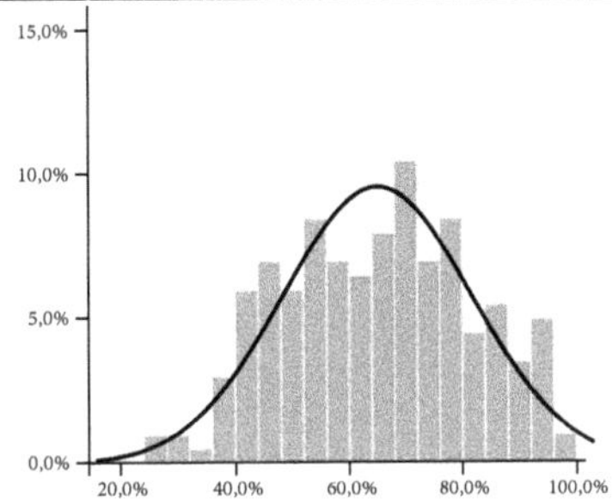

Skewness	–0.0358
Stand error Skewness	0.1719
Kurtosis	–0.7485
Standard error Kurtosis	0.3422

Outside financial expertise

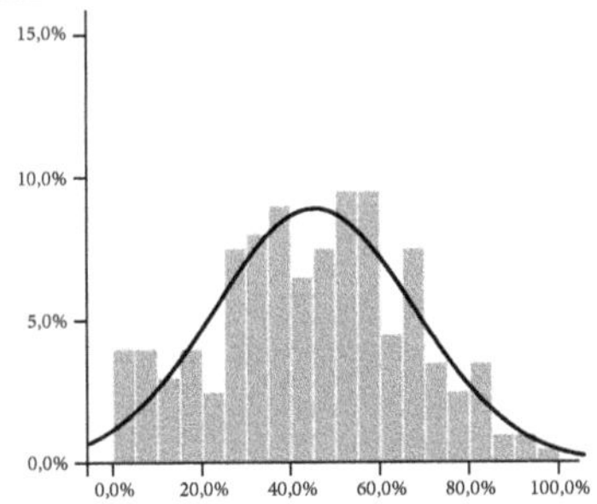

Skewness	0.0009
Stand error Skewness	0.1719
Kurtosis	–0.4034
Standard error Kurtosis	0.3422

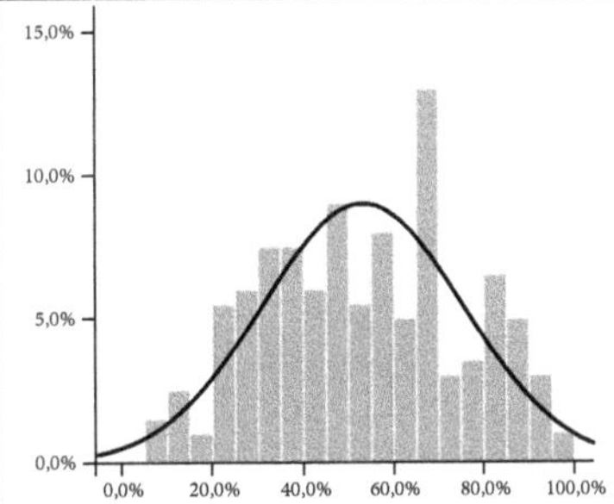

Skewness	–0.0232
Stand error Skewness	0.1719
Kurtosis	–0.8678
Standard error Kurtosis	0.3422

Appendix II.7.17: Distribution average (outside) financial expertise per sector, Top 150 banks

Financial expertise

Cooperative banks (Top 150)

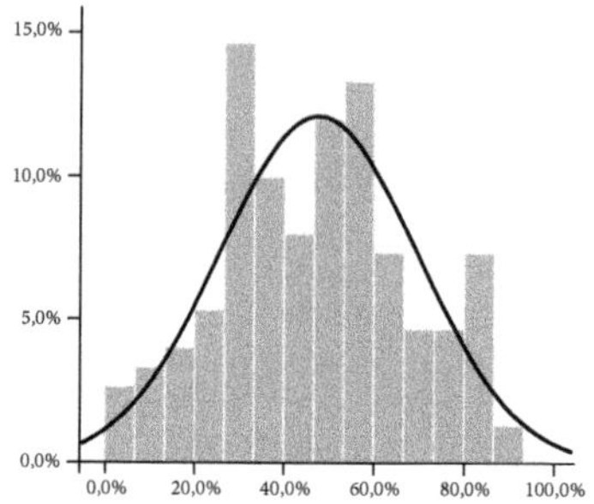

Skewness	0.0979
Stand error Skewness	0.1980
Kurtosis	–0.4022
Standard error Kurtosis	0.3936

Savings banks (Top 150)

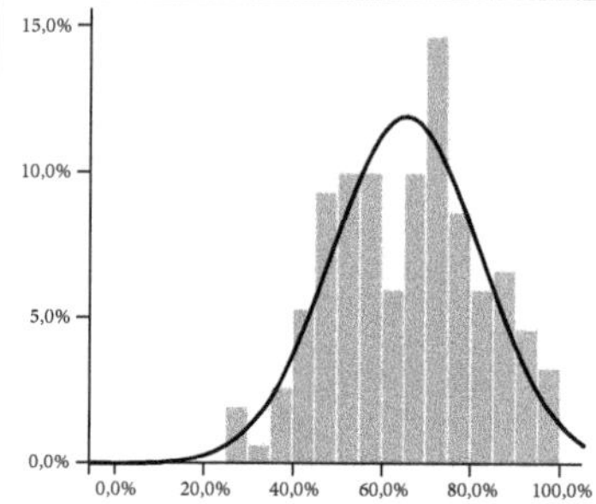

Skewness	–0.0852
Stand error Skewness	0.1980
Kurtosis	–0.6285
Standard error Kurtosis	0.3936

Outside financial expertise

Cooperative banks (Top 150)

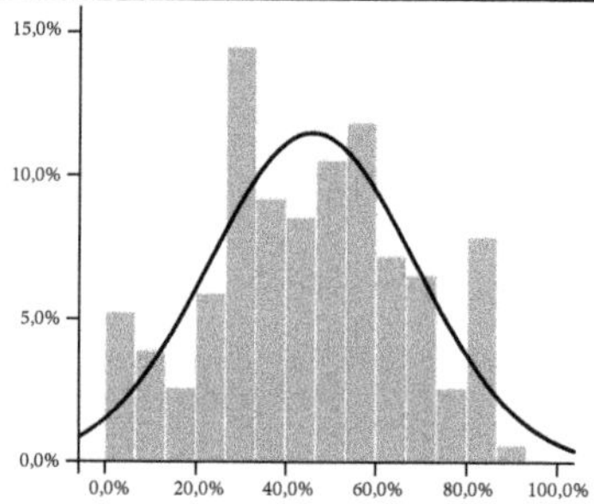

Skewness	0.0259
Stand error Skewness	0.1980
Kurtosis	–0.4375
Standard error Kurtosis	0.3936

Savings banks (Top 150)

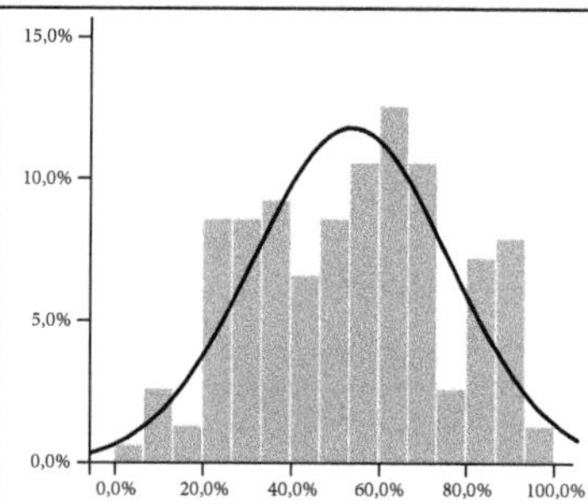

Skewness	–0.0770
Stand error Skewness	0.1980
Kurtosis	–0.8150
Standard error Kurtosis	0.3936

III Impact of Supervisory Board Members' Professional Background on Regional Banks' Risk-Taking

Abstract This paper examines the impact of financial expertise of supervisory board members on the risk-return profile of German regional banks. The data indicate that with more financial expertise bank performance declines and risk goes up. These results induce concerns that mandating financial expertise on boards is not beneficial for the risk-return profile of regional banks. This may suggest that the overconfidence of entrepreneurs leads to this unfavorable development since they represent the largest fraction of professionals within our sample.

III.1 Introduction

European banking markets became increasingly integrated and more competitive subsequent the implications of deregulation and innovation in the financial markets over the two decades prior to the credit crisis that started in late 2007. Consequently banks have expanded, changed, and discarded various business models in recent years due to shifts between regulation and deregulation, macroeconomic and political trends, industry competition, changing customer demands as well as domestic, foreign, and state ownership (A. N. Berger, Clarke, Cull, Klapper, and Udell, 2005; e.g., Dermine, 2003; DeYoung, Hunter, and Udell, 2004; Goddard, Molyneux, Wilson, and Tavakoli, 2007). On the back of this evidence bank managers have constantly adjusted their banks' risk-return profile through policies with respect to financing, investment, organization, and stock returns and merger decisions (R. Adams, Almeida, and Ferreira, 2005; Bertrand and Schoar, 2003; Malmendier and Tate, 2005; Manove and Padilla, 1999). So far, theoretical evidence has not provided a clear picture concerning the ultimately optimal business model, and the in 2007 starting banking crisis has proved that not all business models and their risk-return profiles are equally feasible and sustainable (Altunbas, Manganelli, and Marques-Ibanez, 2011; Demirgüç-Kunt and Huizinga, 2010; Diamond, 1991; Giammarino, Lewis, and Sappington, 1993; R. G. Rajan, 1992; Santos, 2001; Stein, 2002).

Financial institutions exert a powerful influence on economic development, poverty alleviation, and economic stability since they either expand economic opportunities, and foster growth in case of efficient resources allocation or tend to hinder economic growth, curtail economic opportunities, and destabilize economies if the financial system performs poorly (Cihak, Demirguc-Kunt, Feyen, and Levine, 2012; Levine, 2006). Consequently, healthy risk-return profiles are not only important for the stability and profitability of individual banks, but also for the whole financial system. Failures of single firms in the banking industry have a systemic dimension in contrast to other industries. Based on that both regulatory bodies and academic research came to the conclusion to differentiate between the pure size of a financial institution and the systemic importance it has. New terms are focusing on the potential systemic impact if a particular institution fails. This systemic importance of financial institutions is the key issue in both financial stability assessments (Zhou, 2010b). Previous theoretical considerations state either that large banks, which are perceived "too big to fail," require rescue measures by governments as their failures are likely to result in the collapse of the whole financial system (Hoggarth, Reidhill, and Sinclair, 2004; Kaufman, 2002). On the other hand in the case of the simultaneously failure of several weak, and not necessarily large banks, regulators might face a "too many to fail" problem, which could end in a systemic collapse as well (Acharya and Yorulmazer, 2007; Brown and Dinç, 2011).

Given the economic relevance and interaction banks can hardly be fully crisis resilient. Their business models are associated with uncertainty about liquidity needs and a maturity mismatch between assets and liabilities which is seen as substantial systematic-risk exposure yielding towards the fragility of institutions (Bhattacharya, Boot, and Thakor, 1998; Diamond and Rajan, 2001; Farhi and Tirole, 2012). Albeit risk-taking has significant ramification for the economy it is desirable that banks take some risks to bolster the economy (Levine, 2006; R. G. Rajan and Zingales, 1998). Financial intermediaries have fundamental channels which are linked to wealth-increasing projects of the private sector, banks facilitate the capital accumulation, trading, hedging, and pooling of risks (Beck, Levine, and Loayza, 2000; Dell'Ariccia, Detragiache, and Rajan, 2008; Kroszner, Laeven, and Klingebiel, 2007; Levine, 1997; Pang and Wu, 2009).

Supervisory entities and government bodies reform financial regulations regularly to empower bank governance structures with the intention to ensure balanced risk-return profiles and to keep the banking system stable. Consequently a bank manager is calibrating a banks' risk-return profile within the limitations set by the regulation such as bank activities as well as capital and funding requirements (Barth, Caprio, and Levine, 2008). During and post financial crisis, the lack of sufficient industry expertise and effective framework have been recognized as an important shortcoming of internal bank governance mechanisms (Ard and Berg, 2010; Choundhry, 2011; Hau and Thum, 2009a; Kirkpatrick, 2009; Peni and Vähämaa, 2012; Spong and Sullivan, 2010). Furthermore, the business model itself has become more complex and more opaque since the banks grew significant and started expanding into other business areas creating unregulated exposure (Mehran, et al., 2011a).

On the back of this evidence, superior financial expertise of board members is considered as a potential framework to assess and manage risks better as well as to create more stable banks with balanced risk-return profiles from inside. Regulators imposed comprehensive risk management frameworks in combination with recommended governance structures focusing on the overall balance of the board in relation to the risk strategy of the business, taking into account the experience, behavioral and other qualities of individual directors (Aebi, et al., 2012; Walker, 2009). The supervision of bank management and the risk-return profile of the bank are being performed through mandating independent directors in a one-tier system and supervisory board members in a two-tier system (Hopt and Leyens, 2004; John and Senbet, 1998; Jungmann, 2006). Especially the mandate holds for the latter one since this system separates management board and explicitly assigned management monitoring. Despite of the recent research and compiled frameworks the question has not been analyzed in-depth yet what the impact of greater financial expertise in internal governance on a banks' risk-return profile is.

The purpose of this paper is to examine how financial expertise in internal governance mechanisms influences a bank's risk-return profile. It is challenging to divulge the actual influence of financial experts on the risk-return profile of a bank. Factors such as regulatory environment, business models, and competition in the banking industry have direct influence on the performance and the risk of banks. Furthermore, banks are characterized by different governance structures with either a one- or two-tier system across borders. These two factors are of high relevance since they result in a distortion of the analysis with regards to whom or what mainly affected a banks' risk-return profile.

For the purpose of the intended analysis the German cooperative banks as an important pillar of the regional banking sector displays an unique field of data. Since all banks within the sector operate in the same regulatory environment, and have similar business models, comparable regional reach, strategies, and organizational structures this sector provides a homogeneous object of investigation. The competitive advantage of the relatively small regional banks results from the concentration on selected market segments with two main roles, lending to small and midsized companies as well as to private households (Mercieca, Schaeck, and Wolfe, 2007).

The typical German two-tier board system that separates management and supervision also applies to regional banks including the general regulations on supervisory board members and labor co-determination (Hopt and Leyens, 2004). With regards to the governance perspective, the managers of these credit institutions have a particular characteristic compared to exchange-listed commercial banks since they are not confronted with a market for corporate control (Manne, 1965). Consequently, the absence of one governance instrument increases the importance of all other governance mechanisms. Following the ignorance of the financial expertise of supervisory board members and in response to the financial crisis, modifications of the German legislation have been implemented to increase the quality of internal control and stability of the banking system. Since 2009, new elected members of supervisory boards of financial institutions such as banks and insurance companies in Germany have to meet new legal requirements in terms of financial expertise. In the future prospective members' competence will be checked by BaFin in order to make sure that the supervisory board can exercise its tasks (BaFin and Deutsche Bundesbank, 2010).

For our examination on the influence of the financial expertise of supervisory board members on the risk-return profile of German regional banks the present study relies on a unique, manually collected sample with more than 200 institutions comprising only entities being cooperative banks in its legal form. The size of the data set, the focus on a two-tier board structure as well as the proprietary compilation of data including the granularity is unrivaled given access to non-public data provided by Deutsche Bundesbank. The paper identifies two important areas to discuss for the German banking sector and its regulator which we want to highlight at this point. Is financial expertise beneficial for the development of a German regional bank and it is risk-return profile? It is evident that in a sector where risk taking is at the core of each company's business model, financial expertise should display a particularly important factor for the bank's risk-taking behavior. Based on the results showing that financial expertise does not lead to a favorable development of a risk-return profile of a bank it remains open what the optimal composition of a supervisory board of a regional banks is. In particular, the large fraction of entrepreneurs within a supervisory board has presumably a significant contribution to the deteriorated risk-return profile through their overconfidence.

The remainder of this paper is structured as follows: Chapter III.2 provides an overview of the related literature with a particular focus on the influence of the financial expertise of board members, board composition and performance on regional banks' operations. Chapter III.3 introduces the data, sources and empirical model. In Chapter III.4, summary statistics and results of the regression analysis are portrayed. This section also exhibits the results based on different measures and outlier treatments for robustness checks. Section 5 concludes the paper.

III.2 Related Literature

Studies with regards to the impact of financial expertise on risk-taking and performance can be classified into three segments: (i) board competence and expertise, (ii) board size and composition, and (iii) the performance, efficiency and stability of cooperative banks.

Board competence and expertise is mainly characterized by the professional experience of the board members. Positive relationships between financial expertise and performance measures has been identified for example by Cunninham (2007), Davidson, Xie, and Xu (2004), DeFond, Hann, and Hu (2005), Dhaliwal, Naiker, and Navissi (2006), Fernandes and Fich (2009), and Lee, Rosenstein, and Wyatt (1999). Davidson, Xie, and Xu (2004), DeFond, Hann, and Hu (2005), Fernandes and Fich (2009), and Lee, Rosenstein, and Wyatt (1999) apply financial market information using stock price movement and abnormal returns as key metrics. They conclude that capital markets reward competence on the boards following the positive reaction of capital markets after the announcement of appointing financial experts. A different approach for performance measures is applied by Dhaliwal, Naiker, and Navissi (2006) who find a positive correlation between accounting expertise and accruals quality based on the definition of three types of expertise: accounting, finance, and supervisory. This finding is underpinned by Cunningham (2007) pointing out that particular accounting expertise is more important than any other kind of financial expertise.

Mixed resuls are provided by Carcello, Hollingsworth, Klein, and Neal (2008), Güner, Malmendier, and Tate (2008), Rosenstein and Wyatt (1990), and Minton, Taillard, and Williamson (2010). Güner, Malmendier, and Tate (2008) focusing on bankers as board members conclude that there is no significant impact on appointment decisions as far as there are no conflicts of interest between the bankers and the concerned company. Bankers can be detrimental to shareholder wealth in such incidents. According to Rosenstein and Wyatt (1990), all occupations are equally valuable to shareholders, with regard to share price reactions. Based on the findings of Carcello, Hollingsworth, Klein, and Neal (2008), expertise is not beneficial for real earnings management since other governance mechanisms are as good as financial expertise and having a positive impact on the quality of financial reporting. Focusing on the recent banking crisis Minton, Taillard, and Williamson (2010) analyze a sample of more than 650 unique firms consisting of over 300,000 board members over the 2000 to 2007 period the impact of financial expertise on bank risk and conclude that bank risk-taking is positively associated with greater financial expertise.

Focused on the peculiarities of the German two-tier system, only two studies investigated the relationship between expertise and effectiveness of supervisory boards to our knowledge. Kaplan (1994) shows that supervisory board monitoring works efficiently, as indicated by management turnover, resulting from poor firm performance. The quality of supervision in banking is addressed in an empirical analysis comprising a sample of the 29 largest German banks (Hau and Thum, 2009b). For the analysis the authors define 14 biographical criteria to assume competence by the members of the supervisory board. The results suggest that the financial fragility of the banks in the sample correlates with the monitoring ability of the supervisory board members. Delegating supervisory mandates to individuals with financial expertise is considered an option to stabilize the banking system.

The second strand of related literature addresses the impact of board composition and board size on performance. Lipton and Lorsch (1992) and Jensen (1993) suggest that larger boards tend be less effective due to co-ordination problems and director free-riding which might have adverse effects on performance and risk-taking. Empirical studies support this view (Eisenberg, Sundgren, and Wells, 1998; Yermack, 1996). Another study portrays a U-shaped relation between the size of Monetary Policy Committes and inflation, implying that lowest level of inflation will be reached at an optimum level of committee members. Research with focus on the banking industry does not necessarily support the theory that larger boards are less effective. A more recent study shows that that strong bank boards (boards representing more of bank shareholders interest) particularly small and less restrictive boards positively affect bank risk-taking (H. Berger and Nitsch, 2011; Pathan, 2009). This supports other views that larger boards tend to increase in supervision and in advising management (R. B. Adams and Mehran, 2008).

The analysis of the majority of studies related to board composition is focused on the proportion of outside directors - not having the same scope given the peculiarity of the German two tier board structure. Most studies do not find a causal relation between board composition and firm performance (Hermalin and Weisbach, 2003; Wintoki, Linck, and Netter, 2012). Whereas Harris and Raviv (2008) develop theoretical models of board structure finding that optimal boards will employ large numbers of outside directors, and can be larger in overall size. Bermig and Frick (2010) confirm the missing consistent link between board composition and valuation and performance based on a sample of listed German firms in the period between 1998 and 2007. In contrast to Berger, Kick and Schaeck (2012) who find a clear relationship between the socio-economical compositions of a board structure and bank's risk-taking. They analyze a data set for the entire board composition of German banks for the timeframe 1994–2010 and find that boards represented by younger executive teams and female executives tend to take on more risk, contrary to boards with a higher representation of Ph.D degree holders where risk-taking declines.

The third related category of literature focuses on risk-taking, performance, and stability of regional banks with a focus on cooperative banks. The studies analyze these factors on national as well as the international level (Altunbas, Evans, and Molyneux, 2001; Ayadi, Llewellyn, Schmidt, Arbak, and Groen, 2010; Beck, Hesse, Kick, and Westernhagen, 2009; Cihák and Hesse, 2007; Hasan, Schmiedel, and Song, 2012; Iannotta, Nocera, and Sironi, 2007; Lang and Welzel, 1996; Westman, 2010). Overall, the evidence suggests that regional banks tend to be more stable than commercial banks. This finding can be confirmed for the German regional bank sector. Beck, Hesse, Kick, and Westernhagen (2009) show, using the z-score as metric for financial soundness, that German regional banks are more stable than German commercial banks due to the lower earnings volatility. International comparisons confirm that regional banks are more stable than commercial banks, underlined by the better loan quality and lower asset risk of cooperative banks (Cihák and Hesse, 2007; Iannotta, et al., 2007; Westman, 2010). In terms of efficiency and performance the results are mixed. Iannotta, Nocera and Sironi (2007) exhibit that regional banks are slightly more efficient than other banks, however exhibiting lower profits than commercial banks. In this respect Altunbas, Evans, and Molyneux (2001) can confirm the results only partially, since they demonstrate that cooperative have slight cost but also profit advantages over privately owned banks. Ayadi, Llewellyn, Schmidt, Arbak, & Groen (2010) conducting an european wide study can confirm these mixed picture, with respect to Germany they find that regional banks are more profitable in terms of ROE and ROA, while being less efficient due a higher cost-to-income ratio than other banks.

It can be concluded that existing findings exhibit that financial expertise of board members is one of the factors influencing the risk-return profile of firms. Although, previous studies mainly focus on issues of board composition and board size in jurisdictions where a one-tier board system is in place. Further, the majority of studies, investigating the relationship between financial expertise and firm performance, do not deal with banks in particular. Finally, the quality of supervision in terms of financial expertise in two-tier board systems was largely neglected. The study of Hau and Thum (2009a) can be considered as the most similar to our analysis, but their focus is slightly different. It deals with a relatively small sample of 29 large-scale German banks and bank losses only during the banking crisis years. The results suggest that the financial fragility of the banks in the sample correlates with the monitoring ability of the supervisory board members. Delegating supervisory mandates to individuals with financial expertise is considered an option to stabilize the banking system.

III.3 Data and Methodology

III.3.1 Sample and Data

The data are based on the 200 largest regional banks in terms of total assets at the end of 2009 (Top 200) being in the legal form of cooperative banks. Cooperative banks that are not of the legal form of a cooperative firm are excluded from the dataset. In order to increase the explanatory power of the sample, the data set has to comply with several requirements. Given the category "other" where no assessment regarding financial expertise of an individual can be made, a maximum threshold of 10% for this category per bank has been defined. Consequently a maximum of 10% of the overall supervisory board, or one individual for supervisory boards of up to nine individuals, is allowed to be classified as "other". If a cooperative has not been included in the analysis due to lack of data or a too high representation of individuals who could not clearly be labeled, the institution ranking subsequent in size is included, instead.

The present paper analyses two samples. Besides, the Top 200 which consists of the largest 200 cooperative banks, we run our analysis on the 150 largest cooperative banks which have not been involved in any mergers activities over the panel horizon and the two years preceding this horizon in order to control for potential distortions for merger activities. In total, 257 cooperative banks have been considered in this study.

Our Top 200 sample covers 57% of the total assets of the German cooperative bank sector as of the end of 2009. The average cooperative bank in the sample has total assets of EUR 1.9 billion. The largest cooperative bank has total assets of EUR 41.4 billion, while the smallest bank has EUR 0.7 billion. The merger-controlled banks account for 35% of the cooperative bank sector's total assets. The average of total assets in the merger-controlled sample is EUR 1.6 billion for cooperative banks. The total assets of cooperative banks range from EUR 0.5 billion to EUR 41.4 billion.

Given the lack of a public available data base for the supervisory board composition, individual data on the supervisory board members is collected manually from each bank's annual report (published by the Bundesanzeiger and accessed via the Unternehmensregister or LexisNexis databases). Balance sheet and profit and loss statement data comes from the *Deutsche Bundesbank (BAKIS database)*. BAKIS is the joint information system of the Federal

Financial Supervisory Authority (BaFin) and Deutsche Bundesbank, and it contains bank-specific data. The *Hoppenstedt Banken* database was used to access the merger history of each cooperative bank. Data for macroeconomic and structural control variables have been provided by the Regionaldatenbank Deutschland of the German Federal Statistical Office.

III.3.2 Hypotheses and Model

In the present study we address with our empirical model the following research questions: "How are the risk, stability, and performance of regional banks impacted by (outside) financial expertise." In the course of this research question, we test the following two hypotheses:

Hypothesis 1: (Risk-adjusted) performance of a regional bank is unrelated to the (outside) financial expertise of the supervisory board members.

Hypothesis 2: The stability and risk of a regional bank is not driven by the (outside) financial expertise of the supervisory board members.

The empirical examination is based on a panel analysis via a random effects regression model of the following general form:

$$DV_{it} = \alpha + \beta FE_{it} + \gamma B_{it} + \delta M_{it} + \varepsilon_{it} \qquad \text{(III.1)}$$

where DV is the dependent variable of cooperative bank i at time t. Dependent variables for stability and risk are z-score and non-performing loans (NPL) ratio, whereas the dependent variables for performance are return on risk-weighted assets (RORWA) and return on equity (ROE). FE is the financial expertise, B is a vector of bank-specific variables, M is a vector of macroeconomic and structural control variables, and ε is the error term. Vector B comprises (a) bank size, (b) bank size growth, (c) bank efficiency, (d) bank loan volume growth, (e) bank claims on monetary financial institutions (MFI), (f) bank claims on non-monetary financial institutions (non-MFI), and (g) supervisory board size. Vector M consists of the macroeconomic and structural control variables (h) area, (i) federal state, and (j) local GDP per capita.

III.3.3 Financial Expertise

The financial expertise of supervisory board members is gauged based on their professional backgrounds. This follows previous studies (e.g., Davidson, et al., 2004; Dhaliwal, et al., 2006; Minton, et al., 2010). The following professional backgrounds with assumed financial expertise have been constituted according to occupations with the help of publicly available data in the annual reports. This allows assumptions to be made regarding the financial expertise of the supervisory board members which is defined as outlined in Table III.1:

Table III.1: Professional backgrounds with assumed financial expertise

Level 1: Employment	Self-employed persons with assumed financial expertise	Employed persons with assumed financial expertise	Retired persons with assumed financial expertise
Level 2: Occupation	Entrepreneur, Merchant, Owner	Non-bank employee with assumed financial focus (e.g. member of management board)	Retired self-employed person with assumed financial expertise
	Managing Partner	Bank employee	Retired employed person with assumed financial expertise
	Partner	Public officer with assumed financial focus (e.g. treasurer)	
		Federal and State Minister, State Secretary	
		Local and regional politician	

The main idea behind the applied methodology is the obvious relation to financial issues. For instance, financial expertise is expected in the case of management board members. Further, the definition of financial expertise is mainly on the basis of the German regulatory bodies (BaFin and Deutsche Bundesbank, 2010). For instance, following the regulators' joint bulletin, financial expertise is assumed for potential mandatory members, such as mayors and district administrators. Both regulatory bodies do not explicitly specify the required competence levels, but provide indications concerning occupations and experiences that allow assumptions to be made regarding financial expertise. Professional experience gained in other areas might be also sufficient to justify financial expertise. Additionally, supervisory board members can gain relevant expertise through similar supervisory mandates and professional activities in the banking sector. Furthermore, regulatory bodies consider potential mandatory members, such as mayors and district administrators, whose board presence is legally required, to be financially literate (BaFin and Deutsche Bundesbank, 2010).

Given the fact that details in the annual reports differ between banks, several assumptions concerning tenure, employment classification, and politicians have been applied. To control for the portion of employee representatives on the board the regression analysis is conducted twice for each sample. First, the financial expertise of the total supervisory board and its impact on risk and performance is tested. Second, employee representatives who are employed at the respective bank are excluded in order to analyze the impact on performance and risk of the outside expertise of the free eligible supervisory board members.

III.3.4 Measurement of Performance and Risk

The primary risk measure is the z-score that has widely been used for the analysis of bank risk (Boyd and Runkle, 1993; Laeven and Levine, 2009). We calculate z-scores for each cooperative bank to measure the individual bank's insolvency risk and follow Laeven & Levine (2009) for the calculation. Based on the idea that insolvency is the state in which a bank's capital does not suffice to absorb losses the probability of insolvency is defined as prob(-ROA < CAR) where ROA is the return on assets and CAR is the capital assets ratio (Roy, 1952). Given that profits are normally distributed the probability of insolvency becomes (ROA+CAR)/ σ(ROA), where σ(ROA) is the 10 years standard deviation of ROA (Laeven and Levine, 2009). A higher z-value indicates a more stable bank. The ratio of loan loss provisions to loans serves as alternative risk measure. As we outlined at the beginning lending to small and mid-sized enterprises as well as to private households is one of the main pillars of regional banks' business and therefore represents an important measure for regional banks.

We measure performance with return on equity (*ROE*) and return on risk weighted assets (*RORWA*). *ROE* is defined as income before tax divided by average equity. *RORWA* is defined as income before tax divided by average risk-weighted assets. This allows reflecting the bank specific risk profile. Operating result is used for both performance measures in order to avoid distortions due to undisclosed reserves. These reserves are typically used when banks are in trouble (Beck, et al., 2009).

III.3.5 Control Variables

Our empirical model controls besides bank-specific issues also for macroeconomic as well as structural aspects. To factor in different bank sizes and growth rates, we applied the log of total assets and the annual change in total assets; for different efficiency levels we used the cost income ratio (CIR), which is defined as the ratio of general administrative expenses to operating result. To account for different levels of lending engagements we used the growth rate of the total loan volume. Additionally, the ratios of claims on MFI to total assets and claims on non-MFI to total assets are factored in. Further we control for the size of supervisory boards as larger boards tend to incentivize free-riding and this might lead to a negative effect of the supervisory board size on performance and risk (Jensen, 1993).

As regional banks have legally specified business areas, it is important to control for the region where the bank is located. We capture these structural differences by an index distinguishing between urban and rural areas. Further a binary variable identifying federal states is applied. Regional banks which used to be in the former German Democratic Republic are assigned a value of one. The latter variable is important to control for the long-term business relationships. Regional banks in Eastern German federal states worked in a different structure and business environment under the East German regime until 1990. We measure the difference between urban and rural areas based on population. The differentiation between regional, district, and county centers is captured by an index with five clusters which have been defined. For the discrimination between district and regional centers, areas with up to 1,000,000 inhabitants are divided into four clusters of 250,000 inhabitants each. The fifth cluster is comprised by areas with more than 1,000,000 inhabitants. This allows separating sparsely populated areas from densely populated and metropolitan areas. In order to differentiate the economic development, we considered the local GDP per capita. The population and the GDP per capita are adjusted for mergers during the panel horizon in order to capture the effect of macroeconomic changes. The following Table III.2 gives an overview of the definitions and sources of all control variables.

Table III.2: Definition of control variables and sources

Bank level control variables	**Description**	**Source**
a. Bank size	Ln of total assets	BAKIS (Deutsche Bundesbank)
b. Bank size growth	Year-to-year change in total assets	BAKIS (Deutsche Bundesbank)
c. Bank efficiency	General administrative expenses to operating result (CIR)	BAKIS (Deutsche Bundesbank)
d. Bank loan volume growth	Year-to-year change in total loans	BAKIS (Deutsche Bundesbank)
e. Bank claims on MFI	Claims on MFI divided by total assets	BAKIS (Deutsche Bundesbank)
f. Bank claims on non-MFI	Claims on non-MFI divided by total assets	BAKIS (Deutsche Bundesbank)
g. Bank supervisory board size	Number of supervisory board members	Annual reports
Macroeconomic and structural control variables		
h. East/West	Binary variable separating Eastern and Western federal state	Annual reports
i. GDP per capita	GDP of business area divided by population within business area	Regionaldatenbank Deutschland
j. Population	Index based on population within business area	Regionaldatenbank Deutschland

III.4 Results

III.4.1 Summary Statistics

There is no obvious strong stakeholder group dominating solely the composition of cooperative banks supervisory boards. Rather cooperative banks supervisory boards are characterized by a large fraction of self-employed and employed people, they account for almost the same proportion of the board, comprising 40% and 50% respectively of the supervisory board. Notable is that only 5% of the members of cooperative banks' are employed at the respective bank, suggesting that insiders play a minor role. Further, our analysis reveals that politicians account for approximately 3% of the board members implying that cooperative banks are impacted by few political interest and influence. Other notable fractions are retired individuals which make up almost 10% of the supervisory board. For the merger-controlled cooperative banks, see Appendix III.6.3.

Table III.3: Supervisory board composition, Top 200 cooperative banks

Variables	**Mean**	**Std. Dev.**	**Coeff. of variation**	**Min**	**Max**
Insider (%)	5.20	11.88	228.34	0.00	52.94
Outsider (%)	94.80	11.88	12.53	47.06	100.00
Employment					
Employed individuals (%)	50.22	22.94	45.68	0.00	100.00
Self-employed individuals (%)	39.55	23.49	59.40	0.00	91.67
Retired individuals (%)	9.20	11.86	128.99	0.00	77.78
Others (%)	1.03	2.76	268.43	0.00	14.29
Politicians					
Federal politicians (%)	0.09	0.90	1,020.84	0.00	11.11
Federal state politicians (%)	0.24	1.53	629.23	0.00	20.00
Regional politicians (%)	0.00	0.00	0.00	0.00	0.00
Local politicians (%)	1.83	4.24	231.21	0.00	25.00
Current and retired politicians (%)	2.80	5.53	197.83	0.00	35.29

Despite the same focus and core business, regional banks display a relatively wide range of performance, with coefficients of variation of 65.70% for RORWA and 62.04% for ROE. The distribution range for RORWA is from −1.82% to 6.27% and for ROE from −17.62% to 55.21%. The average performance measured by RORWA is 1.21%, whereas ROW is 12.19%. Risk and stability metrics show a similar pattern and variation, with coefficients of 65.24% for z-score and 74.15% for the NPL ratio. Z-score shows an average of 22.71, ranging in the distribution pattern from 3.61 to 103.23. The minimum NPL ratio in the sample is zero, and reaches a peak of 13.47%. The average NPL ratio is 2.66%.

The analysis reveals that financial expertise at regional banks has a high variation, given the variation coefficient of 47.88. This is underlined by the fact that the distribution of financial expertise ranges from boards with zero financial expertise to boards composed by individuals assigned only with financial expertise. On average a board of a regional bank has a fraction of financial experts of 47.76%. The data sample adjusted for insiders, exclusion of bank employees, shows similar results and not much variation. Besides the board composition also the board size indicates high variation with a coefficient of variation of 35.76. The board size ranges from 5 individuals at the smallest board to 37 individuals at the largest board. On average a supervisory board of a regional bank has 12.42 members.

With regards to other bank-level variables, bank size growth and loan volume growth show the largest variation, whereas bank size has the lowest coefficient of variation within the sample. Our results suggest that, over the years, regional banks shift their focus on the more profitable lending business by allocating their assets without growing in total bank size by the same factor. Whereas average bank growth is 2.61%, the loan volume grows at an average rate of 4.98%. Bank size shows the lowest coefficient of 3.28 indicating that bank size of our sample is nearly comparable. Bank efficiency is relatively homogeneous among all banks as indicated by the relatively low coefficient of variation of 14.37%. The non-MFI engagement by regional banks does not diverge much, as indicated by the low coefficient of variation, regardless of a broad range between minimum and maximum values. In contrast regional banks are rather different in their inter-bank activities as the coefficient of variation for claims on MFI shows. Our findings remain qualitatively identical in the merger-controlled panel (see Appendix III.6.4).

Table III.4: Summary statistics, Top 200 cooperative banks

Dependent variables	Mean	Std. Dev.	Coeff. of variation	Min	Max
RORWA (%)	1.21	0.80	65.70	-1.82	6.27
ROE (%)	12.19	7.56	62.04	-17.62	55.21
z-score	22.71	14.81	65.24	3.61	103.23
NPL ratio (%)	2.66	1.97	74.15	0.00	13.47
Bank level variables					
Financial expertise (%)	47.76	22.87	47.88	0.00	100.00
Outside financial expertise (%)	45.25	23.23	51.34	0.00	100.00
Bank size (ln '000s of EUR)	20.90	0.69	3.28	19.60	24.45
Bank efficiency (%)	66.48	9.55	14.37	15.98	112.92
Bank size growth (%)	2.61	4.61	176.76	-14.80	31.47
Board size	12.42	4.44	35.76	5.00	37.00
Loan growth (%)	4.98	7.44	149.52	-13.19	51.54
Claims on MFI (%)	11.89	6.59	55.47	0.06	45.65
Claims on non-MFI (%)	58.67	11.39	19.41	11.17	83.57
Macroeconomic and structural variables					
Federal state	0.02	0.14	700.29	0.00	1.00
GDP per capita (,000s of EUR)	28.04	7.32	26.12	9.39	62.04
Population	2.67	1.39	52.07	1.00	5.00

All cooperative banks are split into four equal clusters by financial expertise consisting of 50 banks each in order to analyze the linkage between the different levels of financial expertise and the performance, risk, and stability of a bank. Cluster 1 comprises the banks with the highest levels of financial expertise, and Cluster 4 contains those with the lowest levels. The analysis indicates that financial expertise of the supervisory board tends to reduce stability. Regional banks in Cluster 1 and Cluster 2 have a meaningful lower z-score and higher NPL ratio than those in Cluster 3 and 4. The increased risk-taking within Cluster 1 and 2 does not get paid off by higher performance. The performance of regional banks tends to deteriorate with increasing financial expertise. This trend is consistent across both metrics RORWA and ROE from Cluster 1 to 3 whereas Cluster 4 shows a slightly lower performance than Cluster 3 and 2, but still higher than Cluster 1.

Other variables worth looking at it are bank size, efficiency, and loan volume growth. The analysis demonstrates that larger banks have a higher level of financial expertise. This could be traced back to the hypothesis that the larger the bank, the more complex its business model and strategy as well as the range of activities, and the higher the requirement for financial expertise are. In contrast to the size effect the variable bank efficiency shows that regional banks with high expertise reveal significantly higher CIRs than low-expertise regional banks which lead to the hypothesis that larger banks are less efficient. Concerning loan volume growth, Cluster 4, 3 and 2 show higher growth rates than Cluster 1 which might be based on the scale effect since those banks tend to be also smaller in terms of size; this is in contrast to the effect that banks with lower expertise are more stable. The trend on bank size growth is coherent with loan growth. Our analysis might hypothesize that loan growth leads to stability. The top 150 merger-controlled panel confirms these results, see Appendix III.6.5.

Table III.5: Bank level variables, clustered by financial expertise, Top 200 cooperative banks

Dependent variables	**Cluster 1**	**Cluster 2**	**Cluster 3**	**Cluster 4**	**Delta Cluster 1–4**
RORWA (%)	1.05	1.24	1.34	1.22	-0.17
ROE (%)	10.86	12.37	13.54	11.99	-1.13
z-score	19.05	22.18	24.52	25.06	-6.01
NPL ratio (%)	3.14	2.70	2.59	2.22	0.92
Bank level variables					
Financial expertise (%)	76.53	54.89	39.85	19.78	56.75
Outside financial expertise (%)	72.95	53.04	36.87	18.13	54.82
Bank size (ln '000s of EUR)	21.09	20.89	20.88	20.74	0.35
Bank efficiency (%)	67.92	66.54	65.61	65.88	2.04
Bank size growth (%)	1.82	2.96	2.62	3.01	-1.19
Board size	12.65	11.66	12.67	12.69	-0.04
Loan growth (%)	4.08	5.26	5.03	5.54	-1.46
Claims on MFI (%)	12.06	11.97	13.06	10.47	1.59
Claims on non-MFI (%)	59.73	57.06	58.46	59.44	0.29

The following Table III.6 provides evidence of the significance between the clusters (see Appendix III.6.6 for the merger-controlled panel).

Table III.6: Pairwise test of the significance between expertise clusters, Top 200 cooperative banks

Dependent variables	Cluster 1 vs. 2	Cluster 1 vs. 3	Cluster 1 vs. 4	Cluster 2 vs. 3	Cluster 2 vs. 4	Cluster 3 vs. 4
	t (*p-value*)	t (*p-value*)	t (*p-value*)	t (*p-value*)	t (*p-value*)	t (*p-value*)
RORWA	-2.9746*** *0.0032*	-5.1122*** *0.0000*	-2.8960*** *0.0041*	-1.7083* *0.0886*	0.2822 *0.7780*	2.2395** *0.0259*
ROE	-2.4392** *0.0153*	-4.8278*** *0.0000*	-2.0750** *0.0388*	-2.0154** *0.0448*	0.7044 *0.4817*	3.0085*** *0.0028*
z-score	-2.9416*** *0.0035*	-5.1116*** *0.0000*	-5.3941*** *0.0000*	-2.1057** *0.0361*	-2.2044** *0.0283*	-0.3978 *0.6910*
NPL ratio	2.9874*** *0.0031*	4.0449*** *0.0001*	6.0319*** *0.0000*	0.5127 *0.6085*	2.9269*** *0.0037*	2.2893** *0.0228*
Bank level variables						
Financial expertise	36.4796*** *0.0000*	62.4921*** *0.0000*	107.0168*** *0.0000*	31.6913*** *0.0000*	58.9953*** *0.0000*	35.3432*** *0.0000*
Outside financial expertise	25.2058*** *0.0000*	37.7623*** *0.0000*	79.3250*** *0.0000*	20.1509*** *0.0000*	47.0515*** *0.0000*	21.5942*** *0.0000*
Bank size	4.0484*** *0.0001*	3.5593*** *0.0004*	6.9548*** *0.0000*	0.2905 *0.7716*	3.3427*** *0.0009*	2.2812** *0.0232*
Bank efficiency	1.8552* *0.0645*	3.4015*** *0.0008*	3.2641*** *0.0012*	1.2181 *0.2241*	0.8768 *0.3813*	-0.4186 *0.6758*
Bank size growth	-3.3467*** *0.0009*	-1.9672* *0.0502*	-3.2731*** *0.0012*	1.0335 *0.3023*	-0.3325 *0.7397*	-0.8804 *0.3795*
Board size	2.7820*** *0.0057*	-0.0637 *0.9492*	-0.0953 *0.9242*	-3.5862*** *0.0004*	-2.8178*** *0.0052*	-0.0343 *0.9726*
Loan growth	-2.6742*** *0.0080*	-2.0712** *0.0393*	-3.1177*** *0.0020*	0.4078 *0.6837*	-0.4854 *0.6278*	-0.7861 *0.4325*
Claims on MFI	0.1639 *0.8699*	-1.9450* *0.0527*	2.9122*** *0.0039*	-1.9462* *0.0526*	2.8777*** *0.0043*	4.6932*** *0.0000*
Claims on non-MFI	2.8703*** *0.0044*	1.7566* *0.0800*	0.3068 *0.7592*	-1.4140 *0.1584*	-2.4490** *0.0149*	-1.1065 *0.2694*

Confidence level: 95%
* indicates significance at the 10% level, ** at the 5% level, and *** at the 1% level, respectively.

III.4.2 Regression Results

Regression analyses confirm that financial expertise on supervisory boards of regional banks in the form of cooperative banks cannot contribute to more bank stability and less loan portfolio risk, rather lead to greater risk taking though. These findings lend support to the evidence from Minton, Taillard, and Williamson

(2010), who show that higher bank risk levels are associated with higher financial expertise. The detrimental impact on risk and stability suggests that financial experts explicitly advocate more risk-taking, which Acharya, Richardson, van Nieuwerburgh, and White (2011) and Wallison (2008) describe as a "race to the bottom" in relation to the mortage quality and ability to increase support for affordable housing. Overall, financial experts tend to deterioate the risk-return profile. Since the negative impact on risk cannot be set off by a higher performance. Our results document that financial expertise reduces profitability and suspends the risk-return trade-off.

As indicated by the Wald-Chi square value, all regressions with RORWA and ROE as dependent variable are significant at the 1% level. The regression results document that financial expertise has a negative impact on the performance of regional banks. This finding is at odds with the corporate finance theory postulating appropriate compensation for risk according to the risk-return trade-off. The coefficients of total board financial expertise and outside financial expertise are not significant for the impact on RORWA and ROE. Loan volume growth is next to board size the only variable which is positively associated with the performance whereas all other variables have a negative impact. This finding suggests that the lending activities as core business and focus of a regional bank are still a meaningful profitability driver.

Interestingly board size is positively related to performance at regional banks. This result is in contrast to the hypothesis that larger boards might lead to members' perceived lower personal responsibility for performance and, therefore, ease free-riding (Harris and Raviv, 2008). There is further evidence as shown by the considerations of Jensen (1993) as well as of Lipton and Lorch (1992) that larger boards are detrimental to performance.

With regards to the negative impact of bank size one could hypothesize that profitable growth of a regional bank is restricted due to the limitations in terms of highly profitable projects. Consequently large regional banks can only underwrite projects at some point with lower profitability leading to shrinking total returns. This might explain the effect that bank size growth reduces profitability. Remarkably, economic strength is the only of the structural variables having a significant impact on performance, neither population density nor the regional aspects have a significant impact on performance.

Table III.7: Random-effect regressions with dependent variables RORWA and ROE, Top 200 cooperative banks

Variable		**RORWA (RE) Financial expertise**		**RORWA (RE) Out. financial expertise**		**ROE (RE) Financial expertise**		**ROE (RE) Out. financial expertise**	
		Coeff.	**SE (robust)**	**Coeff.**	**SE (robust)**	**Coeff.**	**SE (robust)**	**Coeff.**	**SE (robust)**
Financial expertise	Financial expertise	−0.0010	0.0013			−0.0033	0.0139		
	Outside financial expertise			−0.0012	0.0013			−0.0067	0.0136
Bank level	Bank size	−0.2680	0.0598***	−0.2720	0.0575***	−1.9734	0.6668***	−1.9690	0.6355***
	Bank efficiency	−0.0262	0.0033***	−0.0262	0.0034***	−0.2707	0.0345***	−0.2702	0.0345***
	Bank size growth	−0.0408	0.0073***	−0.0409	0.0073***	−0.2505	0.0700***	−0.2515	0.0699***
	Board size	0.0074	0.0068	0.0071	0.0069	0.0835	0.0661	0.0809	0.0667
	Loan growth	0.0433	0.0041***	0.0434	0.0041***	0.2693	0.0334***	0.2692	0.0333***
	Claims on MFI	−0.0088	0.0048*	−0.0088	0.0048*	−0.1319	0.0459***	−0.1318	0.0459***
	Claims on Non-MFI	−0.0144	0.0029***	−0.0145	0.0029***	−0.0634	0.0312**	−0.0639	0.0311**
Macroeconomic and structural environment	Federal state	−0.1279	0.0869	−0.1282	0.0850	0.5330	1.4624	0.5577	1.4346
	GDP per capita	−0.0062	0.0042	−0.0061	0.0042	−0.1055	0.0433**	−0.1047	0.0430**
	Population	0.0054	0.0334	0.0036	0.0332	0.0882	0.3083	0.0700	0.3079
	Constant	9.5131	1.1456***	9.6152	1.1022***	77.9055	13.5145***	78.0171	12.8751***
	Wald Chi^2	279.63	***	282.37	***	179.88	***	181.73	***
	R-sq	0.2548		0.2553		0.1858		0.186	
	No of observations	1,116		1,116		1,116		1,116	

* indicates significance at the 10% level, ** at the 5% level, and *** at the 1% level, respectively.
Standard errors control for clustering at the bank level.

All regression models with z-score and NPL ratio as dependent variables are significant at the 1% level as well - as indicated by the Wald-Chi square value. In contrast to the performance regressions, the financial expertise coefficients are significant in the risk regressions. The results reveal that financial expertise leads to greater risk-taking rather than stabilizing banks. This is supported by the observation that financial expertise tends to increase the loan portfolio risk. These results are remarkable as financial expertise reduces profitabiliy and leads to greater risk taking. The boards of regional banks, in particular cooperative banks, are characterized by a relatively high fraction of entrepreneurs. This group of professionals is supposed to have a solid understand of business risk and selection. Our results show that they tend to overestimate their abilities though and advocate for higher risk taking.

Compared to z-score, most of the bank-level control variables are significant in the regression with the NPL ratio as dependent variable. In this connetion the variables show different impacts on loan portfolio risk and bank stability. Whilst loan growth affects negatively the loan portfolio risk, contributes bank size growth to a lower NPL ratio. Interestingly this effect is conversely on the bank stability. Given the negative effect of loan volume growth on stability, we hypothesize that regional banks can only pririmarly grow by underwriting business which jeopardize the risk profile of the bank and subsequently its loan portfolio.

Concerning the bank size and bank size growth, our analysis shows that these variables have an contrary effect on bank stability and a consistent positive effect on loan portfolio risk given the reduction of the NPL ratio. Whereas regional banks can improve their loan portfolio and stability through economies of scale, our results show that there are not any further diversification effects on the loan portfolio side which help reducing the loan portfolio risk and increasing the bank stability.

The negative impact of board size on the stability and the loan portfolio underlines the free-riding hypothesis from the performance regressions. The perceived lower personal responsibility in large boards might result in a less strict lending policy, which explains the negative impact on performance and the increasing effect on the NPL ratio.

Greater financial expertise does not necessarily lead to greater controlling and monitoring of bank risk as shown by our analysis (e.g., Chuang and Lee, 2006; Fellner, Güth, and Maciejovsky, 2004). Further evidence documents Odean (1998) by showing that the greater expertise individuals have, the more overconfident they tend to be. This theme has been also evaluated by Dittrich, Güth, & Maciejovsky (2005) who demonstrate that overconfidence tend to increase with task complexity.

Table III.8: Random-effect regressions with dependent variables z-score and NPL ratio, Top 200 cooperative banks

Variable		z-score (RE) Financial expertise		z-score (RE) Out. financial expertise		NPL Ratio (RE) Financial expertise		NPL Ratio (RE) Out. financial expertise	
		Coeff.	SE (robust)	Coeff.	SE (robust)	Coeff.	SE (robust)	Coeff.	SE (robust)
Financial expertise	Financial expertise	-0.0719	0.0453			0.0118	0.0041***		0.0039***
	Outside financial expertise			-0.0960	0.0408**			0.0122	
Bank level	Bank size	-1.7478	2.4256	-1.9359	2.4345	-0.5093	0.1680***	-0.4444	0.1633***
	Bank efficiency	-0.0640	0.0254**	-0.0627	0.0257**	-0.0012	0.0059	-0.0011	0.0059
	Bank size growth	0.0492	0.0585	0.0468	0.0578	-0.1578	0.0144***	-0.1576	0.0144***
	Board size	-0.1938	0.2619**	-0.2124	0.2641	0.0442	0.0195**	0.0460	0.0196**
	Loan growth	-0.0926	0.0385	-0.0911	0.0380**	0.0945	0.0106***	0.0941	0.0106***
	Claims on MFI	-0.0067	0.0716	-0.0104	0.0724	0.0338	0.0116***	-0.1576	0.0144***
	Claims on Non-MFI	0.2081	0.1205*	0.2021	0.1201*	0.0292	0.0083***	0.0941	0.0106***
Macroeconomic and structural environment	Federal state	-4.6956	4.8127	-4.5279	4.9777	-0.2500	0.8592	-0.2207	0.8572
	GDP per capita	-0.0359	0.1503	-0.0249	0.1497	-0.0454	0.0139	-0.0459	0.0140
	Population	-0.8731	1.1510	-1.0190	1.1407	-0.2536	0.0815	-0.2458	0.0816
	Constant	60.838	56.2943	66.290	57.1181	12.010	3.4530***	10.580	3.4139***
	Wald Chi^2	65.45	***	64.05	***	268.99	***	269.11	***
	R-sq	0.0959		0.1004		0.2979		0.3005	
	No of observations	1,116		1,116		1,103		1,103	

* indicates significance at the 10% level, ** at the 5% level, and *** at the 1% level, respectively.
Standard errors control for clustering at the bank level.

Overall, these findings are confirmed by the merger-controlled panel Top 150 (see Appendices III.6.7 and III.6.8), only the level of significance differs slightly.

III.4.3 Robustness Checks

In order to run the robustness checks, the panel is adjusted in two ways. All variables are truncated, except for the binary variable (federal state) and the index variable on population (area). First, all observations smaller than the 1st percentile of the distribution are set to the value of the 1st percentile. Observations larger than the 99th percentile are set to the value of the 99th percentile. Second, the same procedures has been applied to all observations smaller than the 5th percentile.

Overall, the outlier-corrected regression results can confirm the same results as per our original data set providing robustness to our findings. The models with outlier-corrected datasets have higher explanatory power with regards to the financial stability and risk than the models without outlier correction, as indicated by the higher R-squared. The significance of the financial expertise coefficients of regional banks increases as the risk regressions indicate.

With regard to performance, all coefficients on financial expertise and a significant part on bank level retain their signs from the original regressions. Despite the outlier correction, the coefficients in the ROE and RORWA remain insignificant (see Appendices III.6.9, III.6.11, III.6.13, and III.6.15).

A comparison with the coeffcients of the outlier-corrected data set underlines our initial findings (see Appendices III.6.10, III.6.12, III.6.14 and III.6.16). There is neither a change in the signs of the expertise coefficients nor a material difference between the Top 200 panel and the merger-adjusted Top 150 panel due to the outlier corrections compared to the original regressions.

III.5 Concluding Remarks

The present study examines the influence of financial expertise of supervisory board members on a bank's risk-return profile based on the example of German regional bank in the form of cooperative banks during the period 2004–2009.

The analysis demonstrates that financial experts on supervisory boards impact the risk-return profile. The risk-return trade off does not work for regional banks in which an increase in performance is associated with an increase in risk. The results are remarkably since financial expertise lead to profitibality reduction and to greater risk-taking. It exhibits that regional banks are not able to benefit from financial experts either way and have a deteriorated risk-return profile. These findings are confirmed by the robustness checks with outlier-corrected datasets at the same high significance level.

Further, the analysis reveals that the selected business strategy of the financial experts by growing the bank size does not lead to a favourable development on the bank's financial performance. The boards of regional banks, in particular cooperative banks, are characterized by a large fraction of self-employed people, making up 40% of the total supervisory board population.

Interestingly, entrepreneurs do not exert a positive influence on the bank performance. Based on their profession and background this group of individuals is supposed to have a solid knowledge and distinctive awarenes of business selection and risk-taking. This phenomen can be explained by a portion of overconfidence with a self-attribution bias where people tend to ascribe any success they in some activity to their own abilities and talents (Barberis and Thaler, 2003). Odean (1998) demonstrates that the greater the expertise individuals have, the more overconfident they tend to be. Further support is exhibited by the analysis of Dittrich, Güth, & Maciejovsky (2005) showing that overconfidence is positively related to the task complexity.

Employed people with an average value of 50% of the total supervisory board represent a large fraction and notable reservoir of financial expertise. Insiders and politicians play a minor role representing 5% and 3% respectively of the board members. Therefore, there is hardly any change between the results for insider and outsider financial expertise.

The results of our analysis are deemed to be valuable for the composition of boards in general, and of supervisory boards in particular. Moreover, it provides evidence to the regulators for their intentions and efforts to improve the stability of the banking system by introducing directives in order to determine optimal board composition and internal governance structures. Overall, it is very remarkable that our findings document that financial expertise suspends the risk-return trade-off and reduces profitibality. Based on that result, it needs to be further investigated whether up to a certain treshold financial expertise is beneficially for the risk-return profile of regional banks and is able to suspend the deteriorated risk-return profile. A subsequent increase of the board needs to be evaluated carefully given diverging effects. While the board size is positively related to the performance of regional banks it leads to a reduction of stability and increase of loan portfolio risk. The performance effect contradicts the theory that larger boards support free-riding incentives leading to lower personal responsibility for performance (Harris and Raviv, 2008; Jensen, 1993; Lipton and Lorsch, 1992).

From a regulator's perspective the results provide evidence that the prescription of universal financial expertise in bank's internal goverance mechanisms does not lead to the desired effect of increasing the stability of the banking system. The results indicate that the new German legislation is not necessarily contributing to an

enhancement of banking system stability as it was intended to. The findings leave the research question what the optimal threshold of the board composition with regards to financial expertise and board size is in order to increase the stability of the banking system.

III.6 Appendix

Appendix III.6.1: Top 200 cooperative banks

No.	Cooperative bank	Rank 2009
1	Deutsche Apotheker- und Ärztebank eG	1
2	Sparda-Bank Baden-Württemberg eG	2
3	Berliner Volksbank eG	3
4	Sparda-Bank Südwest eG	4
5	BBBank eG, Karlsruhe	5
6	Sparda-Bank West eG	6
7	Frankfurter Volksbank eG	7
8	Sparda-Bank Berlin eG	9
9	Volksbank Mittelhessen eG	10
10	Sparda-Bank München eG	11
11	Sparda-Bank Hessen eG	12
12	Mainzer Volksbank eG	13
13	LIGA Bank eG, Regensburg	14
14	KD-Bank eG - die Bank für Kirche und Diakonie	15
15	Sparda-Bank Hannover eG	16
16	Evangelische Kreditgenossenschaft eG	17
17	Hannoversche Volksbank eG	18
18	Bank im Bistum Essen eG	19
19	DKM Darlehnskasse Münster eG	20
20	Dortmunder Volksbank eG	21
21	Bank für Kirche und Caritas eG	22
22	Volksbank Paderborn-Höxter-Detmold eG	23
23	Evangelische Darlehnsgenossenschaft eG	24
24	Sparda-Bank Nürnberg eG	25
25	Bank 1 Saar eG	26
26	Wiesbadener Volksbank eG	28
27	PSD Bank Rhein-Ruhr eG	29
28	Münchner Bank eG	30
29	Sparda-Bank Hamburg eG	31
30	Volksbank eG, Villingen-Schwenningen	32
31	Volksbank Freiburg eG	35
32	Volksbank Pforzheim eG	36
33	Sparda-Bank Münster eG	37
34	Volksbank Bonn Rhein-Sieg eG	38
35	Volksbank Rems eG, Waiblingen	39
36	Volksbank Kur- und Rheinpfalz eG	40
37	Volksbank Oberberg eG	41
38	PSD Bank Nürnberg eG	42
39	Volksbank Ulm-Biberach eG	45
40	Volksbank eG Darmstadt Kreis Bergstraße	46
41	Pax Bank eG	48
42	Volksbank Karlsruhe eG	49
43	Westerwald Bank eG Volks- und Raiffeisenbank	50
44	Volksbank Ludwigsburg eG	51
45	Volksbank Raiffeisenbank Bayern Mitte eG, Ingolstadt	52
46	Volksbank Gütersloh eG	53
47	Vereinigte Volksbank Maingau eG	54
48	Hamburger Volksbank eG	55
49	Volksbank eG Braunschweig Wolfsburg	56
50	Sparda-Bank Regensburg eG	57
51	Volksbank Ruhr Mitte eG	58
52	Volksbank Göppingen eG	59
53	Volksbank Baden-Baden Rastatt eG	60
54	PSD Bank Nord eG	62
55	Volksbank Heilbronn eG	63
56	Volksbank an der Niers eG	64
57	Kasseler Bank eG Volksbank Raiffeisenbank	65
58	VR meine Raiffeisenbank eG, Altötting	67
59	Volksbank RheinAhrEifel eG	69
60	Volksbank Hohenlohe eG, Öhringen	70
61	PSD Bank München eG	71
62	Kölner Bank eG	72
63	Volksbank Kirchheim-Nürtingen eG	73
64	VR-Bank Rhein-Sieg eG	74
65	VR Bank Südpfalz eG	75
66	Volksbank Main-Tauber eG, Tauberbischofsheim	76
67	Volksbank Offenburg eG	77
68	Groß-Gerauer Volksbank eG	79
69	VR Bank HessenLand eG	81
70	Volksbank Gronau-Ahaus eG	83
71	PSD Bank Berlin-Brandenburg eG	84
72	VR Bank Schwäbisch Hall-Crailsheim eG	85
73	Volksbank Neckartal eG, Eberbach	87
74	Volksbank Kurpfalz H + G BANK eG, Heidelberg	88
75	PSD Bank Köln eG	91
76	Volksbank Bad-Oeynhausen-Herford eG	92
77	Volksbank Wiesloch eG	93
78	Volksbank Breisgau Nord eG, Emmendingen	94
79	VR-Bank Rottal-Inn eG, Pfarrkirchen	95
80	Volksbank Raiffeisenbank Dachau eG	96
81	Volksbank Remscheid-Solingen eG	98
82	GLS Gemeinschaftsbank eG	99
83	PSD Bank Karlsruhe-Neustadt eG	101
84	Volksbank eG, Pattensen	102
85	Augusta-Bank eG Raiffeisen-Volksbank, Augsburg	104
86	Volksbank Düsseldorf Neuss eG	105
87	Volksbank Rhein-Ruhr eG	107
88	Sparda-Bank Augsburg eG	109
89	VR-Bank eG, Würselen	111
90	Volksbank Herrenberg-Rottenburg eG	112
91	Volksbank Reutlingen eG	113
92	Volksbank eG, Überlingen	114
93	Volksbank Esslingen eG	118
94	Märkische Bank eG	119
95	Raiffeisenbank Frechen-Hürth eG	120
96	Volksbank Lüneburger Heide eG	121
97	Volksbank Donau-Neckar eG, Tuttlingen	122
98	Raiffeisen-Volksbank Donauwörth eG	123
99	Volksbank Nordheide eG	125
100	Volksbank Plochingen eG	126

Appendix III.6.1: Top 200 cooperative banks (continued)

No.	Cooperative bank	Rank 2009	No.	Cooperative bank	Rank 2009
101	PSD Bank Hannover eG	127	151	Volksbank Hochrhein eG, Waldshut-Tiengen	192
102	Heidenheimer Volksbank eG	128	152	Volksbank eG Bremerhaven-Cuxland	193
103	Volksbank Rhein-Nahe-Hunsrück eG	129	153	GENO BANK ESSEN eG	194
104	Volksbank Hellweg eG	131	154	Volksbank Mönchengladbach eG	195
105	Volksbank Dreiländereck eG, Lörrach	133	155	VR-Bank Werra-Meißner eG	196
106	Bielefelder Volksbank eG	134	156	Volksbank Kaiserslautern- Nordwestpfalz eG	197
107	Volksbank Sauerland eG	135	157	vr bank Untertaunus eG	198
108	Volksbank Hameln-Stadthagen eG	136	158	Raiffeisenbank im Allgäuer Land eG, Altusried	199
109	Volksbank Hunsrück-Nahe eG	137	159	Volksbank Bruhrain-Kraich-Hardt eG, Oberhausen-Rheinhausen	200
110	Volksbank Nordmünsterland eG	141	160	Volksbank Stade-Cuxhaven eG	201
111	Volksbank Dreieich eG	142	161	Raiffeisenbank eG, Heinsberg	202
112	Ostfriesische Volksbank eG	144	162	Volksbank Ahlen-Sassenberg-Warendorf eG	203
113	Volksbank Metzingen-Bad Urach eG	145	163	VR-Bank Memmingen eG	204
114	Volksbank Siegerland eG	146	164	VR-Bank Passau eG	205
115	Volksbank Raiffeisenbank Nürnberg eG	147	165	Waldecker Bank eG	206
116	VR Bank Kaufbeuren-Ostallgäu eG	149	166	Volksbank Büren und Salzkotten eG	207
117	Volksbank Hamm eG	150	167	Volksbank Bad Saulgau eG	208
118	HEIDELBERGER VOLKSBANK eingetragene Genossenschaft	153	168	Dresdner Volksbank Raiffeisenbank eG	209
119	Volksbank Bühl eG	154	169	Vereinigte Volksbank eG im Regionalverband Saarbrücken	210
120	VR Genossenschaftsbank Fulda eG Volksbank Raiffeisenbank seit 1862	155	170	Raiffeisen-Volksbank Ries eG Nördlingen	211
121	Volksbank Niederrhein eG	156	171	Vereinigte Volksbank Raiffeisenbank eG	212
122	Volksbank Münster eG	157	172	VR Bank Flensburg-Schleswig eG	213
123	Volksbank eG, Osterholz-Scharmbeck	158	173	Aachener Bank eG	214
124	VR Bank Hof eG	159	174	Raiffeisenbank Oberpfalz Süd eG, Donaustauf	215
125	VR Bank Ostholstein Nord - Plön eG	160	175	VR Bank Biedenkopf-Gladenbach eG	216
126	VR-Bank Erlangen-Höchstadt-Herzogenaurach eG	161	176	Volksbank Jever eG	217
127	Volksbank Krefeld eG	162	177	Volksbank Allgäu-West eG, Isny	218
128	Volksbank Straubing eG	164	178	Volksbank Forchheim eG	219
129	VR Bank Pinneberg eG	167	179	Genossenschaftsbank Unterallgäu eG, 87719 Mindelheim	220
130	Volksbank Euskirchen eG	168	180	Raiffeisen-Volksbank Miltenberg eG	221
131	VR-Bank Asperg-Markgröningen eG, Möglingen	169	181	Raiffeisenbank Oberallgäu-Süd eG, Sonthofen	222
132	VR-Bank Rhein-Erft eG	170	182	Volksbank Franken eG, Buchen	223
133	Kieler Volksbank eG	171	183	Raiffeisenbank Neumarkt i.d.OPf. eG	224
134	Raiffeisenbank Aschaffenburg eG	172	184	Untertürkheimer Volksbank eG, Stuttgart	227
135	Emsländische Volksbank eG Meppen	173	185	VR-Bank Uffenheim-Neustadt eG Raiffeisen-Volksbank	228
136	Volksbank Marl-Recklinghausen eG	174	186	Volksbank Mainspitze eG	229
137	Volksbank Raiffeisenbank eG, Neumünster	175	187	VR-Bank Neu-Ulm/Weißenhorn eG	230
138	PSD Bank Westfalen-Lippe eG	176	188	Volksbank Weinheim eG	231
139	Volksbank Rhein-Lahn eG	177	189	Raiffeisenbank Rheinbach Voreifel eG	232
140	Volksbank eG, Konstanz	178	190	VBU Volksbank im Unterland eG, Schwaigern	235
141	RV Bank Rhein-Haardt eG	179	191	VR Bank Westthüringen eG	236
142	Raiffeisenbank Cham-Roding-Furth im Wald eG	180	192	Volksbank Bautzen eG	238
143	Raiffeisenbank Weißenburg-Gunzenhausen eG	182	193	Vereinigte Volksbank eG, Telgte	239
144	Volksbank Bocholt eG	183	194	Freisinger Bank eG Volksbank-Raiffeisenbank	240
145	Volksbank Bochum Witten eG	184	195	Volksbank Erft eG	241
146	Volksbank in Schaumburg eG	185	196	Volksbank Ettlingen eG	242
147	Volksbank Lippstadt eG	186	197	VR-Bank in Mittelbaden eG, Iffezheim	244
148	Volksbank-Raiffeisenbank Bayreuth eG	188	198	Volksbank Saaletal eG	245
149	VR Bank eG, Niebüll	189	199	Volksbank Nagoldtal eG	246
150	Volksbank Breisgau-Süd eG, Heitersheim	190	200	Volksbank Südheide eG	247

Appendix III.6.2: Top 150 cooperative banks

No.	Cooperative bank	Rank 2009
1	Deutsche Apotheker- und Ärztebank eG	1
2	Sparda-Bank Baden-Württemberg eG	2
3	Berliner Volksbank eG	3
4	Sparda-Bank Südwest eG	4
5	Sparda-Bank Berlin eG	9
6	Sparda-Bank München eG	11
7	LIGA Bank eG, Regensburg	14
8	Sparda-Bank Hannover eG	16
9	Bank im Bistum Essen eG	19
10	DKM Darlehnskasse Münster eG	20
11	Bank für Kirche und Caritas eG	22
12	Evangelische Darlehnsgenossenschaft eG	24
13	Sparda-Bank Nürnberg eG	25
14	Sparda-Bank Hamburg eG	31
15	Volksbank Pforzheim eG	36
16	Sparda-Bank Münster eG	37
17	Volksbank Bonn Rhein-Sieg eG	38
18	PSD Bank Nürnberg eG	42
19	Pax Bank eG	48
20	Westerwald Bank eG Volks- und Raiffeisenbank	50
21	Volksbank Ludwigsburg eG	51
22	Sparda-Bank Regensburg eG	57
23	Volksbank Baden-Baden*Rastatt eG	60
24	Volksbank Heilbronn eG	63
25	Kasseler Bank eG Volksbank Raiffeisenbank	65
26	PSD Bank München eG	71
27	Kölner Bank eG	72
28	Volksbank Kirchheim-Nürtingen eG	73
29	VR-Bank Rhein-Sieg eG	74
30	Volksbank Offenburg eG	77
31	Groß-Gerauer Volksbank eG	79
32	PSD Bank Berlin-Brandenburg eG	84
33	Volksbank Bad-Oeynhausen-Herford eG	92
34	Volksbank Raiffeisenbank Dachau eG	96
35	Volksbank Remscheid-Solingen eG	98
36	PSD Bank Karlsruhe-Neustadt eG	101
37	Volksbank Düsseldorf Neuss eG	105
38	Volksbank Rhein-Ruhr eG	107
39	Sparda-Bank Augsburg eG	109
40	Volksbank Reutlingen eG	113
41	Volksbank eG, Überlingen	114
42	Volksbank Esslingen eG	118
43	Volksbank Donau-Neckar eG, Tuttlingen	122
44	Volksbank Nordheide eG	125
45	Volksbank Plochingen eG	126
46	PSD Bank Hannover eG	127
47	Volksbank Dreiländereck eG, Lörrach	133
48	Volksbank Nordmünsterland eG	141
49	Volksbank Dreieich eG	142
50	Ostfriesische Volksbank eG	144
51	Volksbank Hamm eG	150
52	HEIDELBERGER VOLKSBANK eingetragene Genossenschaft	153
53	VR Genossenschaftsbank Fulda eG Volksbank Raiffeisenbank seit 1862	155
54	Volksbank Krefeld eG	162
55	Volksbank Straubing eG	164
56	Kieler Volksbank eG	171
57	Volksbank Marl-Recklinghausen eG	174
58	PSD Bank Westfalen-Lippe eG	176
59	Volksbank eG, Konstanz	178
60	Volksbank Bocholt eG	183
61	Volksbank Bochum Witten eG	184
62	Volksbank Lippstadt eG	186
63	Volksbank-Raiffeisenbank Bayreuth eG	188
64	VR Bank eG, Niebüll	189
65	Volksbank Breisgau-Süd eG, Heitersheim	190
66	Volksbank Hochrhein eG, Waldshut-Tiengen	192
67	GENO BANK ESSEN eG	194
68	VR-Bank Werra-Meißner eG	196
69	vr bank Untertaunus eG	198
70	Volksbank Stade-Cuxhaven eG	201
71	Volksbank Ahlen-Sassenberg-Warendorf eG	203
72	VR-Bank Memmingen eG	204
73	Volksbank Büren und Salzkotten eG	207
74	Volksbank Bad Saulgau eG	208
75	Dresdner Volksbank Raiffeisenbank eG	209
76	Vereinigte Volksbank Raiffeisenbank eG	212
77	Aachener Bank eG	214
78	VR Bank Biedenkopf-Gladenbach eG	216
79	Volksbank Jever eG	217
80	Volksbank Allgäu-West eG, Isny	218
81	Genossenschaftsbank Unterallgäu eG, 87719 Mindelheim	220
82	Raiffeisen-Volksbank Miltenberg eG	221
83	Volksbank Franken eG, Buchen	223
84	Untertürkheimer Volksbank eG, Stuttgart	227
85	Volksbank Mainspitze eG	229
86	VR-Bank Neu-Ulm/Weißenhorn eG	230
87	Volksbank Weinheim eG	231
88	Raiffeisenbank Rheinbach Voreifel eG	232
89	VR Bank Westthüringen eG	236
90	Freisinger Bank eG Volksbank-Raiffeisenbank	240
91	Volksbank Erft eG	241
92	Volksbank Ettlingen eG	242
93	Volksbank Nagoldtal eG	246
94	Volksbank Wilferdingen-Keltern eG, Remchingen	248
95	Volksbank Göttingen eG	252
96	Volksbank eG, Waltrop	255
97	Volks- und Raiffeisenbank Neuwied-Linz eG	257
98	Volksbank Rottweil eG	258
99	Volksbank Nordoberpfalz eG	259
100	Volksbank Regensburg eG	262

Appendix III.6.2: Top 150 cooperative banks (continued)

No.	Cooperative bank	Rank 2009
101	Rheingauer Volksbank eG	263
102	Volksbank Lingen eG	264
103	Volksbank Region Leonberg eG	265
104	VR-Bank Mainz eG	267
105	Volksbank Wolfenbüttel-Salzgitter eG	271
106	Volksbank eG Minden-Hille-Porta	277
107	Raiffeisenbank München-Süd eG	278
108	Volksbank Helmstedt eG	279
109	Raiffeisenbank Weiden eG	280
110	Bremische Volksbank eG	281
111	Kulmbacher Bank eG Raiffeisen-Volksbank	282
112	VR Bank Kitzingen eG	283
113	Volksbank Filder eG, Neuhausen	285
114	Volksbank Emmerich-Rees eG	286
115	Volksbank Dill eG -Volksbank und Raiffeisenbank	289
116	Volksbank Tettnang eG	294
117	Leutkircher Bank Raiffeisen- und Volksbank eG	295
118	Volksbank Hohenzollern eG, Hechingen	296
119	Rottaler Volksbank-Raiffeisenbank eG, Eggenfelden	297
120	Volksbank Osnabrück eG	298
121	Volksbank Schwäbisch Gmünd eG	302
122	Raiffeisen-Volksbank Varel-Nordenham eG	303
123	PSD Bank Braunschweig eG	304
124	PSD Bank Koblenz eG	308
125	Rüsselsheimer Volksbank eG	311
126	Volksbank Kirchhellen eG	313
127	Volksbank-Raiffeisenbank eG, Husum	314
128	Volksbank Mittweida eG	315
129	VR Bank Südliche Weinstraße eG	316
130	Volksbank Oldenburg eG	320
131	Vereinigte Volksbank eG Limburg	322
132	Volksbank Magdeburg eG	325
133	VR-Bank Ellwangen eG	328
134	Volksbank Eifel Mitte eG	330
135	Ehinger Volksbank eG, Ehingen	331
136	Volksbank Kinzigtal eG, Wolfach	334
137	Volksbank Zuffenhausen eG, Stuttgart	335
138	Volksbank Brüggen-Nettetal eG	336
139	Volksbank Rhein-Wehra eG, Bad Säckingen	338
140	Volksbank Hildesheimer Börde eG	344
141	Raiffeisenbank Rhein-Berg eG	345
142	Volksbank Strohgäu eG, Korntal-Münchingen	348
143	Volksbank Bad Driburg - Brakel - Steinheim eG	349
144	Volksbank Müllheim eG	350
145	Volksbank Möckmühl-Neuenstadt eG	353
146	Raiffeisenbank Kocher-Jagst eG, Ingelfingen	355
147	Rottaler Raiffeisenbank eG, Pocking	356
148	VR-Bank eG, Regen	357
149	Volksbank Brackenheim-Güglingen eG	360
150	Volksbank Balingen eG	361

Appendix III.6.3: Supervisory board composition, Top 150 cooperative banks (merger-controlled panel)

Variables	Mean	Std. Dev.	Coeff. of Variation	Min	Max
Insider (%)	2.94	9.19	313.05	0.00	52.94
Outsider (%)	97.06	9.19	9.47	47.06	100.00
Employment					
Employed individuals (%)	49.61	23.89	48.16	0.00	100.00
Self-employed individuals (%)	39.70	25.43	64.05	0.00	90.91
Retired individuals (%)	9.74	12.06	123.79	0.00	77.78
Others (%)	0.95	2.91	307.03	0.00	16.67
Politicians					
Federal politicians (%)	0.26	1.52	591.71	0.00	11.11
Federal state politicians (%)	0.15	1.18	771.01	0.00	11.11
Regional politicians (%)	0.00	0.00	0.00	0.00	0.00
Local politicians (%)	1.85	4.44	239.60	0.00	25.00
Current and retired politicians (%)	3.22	6.31	195.77	0.00	35.29

Appendix III.6.4: Summary statistics, Top 150 cooperative banks (merger-controlled panel)

Dependent variables	Mean	Std. Dev.	Coeff. of Variation	Min	Max
RORWA (%)	1.20	0.82	68.27	−1.67	6.27
ROE (%)	12.27	8.10	66.03	−21.43	55.21
z-score	17.69	8.48	47.95	3.95	66.43
NPL ratio (%)	2.69	2.10	77.95	0.00	13.47
Bank level variables					
Financial expertise (%)	47.53	22.74	47.85	0.00	100.00
Outside financial expertise (%)	45.81	23.65	51.63	0.00	100.00
Bank size (ln ’000s of EUR)	20.61	0.72	3.50	19.30	24.45
Bank efficiency (%)	66.51	9.95	14.96	15.98	112.92
Bank size growth (%)	2.52	4.62	183.63	−19.46	30.61
Board size	10.81	3.66	33.88	4.00	33.00
Loan growth (%)	4.90	7.18	146.63	−12.36	39.29
Claims on MFI (%)	12.09	6.66	55.07	0.06	37.92
Claims on Non-MFI (%)	58.57	11.26	19.22	11.17	82.75
Macroeconomic and structural variables					
Federal state	0.03	0.16	604.49	0.00	1.00
GDP per capita (’000s of EUR)	28.42	10.13	35.63	14.76	231.16
Population	2.49	1.41	56.73	1.00	5.00

Appendix III.6.5: Financial expertise clusters, Top 150 cooperative banks (merger-controlled panel)

Dependent variables	**Cluster 1**	**Cluster 2**	**Cluster 3**	**Delta Cluster 1-3**
RORWA (%)	1.15	1.25	1.18	-0.03
ROE (%)	11.59	13.23	11.99	-0.40
z-score	15.62	17.85	19.61	-3.99
NPL ratio (%)	3.20	2.58	2.29	0.91
Bank level variables				
Financial expertise (%)	71.74	47.16	23.70	48.03
Outside financial expertise (%)	70.55	44.60	22.28	48.27
Bank size (ln '000s of EUR)	20.63	20.69	20.51	0.11
Bank efficiency (%)	67.17	65.93	66.42	0.75
Bank size growth (%)	1.87	2.97	2.71	-0.84
Board size	10.52	10.91	11.02	-0.50
Loan growth (%)	4.12	5.37	5.21	-1.09
Claims on MFI (%)	12.11	12.66	11.50	0.62
Claims on Non-MFI (%)	56.93	58.86	59.92	-2.99

Appendix III.6.6: Pairwise test of significance between expertise clusters, Top 150 cooperative banks (merger-controlled panel)

Dependent variables	Cluster 1 vs. 2	Cluster 1 vs. 3	Cluster 2 vs. 3
	t *(p-value)*	t *(p-value)*	t *(p-value)*
RORWA	−1.5285	−0.4669	1.1298
	0.1275	*0.6409*	*0.2595*
ROE	−2.5850**	−0.6422	2.1633**
	0.0102	*0.5213*	*0.0313*
z-score	−3.8227***	−5.2972***	−2.5639**
	0.0002	*0.0000*	*0.0108*
NPL ratio	4.3753***	6.0238***	2.1036**
	0.0000	*0.0000*	*0.0363*
Bank level variables			
Financial expertise	42.2232***	75.5214***	41.0016***
	0.0000	*0.0000*	*0.0000*
Outside financial expertise	32.4137***	70.3125***	26.9993***
	0.0000	*0.0000*	*0.0000*
Bank size	−1.0340	2.2612**	2.8167***
	0.3020	*0.0245*	*0.0052*
Bank efficiency	1.5473	0.9486	−0.6065
	0.1229	*0.3436*	*0.5446*
Bank size growth	−2.9847***	−2.3450**	0.8224
	0.0031	*0.0197*	*0.4115*
Board size	−1.6942*	−1.6502*	−0.3398
	0.0913	*0.1000*	*0.7342*
Loan growth	−3.1168***	−2.5868**	0.4502
	0.0020	*0.0102*	*0.6529*
Claims on MFI	−1.0752	1.1601	2.3587**
	0.2832	*0.2469*	*0.0190*
Claims on Non-MFI	−2.1078**	−3.5104***	−1.0176
	0.0359	*0.0005*	*0.3097*

Confidence level: 95%

* indicates significance at the 10% level, ** at the 5% level, and *** at the 1% level, respectively.

Appendix III.6.7: Correlation matrix, Top 200 cooperative banks

	RORWA	ROE	Z-score	NPL ratio	Financial expertise	Outside financial expertise	ln Total Assets	CIR	Bank size growth	Loan growth	Claims on MFI	Claims on Non MFI	Board size	GDP per capita	Population	Federal state
RORWA	1.0000															
ROE	0.9023*	1.0000														
Z-score	0.1428*	0.0842*	1.0000													
NPL ratio	−0.0610*	−0.0595*	−0.0025	1.0000												
Financial expertise	−0.1008*	−0.0728*	−0.1527*	0.1755*	1.0000											
Outside financial expertise	−0.0800*	−0.0627*	−0.1431*	0.2384*	0.9575*	1.0000										
ln Total assets	−0.0785*	−0.0486	−0.1088*	−0.2792*	0.2010*	0.0085	1.0000									
CIR	−0.3240*	−0.3421*	−0.0240	0.1415*	0.1005*	0.1230*	−0.1898*	1.0000								
Bank size growth	0.0362	0.0379	−0.0560	−0.2707*	−0.0928*	−0.1109*	0.1061*	−0.1050*	1.0000							
Loan growth	0.2621*	0.1778*	−0.0741*	−0.0031	−0.0553	−0.0732*	0.1463*	−0.0624*	0.6166*	1.0000						
Claims on MFI	−0.0589*	−0.1285*	−0.1304*	−0.0354	0.0311	0.0387	0.0615*	0.1001*	0.0970*	0.0052	1.0000					
Claims on Non MFI	−0.1589*	−0.0633*	0.2899*	0.2025*	−0.0059	−0.0025	−0.1987*	0.0887*	−0.1558*	−0.1568*	−0.4040*	1.0000				
Board size	−0.0259	0.0051	0.1771*	0.0602*	−0.0101	−0.0793*	0.2213*	−0.0203	−0.0230	−0.0446	−0.1281*	0.0917*	1.0000			
GDP per capita	−0.0807*	−0.1111*	−0.0671*	−0.1339*	0.0863*	0.0455	0.2971*	0.0071	0.0866*	0.0784*	0.1931*	−0.1029*	−0.1170*	1.0000		
Population	−0.0271	−0.0359	−0.1609*	−0.3973*	−0.0115	−0.1354*	0.6413*	−0.1898*	0.1223*	0.0956*	0.1393*	−0.2820*	0.0000	0.3317*	1.0000	
Federal state	0.0280	0.0236	−0.0815*	−0.0093	0.0549	0.0695*	−0.1280*	0.0849*	−0.0267	−0.0249	0.0601*	−0.2834*	−0.0362	−0.0908*	−0.0517	1.0000

* significant at the 5% level

Appendix III.6.8: Correlation matrix, Top 150 cooperative banks (merger-controlled panel)

	RORWA	ROE	Z-score	NPL ratio	Financial expertise	Outside financial expertise	ln Total Assets	CIR	Bank size growth	Loan growth	Claims on MFI	Claims on Non MFI	Board size	GDP per capita	Population	Federal state
RORWA	1.0000															
ROE	0.9074*	1.0000														
Z-score	0.1069*	0.0355	1.0000													
NPL ratio	–0.0990*	–0.1084*	–0.0410	1.0000												
Financial expertise	–0.0480	–0.0586	–0.1500*	0.2320*	1.0000											
Outside financial expertise	–0.0403	–0.0609	–0.1340*	0.2825*	0.9652*	1.0000										
ln Total assets	–0.0229	0.0170	–0.1788*	–0.3177*	0.0758*	–0.0896*	1.0000									
CIR	–0.3711*	–0.3799*	0.0055	0.1452*	0.0603	0.0867*	–0.1847*	1.0000								
Bank size growth	0.0425	0.0715*	–0.1061*	–0.3152*	–0.1024*	–0.1320*	0.1303*	–0.1364*	1.0000							
Loan growth	0.2459*	0.1932*	–0.0754*	–0.0384	–0.0424	–0.0645	0.1400*	0.0764*	0.6204*	1.0000						
Claims on MFI	–0.0815*	–0.1385*	–0.1834*	–0.0632	0.0389	0.0380	0.0183	0.1127*	0.0967*	–0.0142	1.0000					
Claims on Non MFI	–0.1566*	–0.0674*	0.2769*	0.2208*	–0.0821*	–0.0722*	–0.2462*	0.0898*	–0.1767*	–0.1575*	–0.3700*	1.0000				
Board size	–0.0355	0.0096	0.2010*	0.0559	–0.0709*	–0.1273*	0.2146*	0.0031	–0.0505	–0.0727*	–0.1190*	0.1037*	1.0000			
GDP per capita	0.0144	0.0378	–0.1155*	–0.1094*	–0.0169	–0.0335	0.1091*	–0.0589	0.0807*	0.0655*	0.1404*	–0.0425	–0.0636	1.0000		
Population	0.0973*	0.0793*	–0.1999*	–0.4469*	–0.1029*	–0.2056*	0.6248*	–0.2307*	0.1504*	0.0903*	0.1513*	–0.3101*	–0.0090	0.2231*	1.0000	
Federal state	0.1183*	0.1045*	–0.0217	0.0702*	0.0572	0.0671*	–0.0974*	–0.0440	–0.0060	–0.0143	0.0148	–0.2265*	–0.0631	–0.0649	–0.0670*	1.0000

* significant at the 5% level

Appendix III.6.9: Random-effect regressions with dependent variables RORWA and ROE, Top 150 cooperative banks (merger-controlled panel)

Variable		**RORWA (RE) Financial expertise**		**RORWA (RE) Out. financial expertise**		**ROE (RE) Financial expertise**		**ROE (RE) Out. financial expertise**	
		Coeff.	**SE (robust)**	**Coeff.**	**SE (robust)**	**Coeff.**	**SE (robust)**	**Coeff.**	**SE (robust)**
Financial expertise	Financial expertise	−0.0110	0.0170			−0.0008	0.0015		
	Outside financial expertise			−0.0134	0.0166			−0.0011	0.0015
Bank level	Bank size	−2.0404	0.6844***	−2.0849	0.6603***	−0.2937	0.0630***	−0.2965	0.0609***
	Bank efficiency	−0.2993	0.0389***	−0.2991	0.0389***	−0.0283	0.0037***	−0.0282	0.0037***
	Bank size growth	−0.2776	0.0736***	−0.2790	0.0737***	−0.0435	0.0078***	−0.0436	0.0078***
	Board size	0.1622	0.1056	0.1582	0.1065	0.0094	0.0096	0.0090	0.0097
	Loan growth	0.2688	0.0399***	0.2690	0.0399***	0.0414	0.0045***	0.0415	0.0045***
	Claims on MFI	−0.1873	0.0530**	−0.1875	0.0530**	−0.0132	0.0053***	−0.0132	0.0053***
	Claims on Non-MFI	−0.0540	0.0354***	−0.0556	0.0356***	−0.0137	0.0034	−0.0138	0.0034
Macroeconomic and structural environment	Federal state	3.7231	1.3706	3.7074	1.3594	0.2776	0.2216***	0.2768	0.2214***
	GDP per capita	0.0259	0.0300	0.0260	0.0299	0.0009	0.0028	0.0010	0.0028
	Population	0.5925	0.3859**	0.5757	0.3876**	0.0813	0.0356	0.0796	0.0355
	Constant	75.4903	13.2886***	76.6627	12.9471***	9.6942	1.2090***	9.7778	1.1848***
	Wald Chi²	164.84	***	166.49	***	239.51	***	238.69	***
	R-sq	0.2055		0.2056		0.2663		0.2664	
	No of observations	896		896		896		896	

* indicates significance at the 10% level, ** at the 5% level, and *** at the 1% level, respectively.
Standard errors control for clustering at the bank level.

Appendix III.6.10: Random-effect regressions with dependent variables z-score and NPL ratio, Top 150 cooperative banks (merger-controlled panel)

Variable		z-score (RE) Financial expertise		z-score (RE) Out. financial expertise		NPL Ratio (RE) Financial expertise		NPL Ratio (RE) Out. financial expertise	
		Coeff.	SE (robust)	Coeff.	SE (robust)	Coeff.	SE (robust)	Coeff.	SE (robust)
Financial expertise	Financial expertise	–0.0213	0.0232			0.0115	0.0044***		
	Outside financial expertise			–0.0258	0.0229			0.0116	0.0043***
Bank level	Bank size	–3.4713	1.3903**	–3.4892	1.4183**	–0.4423	0.1557***	–0.3892	0.1580**
	Bank efficiency	–0.0148	0.0079*	–0.0145	0.0080*	–0.0025	0.0065	–0.0025	0.0064
	Bank size growth	–0.0571	0.0171***	–0.0575	0.0170***	–0.1634	0.0161***	–0.1631	0.0161***
	Board size	0.1439	0.1722	0.1368	0.1712	0.0676	0.0301**	0.0696	0.0302**
	Loan growth	0.0022	0.0123	0.0025	0.0123	0.0947	0.0112***	0.0946	0.0112***
	Claims on MFI	–0.0337	0.0197*	–0.0347	0.0197*	0.0180	0.0124	0.0183	0.0124
	Claims on Non-MFI	0.0484	0.0261*	0.0479	0.0259*	0.0370	0.0091***	0.0377	0.0092***
Macroeconomic and structural environment	Federal state	–1.2522	3.1739	–1.2137	3.1599	1.0533	0.7308	1.0720	0.7272
	GDP per capita	0.4232	0.4853	0.3898	0.4798	–0.3939	0.0882***	–0.3882	0.0887***
	Population	0.0137	0.0136	0.0137	0.0138	–0.0122	0.0042***	–0.0123	0.0042***
	Constant	85.9926	27.8159***	86.7101	28.3948***	9.5360	3.3429***	8.3848	3.4395**
	Wald Chi^2	197.97	***	196.09	***	292.94	***	295.91	***
	R-sq	0.0835		0.0876		0.347		0.348	
	No of observations	896		896		885		885	

* indicates significance at the 10% level, ** at the 5% level, and *** at the 1% level, respectively.
Standard errors control for clustering at the bank level.

Appendix III.6.11: Random-effect regressions with dependent variables RORWA and ROE, Top 200 cooperative banks, with 1% outlier-correction

Variable		RORWA (RE) Financial expertise		RORWA (RE) Out. financial expertise		ROE (RE) Financial expertise		ROE (RE) Out. financial expertise	
		Coeff.	SE (robust)	Coeff.	SE (robust)	Coeff.	SE (robust)	Coeff.	SE (robust)
Financial expertise	Financial expertise	–0.0009	0.0013			–0.0038	0.0134		
	Outside financial expertise			–0.0012	0.0012			–0.0067	0.0131
Bank level	Bank size	–0.2862	0.0642***	–0.2891	0.0620***	–1.9926	0.7068***	–1.9890	0.6780***
	Bank efficiency	–0.0245	0.0032***	–0.0245	0.0032***	–0.2609	0.0311***	–0.2604	0.0311***
	Bank size growth	–0.0431	0.0073***	–0.0432	0.0073***	–0.2653	0.0700***	–0.2662	0.0700***
	Board size	0.0064	0.0064	0.0060	0.0065	0.0922	0.0652	0.0897	0.0658
	Loan growth	0.0452	0.0038***	0.0452	0.0038***	0.2770	0.0343***	0.2770	0.0342***
	Claims on MFI	–0.0082	0.0048*	–0.0081	0.0048*	–0.1232	0.0453	–0.1232	0.0453*
	Claims on Non-MFI	–0.0130	0.0030***	–0.0131	0.0030***	–0.0501	0.0308***	–0.0506	0.0307***
Macroeconomic and structural environment	Federal state	–0.0959	0.0914	–0.0956	0.0897	1.0460	1.4699	1.0674	1.4463
	GDP per capita	0.0122	0.0336	0.0103	0.0335	0.0745	0.2920**	0.0573	0.2928**
	Population	–0.0066	0.0043	–0.0065	0.0043	–0.1108	0.0445	–0.1101	0.0443
	Constant	9.6861	1.2367***	9.7658	1.1946***	76.8669	14.2494***	76.9698	13.6463***
	Wald Chi²	306.54	***	308.50	***	197.45	***	199.44	***
	R-sq	0.2439		0.2443		0.1732		0.1735	
	No of observations	1,116		1,116		1,116		1,116	

* indicates significance at the 10% level, ** at the 5% level, and *** at the 1% level, respectively.
Standard errors control for clustering at the bank level.

Appendix III.6.12: Random-effect regressions with dependent variables z-score and NPL ratio, Top 200 cooperative banks, with 1% outlier-correction

Variable		**z–score (RE) Financial expertise**		**z–score (RE) Out. financial expertise**		**NPL Ratio (RE) Financial expertise**		**NPL Ratio (RE) Out. financial expertise**	
		Coeff.	**SE (robust)**	**Coeff.**	**SE (robust)**	**Coeff.**	**SE (robust)**	**Coeff.**	**SE (robust)**
Financial expertise	Financial expertise	–0.0708	0.0454			0.0117	0.0040***		
	Outside financial expertise			–0.0950	0.0408**			0.0122	0.0038***
Bank level	Bank size	–2.3280	2.8984	–2.4601	2.8947	–0.5746	0.1822***	–0.5151	0.1743***
	Bank efficiency	–0.0776	0.0296***	–0.0764	0.0297***	–0.0039	0.0064	–0.0039	0.0063
	Bank size growth	0.0378	0.0624	0.0352	0.0616	–0.1667	0.0136***	–0.1664	0.0136***
	Board size	–0.1342	0.2401	–0.1550	0.2424	0.0425	0.0199**	0.0447	0.0199**
	Loan growth	–0.0885	0.0404**	–0.0875	0.0399**	0.1017	0.0098***	0.1013	0.0098***
	Claims on MFI	–0.0001	0.0763	–0.0040	0.0771	0.0339	0.0110***	0.0338	0.0109***
	Claims on Non-MFI	0.2062	0.1267	0.2007	0.1263	0.0301	0.0086***	0.0310	0.0086***
Macroeconomic and structural environment	Federal state	–4.8049	5.0243	–4.6030	5.1849	–0.2355	0.8729	–0.2094	0.8707
	GDP per capita	–0.8159	1.1772	–0.9733	1.1689	–0.2330	0.0822***	–0.2236	0.0821***
	Population	–0.0028	0.1491	0.0073	0.1488	–0.0460	0.0138***	–0.0464	0.0138***
	Constant	72.0085	65.5405	76.3514	66.0691	13.4768	3.7947***	12.1492	3.6824***
	Wald Chi^2	71.08	***	69.42	***	340.25	***	342.74	***
	R-sq	0.1006		0.1051		0.3059		0.3091	
	No of observations	1,116		1,116		1,103		1,103	

* indicates significance at the 10% level, ** at the 5% level, and *** at the 1% level, respectively.
Standard errors control for clustering at the bank level.

Appendix III.6.13: Random-effect regressions with dependent variables RORWA and ROE, Top 200 cooperative banks, with 5% outlier-correction

Variable		RORWA (RE) Financial expertise		RORWA (RE) Out. financial expertise		ROE (RE) Financial expertise		ROE (RE) Out. financial expertise	
		Coeff.	SE (robust)	Coeff.	SE (robust)	Coeff.	SE (robust)	Coeff.	SE (robust)
Financial expertise	Financial expertise	–0.0006	0.0012			–0.0020	0.0118		
	Outside financial expertise			–0.0009	0.0011			–0.0059	0.0109
Bank level	Bank size	–0.2619	0.0639***	–0.2613	0.0622***	-1.7002	0.6371***	-1.6715	0.6211***
	Bank efficiency	–0.0229	0.0030***	–0.0228	0.0030***	–0.2472	0.0291***	–0.2463	0.0291***
	Bank size growth	–0.0389	0.0063***	–0.0390	0.0063***	-0.2781	0.0618***	-0.2794	0.0619***
	Board size	0.0043	0.0062	0.0040	0.0062	0.0638	0.0637	0.0608	0.0641
	Loan growth	0.0408	0.0033***	0.0408	0.0033***	0.2514	0.0315***	0.2514	0.0315***
	Claims on MFI	–0.0076	0.0047	–0.0076	0.0047	–0.1075	0.0445**	–0.1075	0.0445**
	Claims on Non-MFI	–0.0118	0.0027***	–0.0118	0.0027***	–0.0305	0.0272	–0.0306	0.0272
Macroeconomic and structural environment	Federal state	–0.0513	0.0992	–0.0484	0.0977	1.1716	1.3137	1.2140	1.3026
	GDP per capita	0.0116	0.0285*	0.0094	0.0286*	0.0353	0.2398***	0.0141	0.2425***
	Population	–0.0087	0.0051	–0.0086	0.0051	–0.1490	0.0482	–0.1481	0.0481
	Constant	9.0736	1.2449***	9.0785	1.2115***	70.0817	12.6840***	69.6634	12.3609***
	Wald Chi²	365.11		366.70		236.93	***	238.21	***
	R-sq	0.2267		0.2273		0.1614		0.1617	
	No of observations	1,116		1,116		1,116		1,116	

* indicates significance at the 10% level, ** at the 5% level, and *** at the 1% level, respectively.
Standard errors control for clustering at the bank level.

Appendix III.6.14: Random-effect regressions with dependent variables z-score and NPL ratio, Top 200 cooperative banks, with 5% outlier-correction

Variable		**z-score (RE) Financial expertise**		**z-score (RE) Out. financial expertise**		**NPL Ratio (RE) Financial expertise**		**NPL Ratio (RE) Out. financial expertise**	
		Coeff.	**SE (robust)**	**Coeff.**	**SE (robust)**	**Coeff.**	**SE (robust)**	**Coeff.**	**SE (robust)**
Financial expertise	Financial expertise	–0.0692	0.0429			0.0120	0.0037***		
	Outside financial expertise			–0.1036	0.0431**			0.0125	0.0035***
Bank level	Bank size	–0.3548	3.0408	–0.3258	3.0967	–0.6075	0.1978***	–0.5557	0.1917***
	Bank efficiency	–0.1094	0.0396***	–0.1056	0.0393***	–0.0089	0.0062	–0.0091	0.0062
	Bank size growth	0.0315	0.0785	0.0267	0.0769	–0.1756	0.0142***	–0.1749	0.0142***
	Board size	–0.1400	0.2156	–0.1658	0.2175	0.1045	0.0102*	0.0424	0.0213**
	Loan growth	–0.1207	0.0497**	–0.1190	0.0491**	0.0301	0.0111***	0.1040	0.0101***
	Claims on MFI	0.0207	0.0792	0.0142	0.0814	0.0291	0.0088***	0.0301	0.0111***
	Claims on Non-MFI	0.2267	0.1388	0.2221	0.1383	0.0399	0.0211***	0.0299	0.0089***
Macroeconomic and structural environment	Federal state	–4.0576	4.8917	–3.6636	5.0936	–0.3751	0.8744	–0.3590	0.8719
	GDP per capita	–1.4701	1.2028	–1.6768	1.2294	–0.2383	0.0774***	–0.2246	0.0777***
	Population	0.0184	0.1635	0.0334	0.1607	–0.0524	0.0134***	–0.0533	0.0133**
	Constant	32.7271	68.4242	34.0038	69.6091	14.7598	4.1286***	13.6133	4.0341***
	Wald Chi^2	68.29		63.34		385.63		397.83	
	R-sq	0.1127		0.1192		0.3161		0.3215	
	No of observations	1,116		1,116		1,103		1,103	

* indicates significance at the 10% level, ** at the 5% level, and *** at the 1% level, respectively.
Standard errors control for clustering at the bank level.

Appendix III.6.15: Random-effect regressions with dependent variables RORWA and ROE, Top 150 cooperative banks (merger-controlled panel), with 1% outlier-correction

Variable		RORWA (RE) Financial expertise		RORWA (RE) Out. financial expertise		ROE (RE) Financial expertise		ROE (RE) Out. financial expertise	
		Coeff.	SE (robust)	Coeff.	SE (robust)	Coeff.	SE (robust)	Coeff.	SE (robust)
Financial expertise	Financial expertise	-0.0008	0.0015			-0.0114	0.0165		
	Outside financial expertise			-0.0010	0.0015			-0.0128	0.0162
Bank level	Bank size	-0.3074	0.0708***	-0.3102	0.0690***	-2.1113	0.7864***	-2.1536	0.7662***
	Bank efficiency	-0.0273	0.0037***	-0.0273	0.0037***	-0.2994	0.0366***	-0.2993	0.0366***
	Bank size growth	-0.0438	0.0081***	-0.0439	0.0081***	-0.2726	0.0782***	-0.2737	0.0782***
	Board size	0.0091	0.0097	0.0088	0.0098	0.1677	0.1012*	0.1637	0.1026
	Loan growth	0.0420	0.0044***	0.0420	0.0044***	0.2687	0.0399***	0.2687	0.0399***
	Claims on MFI	-0.0121	0.0053**	-0.0121	0.0053**	-0.1732	0.0520***	-0.1736	0.0520***
	Claims on Non-MFI	-0.0123	0.0036***	-0.0124	0.0037***	-0.0363	0.0360	-0.0376	0.0362
Macroeconomic and structural environment	Federal state	0.3038	0.2118	0.3029	0.2116	4.1243	1.3211***	4.1081	1.3131***
	GDP per capita	0.0867	0.0409	0.0853	0.0409	0.6204	0.4213	0.6052	0.4235
	Population	-0.0048	0.0051**	-0.0047	0.0051**	-0.0342	0.0593	-0.0336	0.0592
	Constant	9.9596	1.3661***	10.0362	1.3397***	77.3076	15.1394***	78.3601	14.8087***
	Wald Chi^2	271.16	***	270.76	***	194.25	***	195.11	***
	R-sq	0.251		0.251		0.1914		0.1914	
	No of observations	896		896		896		896	

* indicates significance at the 10% level, ** at the 5% level, and *** at the 1% level, respectively.
Standard errors control for clustering at the bank level.

Appendix III.6.16: Random-effect regressions with dependent variables z-score and NPL ratio, Top 150 cooperative banks (merger-controlled panel), with 1% outlier-correction

Variable		**z-score (RE) Financial expertise**		**z-score (RE) Out. financial expertise**		**NPL Ratio (RE) Financial expertise**		**NPL Ratio (RE) Out. financial expertise**	
		Coeff.	**SE (robust)**	**Coeff.**	**SE (robust)**	**Coeff.**	**SE (robust)**	**Coeff.**	**SE (robust)**
Financial expertise	Financial expertise	–0.0241	0.0233			0.0113	0.0045***		
	Outside financial expertise			–0.0292	0.0231			0.0115	0.0043***
Bank level	Bank size	–4.2229	1.9047**	–4.2539	1.9270***	–0.4879	0.1751***	–0.4421	0.1731**
	Bank efficiency	–0.0215	0.0089**	–0.0212	0.0090**	–0.0038	0.0072	–0.0039	0.0072
	Bank size growth	–0.0638	0.0194***	–0.0644	0.0194***	–0.1696	0.0164***	–0.1694	0.0164***
	Board size	0.0452	0.1332	0.0369	0.1302	0.0563	0.0314*	0.0590	0.0316*
	Loan growth	–0.0025	0.0137	–0.0021	0.0137	0.0992	0.0111***	0.0992	0.0111***
	Claims on MFI	–0.0427	0.0216**	–0.0440	0.0217**	0.0217	0.0123*	0.0220	0.0123*
	Claims on Non-MFI	0.0477	0.0271*	0.0472	0.0267*	0.0403	0.0095***	0.0410	0.0095***
Macroeconomic and structural environment	Federal state	–1.2817	3.1911	–1.2312	3.1754	1.0473	0.7695	1.0633	0.7656
	GDP per capita	0.5414	0.4645*	0.5104	0.4550*	–0.3255	0.0873***	–0.3168	0.0874***
	Population	0.1057	0.0643	0.1077	0.0648	–0.0355	0.0121***	–0.0359	0.0122***
	Constant	100.4029	37.2886***	101.3678	37.7437***	10.9317	3.7343***	9.9150	3.7335***
	Wald Chi²	166.60	***	164.77	***	295.94	***	299.24	***
	R-sq	0.0528		0.0555		0.338		0.3394	
	No of observations	896		896		885		885	

* indicates significance at the 10% level, ** at the 5% level, and *** at the 1% level, respectively.
Standard errors control for clustering at the bank level.

Appendix III.6.17: Random-effect regressions with dependent variables RORWA and ROE, Top 150 cooperative banks (merger-controlled panel), with 5% outlier-correction

Variable		RORWA (RE) Financial expertise		RORWA (RE) Out. financial expertise		ROE (RE) Financial expertise		ROE (RE) Out. financial expertise	
		Coeff.	**SE (robust)**	**Coeff.**	**SE (robust)**	**Coeff.**	**SE (robust)**	**Coeff.**	**SE (robust)**
Financial expertise	Financial expertise	–0.0003	0.0013			–0.0060	0.0144		
	Outside financial expertise			–0.0006	0.0013			–0.0093	0.0140
Bank level	Bank size	–0.3070	0.0724***	–0.3068	0.0715***	–2.0619	0.7500***	–2.0648	0.7396***
	Bank efficiency	–0.0272	0.0035***	–0.0271	0.0035***	–0.2946	0.0351***	–0.2941	0.0351***
	Bank size growth	–0.0373	0.0073***	–0.0374	0.0073***	–0.2364	0.0711***	–0.2381	0.0713***
	Board size	0.0067	0.0097	0.0064	0.0098	0.1455	0.0973	0.1412	0.0984
	Loan growth	0.0383	0.0038***	0.0383	0.0038***	0.2328	0.0353***	0.2330	0.0353***
	Claims on MFI	–0.0109	0.0050**	–0.0109	0.0050**	–0.1543	0.0511***	–0.1546	0.0511***
	Claims on Non-MFI	–0.0116	0.0033***	–0.0117	0.0033***	–0.0190	0.0331	–0.0203	0.0333
Macroeconomic and structural environment	Federal state	0.3243	0.1606**	0.3255	0.1605**	4.6213	0.8762*	4.6356	0.8700*
	GDP per capita	0.0829	0.0345	0.0812	0.0349	0.6140	0.3495***	0.5890	0.3579***
	Population	–0.0094	0.0065**	–0.0093	0.0065**	–0.1170	0.0640*	–0.1153	0.0639*
	Constant	10.0354	1.4023***	10.0501	1.3861***	77.0198	14.5793***	77.3304	14.3700***
	Wald Chi^2	314.50	***	313.09	***	275.56	***	276.97	***
	R-sq	0.2393		0.2392		0.1841		0.1845	
	No of observations	896		896		896		896	

* indicates significance at the 10% level, ** at the 5% level, and *** at the 1% level, respectively.
Standard errors control for clustering at the bank level.

Appendix III.6.18: Random-effect regressions with dependent variables z-score and NPL ratio, Top 150 cooperative banks (merger-controlled panel), with 5% outlier-correction

Variable		**z-score (RE) Financial expertise**		**z-score (RE) Out. financial expertise**		**NPL Ratio (RE) Financial expertise**		**NPL Ratio (RE) Out. financial expertise**	
		Coeff.	**SE (robust)**	**Coeff.**	**SE (robust)**	**Coeff.**	**SE (robust)**	**Coeff.**	**SE (robust)**
Financial expertise	Financial expertise	–0.0179	0.0212			0.0119	0.0044***		
	Outside financial expertise			–0.0294	0.0243			0.0125	0.0040***
Bank level	Bank size	–4.8307	2.1420**	–4.8001	2.0941**	–0.5682	0.1826***	–0.5326	0.1809***
	Bank efficiency	–0.0297	0.0112***	–0.0287	0.0114**	–0.0089	0.0072	–0.0091	0.0072
	Bank size growth	–0.0701	0.0241***	–0.0718	0.0235***	–0.1740	0.0163***	–0.1733	0.0163***
	Board size	0.0359	0.1479	0.0248	0.1417	0.0605	0.0287***	0.0635	0.0287***
	Loan growth	–0.0083	0.0149	–0.0073	0.0151	0.1047	0.0107**	0.1046	0.0107**
	Claims on MFI	–0.0456	0.0225**	–0.0481	0.0227**	0.0184	0.0122	0.0187	0.0122
	Claims on Non-MFI	0.0541	0.0286*	0.0524	0.0283*	0.0366	0.0102***	0.0375	0.0101***
Macroeconomic and structural environment	Federal state	–1.5739	3.2055	–1.4521	3.1796	0.9111	0.8135	0.9150	0.8087
	GDP per capita	0.4549	0.4090*	0.4113	0.3901*	–0.3147	0.0779***	–0.2972	0.0776***
	Population	0.1391	0.0800	0.1434	0.0813	–0.0428	0.0147***	–0.0436	0.0147***
	Constant	112.2140	41.2909***	112.2367	40.6225***	13.1621	3.8876***	12.3387	3.8673***
	Wald Chi²	136.13	***	133.52	***	357.48	***	363.8	***
	R-sq	0.0649		0.0702		0.366		0.3715	
	No of observations	896		896		885		885	

* indicates significance at the 10% level, ** at the 5% level, and *** at the 1% level, respectively.
Standard errors control for clustering at the bank level.

IV Bank Governance Structures, Financial Expertise of Supervisory Board Members, Overconfidence, and Bank Risk Taking[9]

Abstract In this study, we analyze whether financial expertise in internal bank governance benefits the financial institution by reducing risk and increasing stability. Whereas behavioural finance theory scrutinizes the benefit of financial expertise, empirical studies substantiate that financial experts do add value. Based on a study of more than 400 German banks, we observe that the financial expertise of supervisory board members reduces stability and increases loan portfolio risk. This finding is robust across ownership types. With regard to performance, the results demonstrate that supervisory board competence impacts banking groups in different ways. In general, our results lead to the question how effective universal expertise in internal governance is; therefore, we propose that financial institutions should have experts for specific responsibilities and areas on their supervisory boards.

IV.1 Introduction

In 1999 and 2006, the Basel Committee on Banking Supervision had already emphasized the high relevance of board competence for an effective governance system (Basel Committee on Banking Supervision, 1999b, 2006a). As one of its principles for an effective governance system, the committee demands that "board members should be qualified for their positions, have a clear understanding of their role in corporate governance and be able to exercise sound judgment about the affairs of the bank" (Basel Committee on Banking Supervision, 2006a). The recent 2008 banking crisis sheds additional light on the significance of governance structure in general and board expertise in particular: inappropriate risk management, incomplete risk information, and insufficient industry expertise were identified as major shortcomings in bank risk governance (Ard and Berg, 2010; Choundhry, 2011; Kirkpatrick, 2009). As a consequence, increasing industry expertise on boards is considered an important and necessary measure to deal with banks' increasingly complex and wide reaching business (Mehran, et al., 2011a). Even though it appears perfectly coherent that increasing expertise

9 This chapter is based on a joint working paper (Böhm, Froneberg, and Schiereck, 2012a).

should allow managing these shortcomings, it remains open whether this is the case in reality. Theoretical evidence and empirical studies provide contradictory findings to this question.

Previous research has shown that individuals tend to be overconfident (e.g., Fischhoff, Slovic, and Lichtenstein, 1977). Such overconfidence can be expressed in different ways: overestimating one's own abilities, rating oneself better than others, or overstating the accuracy of one's own beliefs (Moore and Healy, 2007). These factor may lead to situations where decision-makers wrongly estimate and trade-off risks as well as opportunities (e.g., Chuang and Lee, 2006; Cooper, Woo, and Dunkelberg, 1988; Fellner, et al., 2004). Furthermore, Odean (1998) demonstrates that increasing expertise levels does not resolve the problem but can even hamper it, since expertise can accelerate overconfidence. It can be concluded that behavioural finance theory suggests that financial expertise is not necessarily valuable in respect of improving risk governance.

Fama and Jensen (1983) consider outside directors as a source of knowledge. As a consequence, increasing expertise could be beneficial. Empirical studies analyzing the influence of financial expertise on firm performance substantiate this thought and indicate positive relationships. Better stock performances and higher abnormal returns can be demonstrated by firms with more financial experts on their boards than with fewer experts (e.g., Davidson, et al., 2004; Lee, et al., 1999). In addition to that, some studies with accounting-based measures also support these findings (e.g., Dhaliwal, et al., 2006).

In this study, we examine whether a higher share of financial expertise enhances internal bank governance and has a positive influence on bank's risk-return profile. Analyzing if and how financial experts influence risk and stability of banks makes great demands on the database in terms of homogeneity and consistency to ensure comparability across a large number of banks. Different regulatory requirements, business models, and organizational structures affect bank risk and stability as well and may hide the actual influence of board members' financial expertise. However, for the robustness of the analysis, it is important to have comparable banks across different ownership types.

The German three-pillar banking system provides a unique object of investigation. All banks operate under the same regulatory regime, have the common German two-tier board structure, and provide a large reservoir of comparable banks. From a governance perspective, two of the sectors, cooperative and savings banks together the regional banks, are characterized by an emiment similarity that is highly relevant for the present analysis. Regional banks do not have a so-called "market for corporate control" as they are not tied to capital markets for equity funding (Manne, 1965). This leads to contrary observations since there is a lack of control by investors, as in large exchange-listed commercial banks. Otherwise, regional banks are not being distorted by capital markets.

Regional banks are not exchange-listed and have a completely different ownership structure, which is probably the most striking difference within the regional banking groups, at least from a governance perspective. Savings banks are publicly owned, whereas cooperative banks are strictly in privately ownership (Hackethal, 2004; Schmidt, 2009). Cooperative banks are owned by their members, resulting in a widely dispersed ownership structure. On the other hand in the case of savings banks, this leads into a single shareholder ownning the bank.[10] Due to their public ownership, savings banks are closely tied to local and regional authorities (Fischer and Pfeil, 2004). Consequently, the governance mechanisms of cooperative banks are mainly based on social control among members due to their highly fragmented structure and the "one member, one vote" principle (Hackethal and Schmidt, 2005).

Furthermore, the supervisory boards of both regional banking groups are authorized with different decision-making powers and responsibilities, which allows to test the actual impact of financial expertise for robustness and to be separated from structural aspects. Federal state laws on savings banks provide the supervisory boards of these banks with far-reaching responsibilities, leading to more power for savings banks than banks with other legal statuses, e.g., through the credit committee (Hackethal, 2004). Thus, the supervisory board influences the overall banking strategy at savings banks significantly. Additionally, the laws allow the supervisory board to influence the bank management directly, such as by assigning instructions to the management. Examples of these instructions and approvals include the closure of branches, the acquisition of equity stakes in other companies, the employment of executive employees, and the distribution of profits (Kleff and Weber, 2005; Vins, 2008).[11] In contrast to savings banks laws, the Cooperatives Act (GenG) does not provide such opportunities for the supervisory board to influence the operating decisions of bank management directly.

Regional banks have a similar business model that guarantees a high degree of comparability. They are main competitors at the local and regional levels (Engerer and Schrooten, 2004; Fischer and Pfeil, 2004). The charters of cooperative banks and the savings bank laws of the federal states undermine the similarity. The overall objective of cooperative banks is to serve their members with self-aid

10 In cases where several cities or counties have a savings bank together, there is an association that owns the bank.

11 See, for example, the savings banks law of the state of Baden-Wuerttemberg.

and self-responsibility as guiding principles (Hackethal, 2004). They operate on a regional level and provide universal banking service with focus on typical deposit taking and lending business. The business focus of savings banks is dominated by a public mandate which requires them to operate regionally and foster regional economic development (Hackethal, 2004; Hakenes, Schmidt, and Xie, 2009; Schmidt, 2009). Like cooperative banks, the core business of savings banks is deposit taking and lending. At the end of 2009, the 1,939 German banks included 1,157 cooperative banks and 431 savings banks (Deutsche Bundesbank, 2011).

Overall, German regional banks provide a suitable basis for the analysis. The sample of the present study comprises more than 400 German regional banks in the form of cooperative and savings banks, with more than 39,365 observations at the individual level. This study addresses the following two main questions: "Does more financial expertise of supervisory board members improve bank performance, risk and stability?" and "Are these impacts significantly different across ownership types?"

The remainder of this study is structured as follows: Chapter IV.2 presents related literature on board composition and the financial expertise of board members as well as on the risk-taking and performance of regional banks. Chapter IV.3 introduces the data, sources, and the empirical model. Chapter IV.4 provides descriptive results and presents the outcome of the regression analysis. Chapter IV.5 concludes the study with an evaluation of the findings.

IV.2 Literature Review

The empirical related literature can be classified into three categories. The first category deals with the impact of boards' financial expertise on performance and risk. The second category comprises studies that analyze the influence of board composition and size on firm performance. The third category focuses on the efficiency, performance, and stability of regional banks.

The most related strand of literature is the first, which illustrates the influence of financial expertise on banks' risk-return profile. The studies conclude that higher levels of competence may pay off. However, these results are not consistent. The following strand of literature holds that professional experience of the individuals determines mainly the financial expertise.

Most related studies analyzing the influence of competence on the risk-return profile have a similar conceptual ground but differ to a certain degree, such as in their focus on non-banks and one-tier boards. The results of several studies reflecting accounting-based performance indicators are mixed. Carcello, Hollingsworth, Klein, and Neal (2008) cannot demonstrate that expertise is exclusively beneficial, since there are substitutes for expertise that can lead to the same positive effect on financial reporting. Dhaliwal, Naiker, and Navissi (2006) document a positive relationship between accounting expertise and accruals quality, indicating that expertise in general positively impacts firm performance. Güner, Malmendier, and Tate (2008) examines the impact of bankers on the boards and on investments. They exhibit that bankers do exert influence but not always in the interest of shareholders, especially if there are conflicts of interest between the bankers and the shareholders. Studies with market-based measures indicate that capital markets also reward financial expertise. Positive stock price reactions and abnormal returns can be observed in the context of the appointment of financial experts to boards (Davidson, et al., 2004; DeFond, et al., 2005; Fernandes and Fich, 2009; Lee, et al., 1999). Focusing on the recent banking crisis, Minton, Taillard, and Williamson (2010) demonstrate that bank risk is positively linked to financial expertise.

Apart from the analysis of the explicit influence of board competence, studies analyze generally the effect of board size and composition on firm performance. The results indicate that firm value tend to be reduced by larger boards (Eisenberg, et al., 1998; Yermack, 1996). This undermines the theory that free riding is incentivized by larger boards leading to adverse effects on performance (Jensen, 1993). Conversely, a more recent study documents that value can be enhanced through board size, depending on the complexity of the firm (Coles, Daniel, and Naveen, 2008). Studies concentrating in particular on banks find that banks with larger boards do underperform banks with smaller boards, and that larger boards can lead to a positive effect on bank performance (R. B. Adams and Mehran, 2008; Andres and Vallelado, 2008). Concerning board composition, most studies reveal no link to firm performance (Hermalin and Weisbach, 2003). The fraction of outsiders on the boards was mostly used to proxy board composition. Insignificant relationships were reported regardless of the use of Tobin's q or accounting measures (Bhagat and Black, 2000; Hermalin and Weisbach, 1991; Klein, 1998; Mehran, 1995).

The third category of literature deals with the comparison of performance and risk across the banking sectors. These studies find that savings banks and cooperative are less risky and more stable than are commercial banks. However, the results do not provide evidence whether savings banks are more stable and less risky than cooperative banks, or vice versa. Similar to the present study, Beck, Hesse, Kick, and Westernhagen (2009) concentrate on the German banking sector in order to examine the stability across the three pillars. This allows running meaningful comparisons between banking sectors, as no diverging cross-country effects between banking groups need to be considered. The study finds that commercial banks are less stable than are banks in the other two sectors. The comparison between savings and cooperative banks shows that savings banks face higher insolvency risk than cooperative banks do. However, regarding distress probability, the result is the opposite. Evidence on lending risk is not consistent. Commercial banks show higher profitability than both groups whil being savings banks more profitable than cooperative banks. Goddard, Molyneux, and Wilson (2004) confirm weaker performance for German cooperative and savings banks based on an international sample of 665 banks.

Concerning international banks, Westman (2010) demonstrates, without controlling for operational and ownership characteristics, that cooperative and savings banks are less risky but also less profitable than commercial banks. For international cooperative banks, Cihák and Hesse (2007) find that these banks are more stable than commercial banks in terms of z-score. To a lower degree, the same finding applies to savings banks as well. The aforementioned study covers nearly 17,000 banks from 29 countries. By going beyond mere comparison, the study reveals that the stability of the overall banking system can be increased by cooperative banks. However, the study also concludes that non-profit banks such as cooperative banks can threaten weak commercial banks in the retail market because they initiate cut-throat competition, forcing the commercial banks to focus on more volatile business segments such as corporate and investment banking. The results of Cihák and Hesse (2007) are underpinned by those of another study, which exhibit that earnings stability is higher for both savings and cooperative banks than it is for commercial banks and that cooperative banks are less stable than savings banks (Ayadi, et al., 2010). With regard to efficiency, there is hardly any evidence of significant differences between German regional banks during the 1989–1996 period (Altunbas, et al., 2001).

IV.3 Data set and Methodology

IV.3.1 Sample and Data set

The present study is based on the 400[12] largest savings and cooperative banks as at the end of 2009. Savings banks that are not publicly owned and cooperative banks that are not of the legal form of a cooperative firm are excluded from the dataset. If financial expertise cannot be derived individuals have been allocated to the category "other". Therefore, all banks considered in the panel must be below the following "other" threshold in order to increase the explanatory power

12 The 200 largest banks of each sector are included if the study criteria are satisfied.

of the underlying examination. A maximum of 10% of the overall supervisory board, or one individual for supervisory boards of up to nine individuals, is allowed to be classified as "other". The institution that ranks next in size is included if a savings bank or cooperative has not been included in the analysis due to lack of data or too high a representation of individuals who could not clearly be labeled either financially literate or not literate.

Two samples are analyzed in the present study; thereof the first sample lalled as "Top 200" comprising the 200 largest banks in each sector. The second sample "Top 150" sample includes the 150 largest banks in each sector that were not involved in mergers over the panel horizon and the two years preceding this horizon. Overall, 257 cooperative and 209 savings banks have been included in this study. The Top 200 sample covers 21% of all German banks and accounts for 15% of the German banks' total assets.[13] In the savings banking sector, the largest 200 savings banks account for 71% of the sector's total assets. The largest savings bank in the sample has total assets of EUR 29.3 billion, and the smallest savings bank has EUR 1.5 billion. The mean of total assets is EUR 3.8 billion. With regard to the cooperative banking sector, the largest 200 banks included in the analysis account for 57% of the total assets. The average cooperative bank in the sample has total assets of EUR 1.9 billion. The largest cooperative bank has total assets of EUR 41.4 billion, while the smallest bank has EUR 0.7 billion. The merger-controlled banks (Top 150) account for 45% of the savings bank sector's total assets and for 35% of the cooperative bank sector's total assets and. The average of total assets in the merger-controlled sample is EUR 3.2 billion for savings banks and EUR 1.6 billion for cooperative banks. The total assets of savings banks from EUR 1.4 billion to EUR 15.6 billion and that of cooperative banks range from EUR 0.5 billion to EUR 41.4 billion.

Data on supervisory board members were manually collected from each bank's annual report (published by the Bundesanzeiger and through access via the Unternehmensregister or LexisNexis databases). The merger history of each bank was accessed through the Hoppenstedt Banken database. Balance sheet and Profit & Loss statement data were taken from the BAKIS database. BAKIS is the joint information system of the German Federal Financial Supervisory Authority (BaFin) and Deutsche Bundesbank, and it contains bank-specific data. The Regionaldatenbank Deutschland of the German Federal Statistical Office provided data for macroeconomic and structural control variables.

13 As of the end of 2009.

IV.3.2 Hypotheses and Model

With our empirical model, we test two hypotheses on the influence of supervisory board financial expertise on the risk-return profile of banks. First, we analyze whether the (outside) financial expertise of the supervisory board has an influence on the risk and performance of savings and cooperative banks. Second, we test whether the impact of (outside) financial expertise is the same across ownership types.

Hypothesis 1: *The (outside) financial expertise of the supervisory board members is unrelated to bank risk and performance.*

Hypothesis 2: *The impact of the (outside) financial expertise of the supervisory board on bank risk and performance is equal in cooperative and savings banks.*

The influence of the financial expertise of supervisory boards on bank performance and risk is analyzed based on a panel analysis via a random-effect regression model of the following general form:

$$DV_{it} = \alpha + \beta FE_{it} + \gamma B_{it} + \delta M_{it} + \theta SD_{i} + \varepsilon_{it} \qquad \text{(IV.1)}$$

where *DV* is the dependent variable of bank *i* at time *t*. Dependent variables for stability and risk are z-score and non-performing loans (NPL) ratio. The dependent variables for performance are return on risk-weighted assets (RORWA) and return on equity (ROE). *FE* is the financial expertise of the supervisory board, *B* comprises bank-level control variables, *M* comprises macroeconomic and structural control variables, *SD* is a dummy variable for savings banks, and ε is the error term. For a comparison of the coefficients across the two sectors, interaction effects are included in the regression model. Therefore, *FE*, *B*, and *M* are made to interact with dummy variables for savings and cooperative banks. *B* comprises (a) bank size, (b) bank size growth, (c) bank efficiency, (d) bank loan volume growth, (e) claims on monetary financial institutions (MFI), (f) claims on non-monetary financial institutions (non-MFI), and (g) supervisory board size. *M* comprises (h) East/West dummy, (i) local Gross Domestic Product (GDP) per capita, and (j) population.

The equality of the coefficients across the banking sectors is tested with the following null hypothesis (H_0):

$$H_0 : \beta_{cv} - \beta_{sv} = 0 \qquad \text{(IV.2)}$$

where β is the regression coefficient of variable *v*. *s* indicates the coefficient of the savings banks sector and *c* indicates the regression coefficient of the cooperative banking sector. These coefficients are tested with a Wald parameter test.

IV.3.3 Financial Expertise

The financial expertise of supervisory board members is gauged based on their professional backgrounds. This approacj follows previous studies (e.g., Davidson, et al., 2004; Dhaliwal, et al., 2006; Minton, et al., 2010). The financial expertise of supervisory board members is defined as outlined in Table IV.1:

Table IV.1: Professional backgrounds with assumed financial expertise

Level 1: Employment	Self-employed persons with assumed financial expertise	Employed persons with assumed financial expertise	Retired persons with assumed financial expertise
Level 2: Occupation	Entrepreneur, Merchant, Owner	Non-bank employee with assumed financial focus (e.g. member of management board)	Retired self-employed person with assumed financial expertise
	Managing Partner	Bank employee	Retired employed person with assumed financial expertise
	Partner	Public officer with assumed financial focus (e.g. treasurer)	
		Federal and State Minister, State Secretary	
		Local and regional politician	

The main idea behind the applied methodology is the obvious relation to financial issues. For instance, financial expertise is expected in the case of the managing directors of companies. Additionally, the definition of financial expertise mainly follows that of the German regulatory bodies (BaFin and Deutsche Bundesbank, 2010). For example, following the regulators' joint bulletin, financial expertise is assigned to potential mandatory members, such as mayors and district administrators.

Taking into account the differences of details in the annual reports between banks, several assumptions concerning tenure, employment classification, and politicians have been maade. A more detailed methodology has been applied for the identification of local and regional politicians, taking into consideration full-time employment vs. voluntary service and the authorization to give instructions (for further details see Appendix IV.6.1).

Whereas the federal savings bank laws ensure a constant level of employee representation on the supervisory boards of savings banks, cooperative banks have different legal requirements that do not demand a comparable level of employee representation on the supervisory board. For this reason, regression analysis is conducted twice for each sample. First, the financial expertise of the total supervisory board and its influence a bank's risk-return profile is tested. Second, employee representatives who are employed at the respective bank are excluded from the sample to analyze the influence on performance and risk of the outside expertise of the "freely eligible" supervisory boxard members. This enhances comparability in two ways: first, between savings banks located in different federal states and, second, between cooperative and savings banks.

IV.3.4 Measurement of Risk and Return

Risk is measured in two ways. Z-score is applied as a stability measure indicator the risk of insolvency. This indicator has become a widely used method to measure risk (e.g., Boyd and Runkle, 1993; Laeven and Levine, 2009). Insolvency is defined as the state in which a bank's capital is insufficient to absorb losses (Roy, 1952). The probability of insolvency is defined as prob(-ROA<CAR), where ROA is the return on assets and CAR is the capital assets ratio. Assuming that profits are normally distributed, the probability of insolvency becomes (ROA+CAR)/ σ(ROA), where σ(ROA) is the standard deviation of ROA (Boyd and Runkle, 1993). A more stable bank is characteriszed by a higher z-value. ROA is calculated as operating result divided by total assets. The standard deviation of ROA is calculated over the years, from 1994 to the year under consideration. CAR is defined as Tier 1 equity divided by total assets. The loan portfolio risk is measured by the ratio of non-performing loans to total assets. This risk measure is highly important to savings and cooperative banks due to large engagements in the lending business.

The primary performance measure is RORWA and is defined as operating result divided by risk-weighted assets. RORWA performance is risk-adjusted, because a bank's risk-weighted assets are based on its specific risk profile. ROE is used for robustness checks and is defined as operating result divided by equity. We use operating result for both performance measures to avoid distortions due to undisclosed reserves. These reserves are already accounted for in the annual net profit (Beck, et al., 2009).

IV.3.5 Control Variables

The present study controls for bank-specific issues as well as macroeconomic and structural aspects. The log of total assets and the year-to-year change in total assets are used to account for differences in bank size and bank growth. We use the cost-income ratio (CIR), which is defined as general administrative expenses divided by operating results, to control for different efficiency levels. We use the annual change in total loans to account for different levels of lending engagement. In addition, the difference in activities between savings and cooperative banks is reflected by the ratios of claims on MFI to total assets and claims on non-MFI to total assets. Different board sizes may affect performance and risk due to free-riding incentives in different ways (Jensen, 1993). Accordingly, the size of the supervisory board is accounted for in the empirical analysis.

The region in which the bank is located is very important since both banking groups have clearly defined business areas. Structural issues are captured by an index variable that separates urban and rural areas, and with a binary variable that separates federal states that used to be in the former German Democratic Republic from other federal states. Banks in the federal states of the former German Democratic Republic are assigned a value of one. The difference between urban and rural areas is based on population. An index is applied to separate sparsely populated areas from densely populated and metropolitan areas in order to differentiate between regional, district, and county centers. Five clusters have been defined. Areas with up to 1,000,000 inhabitants are divided into four clusters of 250,000 inhabitants each. The fifth cluster is composed of areas with more than 1,000,000 inhabitants. Regional economic development is gauged by the GDP per capita of the business area. The population and the GDP per capita are adjusted for mergers during the panel horizon in order to capture the effect of macroeconomic changes. The following Table IV.2 gives an overview of the definitions and sources of all control variables.

Table IV.2: Definition of control variables and sources

Bank level control variables	Description	Source
a. Bank size	Ln of total assets	BAKIS (Deutsche Bundesbank)
b. Bank size growth	Year-to-year change in total assets	BAKIS (Deutsche Bundesbank)
c. Bank efficiency	General administrative expenses to operating result (CIR)	BAKIS (Deutsche Bundesbank)
d. Bank loan volume growth	Year-to-year change in total loans	BAKIS (Deutsche Bundesbank)
e. Bank claims on MFI	Claims on MFI divided by total assets	BAKIS (Deutsche Bundesbank)
f. Bank claims on non-MFI	Claims on non-MFI divided by total assets	BAKIS (Deutsche Bundesbank)
g. Bank supervisory board size	Number of supervisory board members	Annual reports
Macroeconomic and structural control variables		
h. East/West	Binary variable separating Eastern and Western federal state	Annual reports
i. GDP per capita	GDP of business area divided by population of business area	Regionaldatenbank Deutschland
j. Population	Index based on population within business area	Regionaldatenbank Deutschland

IV.4 Results

IV.4.1 Summary Statistics

Predominantly employed people are on savings banks' supervisory boards; this is mainly driven by the large fraction of insiders who account on average for 25% of the board. On the contrary, only 5% of the members of cooperative banks' supervisory boards are employed at the respective bank. Cooperative banks' supervisory boards are rather dominated by a large fraction of self-employed people accounting for almost 40% of the supervisory boards and exceeding the number of self-employed people at savings banks by far. In line with insiders, politicians only play a role in savings banks. Due to the public ownership of savings banks they represent as expected a notable fraction of the supervisory boards.

In summary, the supervisory board composition of the banks is quite different despite the similar business model. Therefore, the assignment of financial expertise in the two regional banking groups is driven by different employment groups, which adds robustness to the analysis of the impact of financial experts on risk and stability.

Table IV.3: Supervisory board composition, Top 200

Variables		Mean	Std. Dev.	Coeff. of Variation	Min	Max
Insider (%)	Cooperative banks	5.20	11.88	228.34	0.00	52.94
	Savings banks	24.71	12.33	49.90	0.00	41.67
Outsider (%)	Cooperative banks	94.80	11.88	12.53	47.06	100.00
	Savings banks	75.29	12.33	16.38	58.33	100.00
Employment						
Employed individuals (%)	Cooperative banks	50.22	22.94	45.68	0.00	100.00
	Savings banks	73.32	12.24	16.70	36.36	100.00
Self-employed individuals (%)	Cooperative banks	39.55	23.49	59.40	0.00	91.67
	Savings banks	12.62	9.57	75.80	0.00	47.37
Retired individuals (%)	Cooperative banks	9.20	11.86	128.99	0.00	77.78
	Savings banks	12.71	9.95	78.25	0.00	55.56
Other (%)	Cooperative banks	1.03	2.76	268.43	0.00	14.29
	Savings banks	1.35	2.77	204.11	0.00	12.50
Politicians (officiating)						
Federal politicians (%)	Cooperative banks	0.09	0.90	1,020.84	0.00	11.11
	Savings banks	0.76	2.29	299.94	0.00	15.38
Federal state politicians (%)	Cooperative banks	0.24	1.53	629.23	0.00	20.00
	Savings banks	2.57	4.22	164.08	0.00	23.08
Regional politicians (%)	Cooperative banks	0.00	0.00	0.00	0.00	0.00
	Savings banks	5.88	4.69	79.74	0.00	28.57
Local politicians (%)	Cooperative banks	1.83	4.24	231.21	0.00	25.00
	Savings banks	15.15	12.57	82.97	0.00	54.55
Officiating and retired politicians (%)	Cooperative banks	2.80	5.53	197.83	0.00	35.29
	Savings banks	28.13	15.19	54.00	0.00	75.00

Comparing risk and stability measures of both regional banking groups does not provide consistent results (see Table IV.4). Cooperative banks are more stable than savings banks in terms of z-score. But at the same time, they have a higher loan portfolio risk than savings banks in terms of the NPL ratio. Savings banks perhaps better realize diversification benefits in their loan portfolio than cooperative banks due to their larger bank size. Performance measures reveal a clear picture contrary to risk and stability. Savings banks' performance exceeds that of cooperative banks in both performance measures.

Savings banks' financial expertise significantly outreaches that of cooperative banks, undermining that they benefit from the legally required employee representation. This leads to the effect that savings banks have an expertise floor at 20%. Controlling for insiders aligns the expertise values but leaves the savings banks' supervisory board more financially literate. Outside financial expertise for both groups is around 50% and ranges from 0% to 100%. This suggests that neither banking sector has fundamentally different preferences with regard to the composition of their "freely eligible" members.

As expected, savings banks are significantly larger than their cooperative competitors. Accordingly, the larger average bank size and the legally required employee representation result in larger supervisory boards of savings banks. Contrary to bank size, as regards both growth rates, cooperative banks are ahead of savings banks. Cooperative banks are more engaged in business development and grow a lot faster than savings banks, in both total assets and loan volume. The stronger focus on growth might be caused by the more entrepreneur-staffed supervisory boards in cooperative banks. Self-employed business people might have a stronger focus on growth and business expansion, which explains the higher growth rates. Another effect stems from the circumstance that savings banks are starting from a different base due to their smaller size. Despite the stronger business expansion, profitability is lower and risk is higher for cooperative banks. The reason might be the monopolistic structures of local markets. Since those markets are limited in size and monopolistically structured, growth comes at the expense of lower profitability and more risk (Claessens and Laeven, 2003; Hempell, 2002). In general, the asset shift toward more profitable lending business as indicated by the higher loan volume growth compared to the total assets growth is consistent in both regional banking sectors.

All differences in the risk, stability, performance, and other bank-level variables between the two groups are significant, except of claims on non-MFI (see Appendices IV.6.5 and IV.6.7). Additionally, the merger-controlled panel confirms these results (see Appendix IV.6.6).

Table IV.4: Summary statistics, Top 200

Dependent variables	**Group**	**Mean**	**Std. Dev.**	**Coeff. of Variation**	**Min**	**Max**
z-score	Cooperative banks	22.71	14.81	65.24	3.61	103.23
	Savings banks	19.40	10.56	54.41	2.87	77.02
NPL ratio (%)	Cooperative banks	2.66	1.97	74.15	0.00	13.47
	Savings banks	2.11	1.51	71.38	0.04	11.56
ROE (%)	Cooperative banks	12.19	7.56	62.04	−17.62	55.21
	Savings banks	13.60	8.45	62.11	-61.76	67.79
RORWA (%)	Cooperative banks	1.21	0.80	65.70	−1.82	6.27
	Savings banks	1.33	0.99	74.08	−2.92	8.65
Bank level variables						
Financial expertise (%)	Cooperative banks	47.76	22.87	47.88	0.00	100.00
	Savings banks	64.98	17.25	26.55	20.00	100.00
Outside financial expertise (%)	Cooperative banks	45.25	23.23	51.34	0.00	100.00
	Savings banks	53.15	22.86	43.01	0.00	100.00
Board size	Cooperative banks	12.42	4.44	35.76	5.00	37.00
	Savings banks	16.81	5.29	31.46	7.00	48.00
Bank size (ln ,000s of EUR)	Cooperative banks	20.90	0.69	3.28	19.60	24.45
	Savings banks	21.78	0.60	2.77	20.56	24.16
Bank size growth (%)	Cooperative banks	2.61	4.61	176.76	−14.80	31.47
	Savings banks	0.25	3.34	1,323.23	−16.29	18.26
Bank efficiency (%)	Cooperative banks	66.48	9.55	14.37	15.98	112.92
	Savings banks	65.29	7.32	11.20	36.00	95.51
Loan growth (%)	Cooperative banks	4.98	7.44	149.52	−13.19	51.54
	Savings banks	2.86	9.80	342.62	−14.70	104.87
Claims on MFI (%)	Cooperative banks	11.89	6.59	55.47	0.06	45.65
	Savings banks	9.85	6.55	66.58	0.00	44.37
Claims on non-MFI (%)	Cooperative banks	58.67	11.39	19.41	11.17	83.57
	Savings banks	58.91	12.00	20.37	24.21	85.36
Macroeconomic and structural variables						
East/West	Cooperative banks	0.02	0.14	700.29	0.00	1.00
	Savings banks	0.13	0.34	258.80	0.00	1.00
GDP per capita ('000s of EUR)	Cooperative banks	28.04	7.32	26.12	9.39	62.04
	Savings banks	27.49	7.62	27.73	14.12	72.20
Population	Cooperative banks	2.67	1.39	52.07	1.00	5.00
	Savings banks	1.73	0.90	51.96	1.00	5.00

All banks are clustered by financial expertise in order to assess how different financial expertise levels within each group are associated with risk, stability, performance, and further bank level characteristics (see Table IV.5). Each cluster in both groups contains 50 banks. Banks with the highest expertise levels are included in Cluster 1, and those with the lowest levels in Cluster 4.

Financial expertise tends to reduce stability. For cooperative banks, this holds consistently across all clusters. With savings banks, stability consistently diminishes from Clusters 4 to 2, but then slightly rises again in Cluster 1. Similar to z-score, the NPL ratio trend in cooperative banks is consistent across all clusters. The larger the number of financial experts on cooperative banks' supervisory boards, the higher the NPL ratio. Savings banks' NPL ratio does not show a similar pro-risk attitude of financial experts. From Cluster 4 to Cluster 3, the ratio rises with higher expertise level, but decreases from Cluster 3 to Cluster 1. Apparently, savings banks' higher performance in the high-expertise clusters is associated with higher loan portfolio risk since Clusters 2 and 3 are above Cluster 4. But since Cluster 1 has the same level as Cluster 4, there is obviously a threshold above which financial expertise has a risk-decreasing effect.

Both regional banking groups display a totally contrarian performance. While the performance of savings banks benefits from rising board expertise, cooperative banks' tends to deteriorate with increasing financial expertise.

It is worth mentioning further the variables bank size, loan volume growth, and efficiency. One could hypothesize that the larger the bank, the more complex its business, which requires higher expertise levels. However, only cooperative banks confirm that hypothesis since their financial expertise increase with bank size. Against the odds, only in savings banks do efficiency levels benefit from higher levels of financial expertise. Savings banks with high expertise levels reveal significantly lower CIRs than low-expertise savings banks. The opposite holds for cooperative banks. With regard to loan volume growth, the analysis exhibits that in both groups, low-expertise banks have higher growth rates. One could assume that banks with low expertise levels are less engaged in expanding their lending activities, which might be the reason for their higher stability compared to high-expertise banks. However, the higher growth rates of low-expertise banks contradict this view. Overall, these findings are confirmed by the merger-controlled panel (see Appendix IV.6.8).

Table IV.5: Summary statistics, clustered by financial expertise, Top 200

Dependent variables	Group	Cluster 1	Cluster 2	Cluster 3	Cluster 4	Delta Cluster 4–1
z-score	Cooperative banks	19.05	22.18	24.52	25.06	–6.01
	Savings banks	18.65	17.38	20.67	20.89	–2.25
NPL ratio (%)	Cooperative banks	3.14	2.70	2.59	2.22	0.92
	Savings banks	2.01	2.11	2.30	2.03	–0.01
ROE (%)	Cooperative banks	10.86	12.37	13.54	11.99	–1.13
	Savings banks	15.20	14.31	13.07	11.82	3.37
RORWA (%)	Cooperative banks	1.05	1.24	1.34	1.22	–0.17
	Savings banks	1.42	1.50	1.26	1.13	0.29
Bank level variables						
Financial expertise (%)	Cooperative banks	76.53	54.89	39.85	19.78	56.75
	Savings banks	86.38	71.28	58.69	43.56	42.81
Outside financial expertise (%)	Cooperative banks	72.95	53.04	36.87	18.13	54.82
	Savings banks	81.12	61.24	43.70	26.56	54.56
Board size	Cooperative banks	12.65	11.66	12.67	12.69	–0.04
	Savings banks	17.37	16.39	16.67	16.80	0.57
Bank size (ln ,000s of EUR)	Cooperative banks	21.09	20.89	20.88	20.74	0.35
	Savings banks	21.74	21.87	21.68	21.84	–0.10
Bank size growth (%)	Cooperative banks	1.82	2.96	2.62	3.01	–1.19
	Savings banks	0.67	0.17	0.25	–0.07	0.73
Bank efficiency (%)	Cooperative banks	67.92	66.54	65.61	65.88	2.04
	Savings banks	64.05	64.69	65.64	66.78	–2.74
Loan growth (%)	Cooperative banks	4.08	5.26	5.03	5.54	–1.46
	Savings banks	2.46	2.28	2.69	4.02	–1.56
Claims on MFI (%)	Cooperative banks	12.06	11.97	13.06	10.47	1.59
	Savings banks	11.58	9.72	10.06	8.03	3.55
Claims on non-MFI (%)	Cooperative banks	59.73	57.06	58.46	59.44	0.29
	Savings banks	53.55	58.24	59.75	64.11	–10.56

Table IV.6 provides the significance of pairwise tests between the clusters in both groups (see Appendix IV.6.9 for the merger-controlled panel).

Table IV.6: Pairwise test of significance between expertise clusters, Top 200

Dependent variables		Cluster 1 vs. 2	Cluster 1 vs. 3	Cluster 1 vs. 4	Cluster 2 vs. 3	Cluster 2 vs. 4	Cluster 3 vs. 4
		t (*p-value*)	t (*p-value*)	t (*p-value*)	t (*p-value*)	t (*p-value*)	t (*p-value*)
z-score	Cooperative banks	-2.9416***	-5.1116***	-5.3941***	-2.1057**	-2.2044**	-0.3978
		0.0035	*0.0000*	*0.0000*	*0.0361*	*0.0283*	*0.6910*
	Savings banks	1.7932*	-2.0026**	-2.6364***	-3.5476***	-4.6260***	-0.2238
		0.0740	*0.0461*	*0.0088*	*0.0005*	*0.0000*	*0.8230*
NPL ratio	Cooperative banks	2.9874***	4.0449***	6.0319***	0.5127	2.9269***	2.2893**
		0.0031	*0.0001*	*0.0000*	*0.6085*	*0.0037*	*0.0228*
	Savings banks	-0.8212	-2.3812**	0.0338	-1.8113*	0.9519	2.8269***
		0.4122	*0.0179*	*0.9730*	*0.0711*	*0.3419*	*0.0050*
ROE	Cooperative banks	-2.4392**	-4.8278***	-2.0750**	-2.0154**	0.7044	3.0085***
		0.0153	*0.0000*	*0.0388*	*0.0448*	*0.4817*	*0.0028*
	Savings banks	1.5491	2.9093***	6.0121***	1.7952*	4.3481***	1.8871*
		0.1224	*0.0040*	*0.0000*	*0.0736*	*0.0000*	*0.0601*
RORWA	Cooperative banks	-2.9746***	-5.1122***	-2.8960***	-1.7083*	0.2822	2.2395**
		0.0032	*0.0000*	*0.0041*	*0.0886*	*0.7780*	*0.0259*
	Savings banks	-1.1722	2.0085**	4.5434***	2.9031***	4.8021***	1.7949*
		0.2420	*0.0455*	*0.0000*	*0.0040*	*0.0000*	*0.0737*
Bank level variables							
Financial expertise	Cooperative banks	36.4796***	62.4921***	107.0168***	31.6913***	58.9953***	35.3432***
		0.0000	*0.0000*	*0.0000*	*0.0000*	*0.0000*	*0.0000*
	Savings banks	38.6471***	72.3544***	97.5500***	31.8934***	61.9574***	32.0524***
		0.0000	*0.0000*	*0.0000*	*0.0000*	*0.0000*	*0.0000*
Outside financial expertise	Cooperative banks	25.2058***	37.7623***	79.3250***	20.1509***	47.0515***	21.5942***
		0.0000	*0.0000*	*0.0000*	*0.0000*	*0.0000*	*0.0000*
	Savings banks	29.4410***	54.4313***	68.7638***	22.6287***	42.3762***	20.1752***
		0.0000	*0.0000*	*0.0000*	*0.0000*	*0.0000*	*0.0000*
Bank size	Cooperative banks	4.0484***	3.5593***	6.9548***	0.2905	3.3427***	2.2812**
		0.0001	*0.0004*	*0.0000*	*0.7716*	*0.0009*	*0.0232*
	Savings banks	-3.0146***	1.3804	-1.9940**	4.2496***	0.7161	-2.9528***
		0.0028	*0.1685*	*0.0471*	*0.0000*	*0.4745*	*0.0034*
Bank efficiency	Cooperative banks	1.8552*	3.4015***	3.2641***	1.2181	0.8768	-0.4186
		0.0645	*0.0008*	*0.0012*	*0.2241*	*0.3813*	*0.6758*
	Savings banks	-1.0181	-2.6110***	-4.4523***	-1.8035*	-3.6803***	-2.1189**
		0.3094	*0.0095*	*0.0000*	*0.0723*	*0.0003*	*0.0349*
Bank size growth	Cooperative banks	-3.3467***	-1.9672*	-3.2731***	1.0335	-0.3325	-0.8804
		0.0009	*0.0502*	*0.0012*	*0.3023*	*0.7397*	*0.3795*
	Savings banks	1.7965*	1.4950	2.6986***	-0.0661	0.9662	1.1114
		0.0735	*0.1361*	*0.0074*	*0.9473*	*0.3348*	*0.2674*
Board size	Cooperative banks	2.7820***	-0.0637	-0.0953	-3.5862***	-2.8178***	-0.0343
		0.0057	*0.9492*	*0.9242*	*0.0004*	*0.0052*	*0.9726*
	Savings banks	2.0786**	1.5048	1.3134	-0.8163	-1.2133	-0.3118
		0.0385	*0.1334*	*0.1900*	*0.4150*	*0.2260*	*0.7554*

Dependent variables		Cluster 1 vs. 2	Cluster 1 vs. 3	Cluster 1 vs. 4	Cluster 2 vs. 3	Cluster 2 vs. 4	Cluster 3 vs. 4
		t (*p-value*)	t (*p-value*)	t (*p-value*)	t (*p-value*)	t (*p-value*)	t (*p-value*)
Loan growth	Cooperative banks	−2.6742*** *0.0080*	−2.0712** *0.0393*	−3.1177*** *0.0020*	0.4078 *0.6837*	−0.4854 *0.6278*	−0.7861 *0.4325*
	Savings banks	0.3587 *0.7201*	−0.6442 *0.5200*	−2.2038** *0.0284*	−1.0905 *0.2764*	−2.1322** *0.0338*	−1.4634 *0.1445*
Claims on MFI	Cooperative banks	0.1639 *0.8699*	−1.9450* *0.0527*	2.9122*** *0.0039*	−1.9462* *0.0526*	2.8777*** *0.0043*	4.6932*** *0.0000*
	Savings banks	3.4456*** *0.0007*	2.7623*** *0.0061*	7.0218*** *0.0000*	−0.6907 *0.4903*	3.5515*** *0.0004*	4.4932*** *0.0000*
Claims on non-MFI	Cooperative banks	2.8703*** *0.0044*	1.7566* *0.0800*	0.3068 *0.7592*	−1.4140 *0.1584*	−2.4490** *0.0149*	−1.1065 *0.2694*
	Savings banks	−5.0788*** *0.0000*	−6.2691*** *0.0000*	−11.3830*** *0.0000*	−1.6453 *0.1010*	−7.3531*** *0.0000*	−4.7265*** *0.0000*

Confidence level: 95%
* indicates significance at the 10% level, ** at the 5% level, and *** at the 1% level, respectively.

IV.4.2 Regression Results

Regression results display that financial experts on supervisory boards cannot contribute to more stability and less loan portfolio risk but rather lead to greater risk-taking. The results lend support to evidence from behavioural finance theory. Fellner, Güth, and Maciejovsky (2004) demonstrates that such an "illusion of expertise" can result in an overestimation of one's own abilities in trading off risks and expected returns. Hence, the calls for more expertise in supervisory boards could potentially result in a vicious circle. As Odean (1998) points out, overconfidence increases with expertise, which then might aggravate the problem. Furthermore, our finding is consistent across ownership structures and underpins the results of Minton, Taillard, and Williamson (2010), who also reveal that higher levels of expertise are associated with higher levels of bank risk. Financial expertise only pays off for savings banks in terms of bank performance. This is remarkable because both regional banking groups have similar business models and operate in the same regulatory environment. Savings banks are compensated for greater risk, as their performance increases in tandem, in contrast to cooperative banks, where financial expertise reduces profitability.

All regressions with z-score and NPL ratio as dependent variables are significant at the 1% level, as indicated by the Wald chi-square test (see Table IV.7). The impact of financial expertise on stability and risk is similar in savings and cooperative banks as indicated by the financial expertise and outside financial expertise coefficients. Although at first sight the negative impact appears to be stronger at cooperative banks, the effect is only significantly different from savings banks for outside financial expertise (see Table IV.8). Thus, insiders apparently influence both regional banking groups differently. Since the negative effect of expertise on z-score at savings banks is stronger inclusive insiders, the statutory employee representatives do obviously not exert a favourable influence on the other financial experts. Contrary, at cooperative banks where on average much less employee representatives are on the supervisory board, insiders influence the other financial experts positively. The reason why the negative impact of financial expertise on loan portfolio risk is significant at cooperative banks in particular might be due to the different board compositions. Cooperative banks' supervisory boards include a large fraction of entrepreneurs. Although they are supposed to have a sound understanding of business risk, they might also tend to overrate their abilities more than people of different professions.

Only at first sight most bank characteristics affect both regional banking groups' z-score differently. Although except of claims on non-MFI and board size all other variables have different directions, the comparison of the coefficients does not provide evidence for highly significant different effects on both banking groups' stability through most bank characteristics. However, bank size growth and loan volume growth are significantly different between both groups. Given the much higher growth rate of cooperative banks and the negative impact of loan volume growth on stability, this indicates from a stability viewpoint that they primarily grow in more disadvantageous business than savings banks do.

In contrast to z-score, the influence of bank characteristics on the NPL ratio have the same direction but are mainly significantly different between both regional banking groups (see Table IV.8). Bank size and bank size growth are of particular interest. The fact that both variables have a more pronounced negative impact on the NPL ratio at cooperative banks implies that they can better benefit from an increase in banks size than savings banks. Cooperative banks can catch up with savings banks which are larger in size and already better realize diversification benefits within their loan portfolio, whereas savings bank can hardly further improve their loan portfolio through economies of scale

The adverse effect of board size on both measures in both banking groups follows the theory that larger boards tend to ease free riding (Jensen, 1993). In larger boards, individuals might feel less personally responsible. As a result, this might lead to less strict decisions with regard to risk and stability.

Table IV.7: Random-effect regressions with dependent variables z-score and NPL ratio, Top 200

Variable		**z-score (RE) Financial expertise**		**z-score (RE) Out. fin. expertise**		**NPL ratio (RE) Financial expertise**		**NPL ratio (RE) Out. fin. expertise**	
		Coeff.	**SE (robust)**	**Coeff.**	**SE (robust)**	**Coeff.**	**SE (robust)**	**Coeff.**	**SE (robust)**
Financial expertise	Financial expertise*C	−0.0665	0.0486			0.0124	0.0040***		
	Outside financial expertise*C			−0.0933	0.0433**			0.0129	0.0039***
	Financial expertise*S	−0.0126	0.0297			0.0083	0.0041**		
	Outside financial expertise*S			−0.0069	0.0239			0.0034	0.0033
Bank level	Savings	−109.6875	77.4025	−116.0794	79.0390	−9.5294	4.6658**	−7.4002	4.7363
	Bank size*C	−2.3704	2.8477	−2.5019	2.8979	−0.6060	0.1504***	−0.5376	0.1478***
	Bank efficiency*C	−0.0625	0.0253**	−0.0609	0.0256**	−0.0014	0.0059	−0.0014	0.0059
	Bank size growth*C	0.0479	0.0596	0.0459	0.0589	−0.1586	0.0145***	−0.1583	0.0145***
	Loan growth*C	−0.0927	0.0364**	−0.0912	0.0360**	0.0950	0.0106***	0.0946	0.0106***
	Claims on MFI*C	−0.0069	0.0751	−0.0110	0.0760	0.0331	0.0114***	0.0329	0.0113***
	Claims on Non-MFI*C	0.1864	0.1243	0.1807	0.1238	0.0320	0.0080***	0.0329	0.0081***
	Board size*C	−0.2583	0.2650	−0.2780	0.2670	0.0488	0.0190***	0.0509	0.0191**
	Bank size*S	2.4890	2.0066	2.5571	2.0101	−0.0841	0.1835	−0.0926	0.1855
	Bank efficiency*S	0.0210	0.0336	0.0211	0.0338	−0.0228	0.0083***	−0.0233	0.0084***
	Bank size growth*S	−0.1114	0.0230***	−0.1114	0.0230***	−0.0984	0.0125***	−0.0985	0.0125***
	Loan growth*S	0.0370	0.0072***	0.0366	0.0069***	0.0495	0.0062***	0.0497	0.0063***
	Claims on MFI*S	0.0278	0.0401	0.0273	0.0402	−0.0148	0.0086*	−0.0147	0.0086*
	Claims on Non-MFI*S	0.0318	0.0519	0.0331	0.0523	0.0299	0.0105***	0.0284	0.0106***
	Board size*S	−0.0093	0.0767	−0.0106	0.0774	0.0343	0.0107***	0.0365	0.0105***
Macroeconomic and structural environment	East/West	−6.4381	1.9577***	−6.3819	1.9836***	0.5403	0.3142*	0.5537	0.3150*
	GDP per capita	−0.0426	0.0762	−0.0386	0.0760	−0.0285	0.0071***	−0.0283	0.0071***
	Population	−0.7003	1.0528	−0.8073	1.0453	−0.2003	0.0677***	−0.1944	0.0677***
	constant	75.3387	66.4776	79.8147	67.7597	13.1721	3.2084***	11.6559	3.2035***
	Wald chi^2	165.02	***	164.49	***	492.88	***	493.54	***
	R-sq	0.0850		0.0880		0.2788		0.2798	
	No of observations	2,278		2,278		2,259		2,259	

* indicates significance at the 10% level, ** at the 5% level, and *** at the 1% level, respectively.
Standard errors control for clustering at the bank level.

The following Table IV.8 provides the comparison of the coefficients of the z-score and NPL ratio regressions (for the merger-controlled panel, see Appendix IV.6.13).

Table IV.8: Coefficient comparison, random-effect regressions with dependent variables z-score and NPL ratio, Top 200

Variable		**z-score (RE) Financial expertise**		**z-score (RE) Out. fin. expertise**		**NPL ratio (RE) Financial expertise**		**NPL ratio (RE) Out. fin. expertise**	
		chi²	**P>chi²**	**chi²**	**P>chi²**	**chi²**	**P>chi²**	**chi²**	**P>chi²**
Financial expertise	Financial expertise: C vs. S	0.8800	0.3469			0.5100	0.4769		
	Outside financial expertise: C vs. S			3.0200	0.0802*			3.5300	0.0603*
Bank level	Bank size: C vs. S	2.1600	0.1418	2.2300	0.1353	6.8600	0.0088***	4.9200	0.0266**
	Bank efficiency: C vs. S	3.9000	0.0482**	3.7000	0.0543*	4.4800	0.0343**	4.6400	0.0312**
	Bank size growth: C vs. S	6.2600	0.0124**	6.2400	0.0125**	9.8800	0.0017***	9.7700	0.0018***
	Board size: C vs. S	0.8500	0.3574	0.9600	0.3276	0.4500	0.5002	0.4500	0.5015
	Loan growth: C vs. S	12.1100	0.0050***	12.0500	0.0005***	13.6700	0.0002***	13.3100	0.0003***
	Claims on MFI: C vs. S	0.1600	0.6870	0.2000	0.6584	11.2200	0.0008***	11.0500	0.0009***
	Claims on Non-MFI: C vs. S	1.5000	0.2202	1.3900	0.2386	0.0300	0.8742	0.1200	0.7310

* indicates significance at the 10% level, ** at the 5% level, and *** at the 1% level, respectively.

All regression models with RORWA and ROE as dependent variables are significant at the 1% level as well (see Table IV.9). The expertise coefficients show that the impact on cooperative banks is opposite to that on savings banks. Cooperative banks' performance is affected negatively while savings banks' performance is improved. This finding on cooperative banks is contradictory to the corporate finance theory predicting compensation for risk according to the risk-return trade-off. We hypothesize that experts at cooperative banks are overly enthusiastic on growth and business development and therefore disregard the inherent risks of growing by neglecting a careful business risk selection. Similar to loan portfolio risk and stability, insiders hardly make a difference. Overall, banks without merger activities confirm these results (see Appendix IV.6.14).

In contrast to the expertise coefficients most other bank level variables have the same direction. However, the comparisons of the coefficients suggest that both regional banking groups are affected significantly different (see Table IV.10). The negative impact of bank size in both regional banking groups might be due to the limited number of highly profitable projects within each area. Thus, we conclude that larger banks have to switch to more projects with lower profitability and suffer from sinking returns. For this reason it seems logical that bank size growth reduces profitability, as well. Given the coefficients, cooperative banks apparently suffer more from this "switching-effect" than savings banks. The expansion of the loan portfolio has a highly significant positive impact in both regional banking groups what implies that for all banks in the sample, it is beneficial to expand their traditional core business as this still boosts their performance. Whereas cooperative banks' higher loan volume growth rate impacts stability negatively, it pays off for their performance at least.

Board size reveals an ambiguous relationship with performance. Whereas it reduces performance at savings banks, it is positively related to performance at cooperative banks. Since both regional banking groups have significantly different board sizes, this indicates that the optimal board size for performance lies in between. However, the question remains unanswered who should be removed from savings banks' supervisory boards and whether cooperative banks' supervisory boards should be staffed with more financial or with non-financial experts.

Table IV.9: Random-effect regressions with dependent variables RORWA and ROE, Top 200

Variable		RORWA (RE) Financial expertise		RORWA (RE) Out. fin. expertise		ROE (RE) Financial expertise		ROE (RE) Out. fin. expertise	
		Coeff.	**SE (robust)**	**Coeff.**	**SE (robust)**	**Coeff.**	**SE (robust)**	**Coeff.**	**SE (robust)**
Financial expertise	Financial expertise*C	–0.0011	0.0013			–0.0038	0.0135		
	Outside financial expertise*C			–0.0013	0.0012			–0.0067	0.0133
	Financial expertise*S	0.0014	0.0017			0.0309	0.0169		
	Outside financial expertise*S			0.0017	0.0013			0.0290	0.0126
Bank level	Savings	–2.5366	1.5852	–2.7989	1.5820*	–9.3458	17.8275	–10.6689	17.5873
	Bank size*C	–0.2604	0.0555***	–0.2660	0.0534***	–1.8690	0.6220***	–1.8773	0.5917***
	Bank efficiency*C	–0.0268	0.0033***	–0.0268	0.0033***	–0.2728	0.0335***	–0.2722	0.0336***
	Bank size growth*C	–0.0411	0.0072***	–0.0412	0.0072***	–0.2486	0.0688***	–0.2495	0.0688***
	Loan growth*C	0.0433	0.0041***	0.0434	0.0041***	0.2667	0.0331***	0.2670	0.0330***
	Claims on MFI*C	–0.0082	0.0048*	–0.0081	0.0048*	–0.1275	0.0448***	–0.1268	0.0449***
	Claims on Non-MFI*C	–0.0129	0.0027***	–0.0129	0.0027***	–0.0625	0.0292**	–0.0620	0.0291**
	Board size*C	0.0073	0.0069	0.0069	0.0069	0.0797	0.0655	0.0770	0.0660
	Bank size*S	–0.0147	0.0680	–0.0104	0.0683	–0.5022	0.6934	–0.4515	0.6962
	Bank efficiency*S	–0.0473	0.0055***	–0.0471	0.0055***	–0.4785	0.0569***	–0.4775	0.0570***
	Bank size growth*S	–0.0126	0.0105	–0.0128	0.0105	–0.0400	0.0828	–0.0436	0.0826
	Loan growth*S	0.0186	0.0029***	0.0188	0.0029***	0.0898	0.0209***	0.0924	0.0213***
	Claims on MFI*S	–0.0161	0.0049***	–0.0163	0.0049***	–0.1347	0.0437***	–0.1367	0.0439***
	Claims on Non-MFI*S	–0.0263	0.0040***	–0.0259	0.0040***	–0.1231	0.0334***	–0.1198	0.0332***
	Board size*S	–0.0191	0.0057***	–0.0186	0.0056***	–0.1099	0.0546**	–0.1000	0.0534*
Macroeconomic and structural environment	East/West	0.1562	0.1337	0.1666	0.1336	1.1746	1.1299	1.3376	1.1400
	GDP per capita	–0.0029	0.0027	–0.0031	0.0027	–0.0674	0.0321**	–0.0700	0.0322**
	Population	0.0032	0.0287	0.0031	0.0286	0.0120	0.2551	0.0142	0.2541
	constant	9.2151	1.0695***	9.3479	1.0314***	74.9554	12.6401***	75.2761	12.0385***
	Wald chi²	439.16	***	441.53	***	464.54	***	464.13	***
	R-sq	0.3129		0.3135		0.2383		0.2393	
	No of observations	2,278		2,278		2,278		2,278	

* indicates significance at the 10% level, ** at the 5% level, and *** at the 1% level, respectively.
Standard errors control for clustering at the bank level.

The following Table IV.10 provides the comparison of the coefficients of the RORWA and ROE regressions (for the merger-controlled panel, see Appendix IV.6.15).

Table IV.10: Coefficient comparison, random-effect regressions with dependent variables RORWA and ROE, Top 200

Variable		RORWA (RE) Financial expertise		RORWA (RE) Out. fin. expertise		ROE (RE) Financial expertise		ROE (RE) Out. fin. expertise	
		chi^2	$P>chi^2$	chi^2	$P>chi^2$	chi^2	$P>chi^2$	chi^2	$P>chi^2$
Financial expertise	Financial expertise: C vs. S	1.3900	0.2385			2.5100	0.1132		
	Outside financial expertise: C vs. S			2.7500	0.0975*			3.7200	0.0539*
Bank level	Bank size: C vs. S	11.8000	0.0006***	13.0200	0.0003***	3.2500	0.0716*	3.6700	0.0556*
	Bank efficiency: C vs. S	10.3800	0.0013***	10.1600	0.0014***	9.7500	0.0018***	9.6800	0.0019***
	Bank size growth: C vs. S	5.0700	0.0244**	5.0100	0.0252**	3.7800	0.0519*	3.7000	0.0545*
	Board size: C vs. S	8.7200	0.0031***	8.2800	0.0040***	4.9400	0.0263**	4.3300	0.0375**
	Loan growth: C vs. S	24.5300	0.0000***	24.2300	0.0000***	20.2900	0.0000***	19.6400	0.0000***
	Claims on MFI: C vs. S	1.3200	0.2501	1.4000	0.2374	0.0100	0.9092	0.0200	0.8753
	Claims on Non-MFI: C vs. S	8.7600	0.0031***	8.1100	0.0044***	2.2800	0.1314	2.1000	0.1472

* indicates significance at the 10% level, ** at the 5% level, and *** at the 1% level, respectively.

IV.4.3 Robustness Checks

Both panels are adjusted in two ways to validate the robustness of the results. All variables are truncated, except for the binary variable (East/West) and the index variable on population. First, all observations lower than the 1st percentile of the distribution are set to the value of the 1st percentile. Observations higher than the 99th percentile are set to the value of the 99th percentile. Second, all observations lower than the 5th percentile of the distribution are set to the value of the 5th percentile, and observations higher than the 95th percentile are set to the value of the 95th percentile. The adjustments are made for both regional banking groups independently.

In general, both outlier-corrected datasets are in line with the original analyses, but lead to increased explanatory power, as indicated by the higher R-squared. This undermines the robustness of the findings outlined above. Furthermore, the performance regressions with the outlier-corrected samples provide financial expertise coefficients with higher significance for savings banks. Similarly, the significance of the financial expertise coefficients of cooperative banks increases in the risk regressions.

With regard to risk, the outlier-corrected regressions confirm the base regressions (see Appendices IV.6.16, IV.6.17, IV.6.20, IV.6.21, IV.6.24, IV.6.25, IV.6.28, and IV.6.29). On the one hand, the financial expertise coefficients of cooperative banks in the regression with the NPL ratio retain the 1% level of significance. On the other hand, savings banks' coefficients remain insignificant.

Regarding ROE performance, the 5% outlier-corrected dataset results in significance at the 1% level for the (outside) financial expertise of savings banks. The expertise coefficients of savings banks in the RORWA regression become significant at the 10% (total supervisory board expertise) and 5% (outside financial expertise) levels. The cooperative banks' coefficients remain insignificant (see Appendices IV.6.18, IV.6.19, IV.6.22, IV.6.23, IV.6.26, IV.6.27, IV.6.30, and IV.6.31).

Comparing the coefficients with outlier-corrected data confirms the initial hypotheses. Financial expertise influences performance differently in both regional banking groups, whereas risk and stability are affected similarly across the two regional banking groups.

IV.5 Concluding Remarks

The present study examines the influence of supervisory board financial expertise on bank risk, stability, and (risk-adjusted) performance. It further tests the hypothesis of whether the effects are equal across different ownership types and banking groups with differently staffed supervisory boards.

We document that financial experts cannot contribute to more stability and less risk. The study does not provide evidence that this is beneficial to stability and risk despite calls for more expertise in internal bank governance. This result is consistent across bank groups with different ownership types, underlining the explanatory power of this finding. The reason for the disadvantageous impact of financial expertise might be overconfidence (e.g., Fischhoff, et al., 1977; Moore and Healy, 2007). When it comes to assessing bank risks, financial experts may overestimate their individual competences and, consequently, overrate their risk assessment based on their private information (Chuang and Lee, 2006; Fellner, et al., 2004). Odean (1998) shows that overconfidence rises with increasing expertise. Thus, more financial experts on the boards do not lead to an improvement but could even weaken banks' stability as they eventually advocate risky business.

With regard to (risk-adjusted) performance, financial expertise affects both banking groups differently as shown by the robustness checks in particular. The risk-return trade-off apparently works for savings banks, but it does not work for cooperative banks. Whereas financial experts on the supervisory boards of savings banks lead to a compensation for the increase in risk, cooperative banks cannot benefit from financial experts either way. For the sake of growing their bank size and loan volume, supervisory board members in savings banks make the banks' management to follow a more selective strategy, at least as regards profitability. Contrary, cooperative banks' supervisory board members obviously do not put enough emphasis on profitable business development

The analysis of the composition of the supervisory boards shows that employed people dominate savings banks' supervisory boards, and at the same time self-employed people play a minor role. This is different at cooperative banks, where both employed and self-employed people represent the largest portion of the composed supervisory board. The large fraction of self-employed people at cooperative banks might be one reason for the twofold adverse effect of financial expertise. Cooper, Woo, and Dunkelberg (1988) provide a background for this finding. They point out that entrepreneurs generally display a high degree of optimism and overrate their abilities to determine their destiny on their own. This might result in a considerable misestimation of bank risks and profitability since cooperative banks' loan portfolio risk is higher and profitability is lower compared to savings banks. As the results suggest, cooperative banks accept prices at which no other bank would underwrite a business. Similar to entrepreneurs at cooperative banks, insiders at savings banks do not exert a beneficial influence, although they are supposed to understand banking business best. The analysis further demonstrates that not only the composition matters, but that the board size is another relevant factor. The comparison of both regional banking groups suggests that only up to a certain board size threshold, stability, risk, and performance are impacted beneficially. Hence, banks should not only focus on the individuals and their characteristics but also on the board as a whole.

In summary, all banks in our sample experience adverse impacts from financial expertise. The findings of the present study question the effectiveness of more required universal financial expertise of supervisory board members. First, the present study does not document a consistent risk-decreasing or stability-enhancing effect across banking sectors. Second, in the case of cooperative banks, financial expertise is even detrimental to performance. Instead of aiming at having supervisory boards with 100% financial experts whose competences are only broadly defined, it may be better to increase supervisory board knowledge in specific areas. Regulators could consider implementing of key areas to be monitored. These areas should be the core responsibilities for which the supervisory boards are fully accountable. Authorities could then force supervisory boards to have experts in all of these core areas. This would ensure that expertise in clearly defined areas is present on the supervisory board.

Assessing financial expertise on the basis of more detailed information such as education background is an avenue for future research that can contribute significantly to the regulation and supervision of banks. In addition, the issue remains open on whether regulation should prescribe the adequacy of individuals or the composition of bank supervisory boards in order to balance various interests. The tasks the supervisory board has to fulfill and how these tasks can be accomplished by its members or experts in specific areas must be clearly stated.

Further, it remains open whether our results can be confirmed by the private banking sector. Another area for research is to focus and run a separate analysis on the CEO as well as on the chairman of the supervisory board who will be probably the leaders in their respective boards.

IV.6 Appendix

Appendix IV.6.1: Underlying assumptions and definition of local and regional politicians

The following assumptions have been applied for the present analysis:

- For the information merchant, we assume a merchant in terms of § 1, German Commercial Code (HGB).
- For information entrepreneurs, we assume that the person is a managing partner/owner of a company.
- A farmer is treated as self-employed if not otherwise explicitly stated.
- In cases of jobs based on apprenticeships, which could suggest both self-employed and employed, employed is assumed if no further information is available.
- If the academic title is the only available information, no classification is attributed (others).

For the determination of board size, as well as for further analysis, we do not consider the following board members:

- Advisory members
- Honorary members
- Members with tenures of less than half a year.

Ministers, state secretaries, and members of parliament at the federal and federal-state level are federal politicians or federal-state politicians, respectively. The number of members of the European parliament is not material for the dataset, and these members are classified as federal politicians. For the identification of politicians at the regional and local levels, a two-step approach has been applied to differentiate between politicians in the strict sense and holders of political electoral office. This is necessary due to the multitude of administrative bodies at the regional and local levels and the heterogeneity of different federal states.

First, given the difference between full-time and voluntary electoral offices, individuals officiating voluntarily in political electoral offices are not considered politicians. These offices include honorary county councils, city councils, and municipal councils. Second, the hierarchical level of the function is considered. In our analysis, we classify the concerned person as a politician if he or she is the head of the administration. This selection step assures that politicians in our dataset are directly elected, with the exception of county administrators in Baden-Wuerttemberg.

Persons who are subject to directives and who have to report to the head of the administration do not count as politicians in the present analysis. Subsequently, district administrators, lord mayors, and mayors are consistently counted nationwide as politicians. There are a few federal states in which city directors, presidents of regional committees, presidents of local committees, and presidents of regional committees are counted as politicians if all the criteria outlined above are satisfied. Other holders of state-specific functions are not counted as politicians even though they are directly or indirectly elected and represent a political position and/or party, such as full-time city councilors in Bavaria, magistrates in Hessen, and (county) deputies in several federal states. All these persons violate the criterion regarding heading the administration. If the function is exercised full-time, the office holders are typically responsible for particular divisions or departments.

Appendix IV.6.2: Top 200 banks, cooperative banks

No.	Cooperative bank	Rank 2009
1	Deutsche Apotheker- und Ärztebank eG	1
2	Sparda-Bank Baden-Württemberg eG	2
3	Berliner Volksbank eG	3
4	Sparda-Bank Südwest eG	4
5	BBBank eG, Karlsruhe	5
6	Sparda-Bank West eG	6
7	Frankfurter Volksbank eG	7
8	Sparda-Bank Berlin eG	9
9	Volksbank Mittelhessen eG	10
10	Sparda-Bank München eG	11
11	Sparda-Bank Hessen eG	12
12	Mainzer Volksbank eG	13
13	LIGA Bank eG, Regensburg	14
14	KD-Bank eG - die Bank für Kirche und Diakonie	15
15	Sparda-Bank Hannover eG	16
16	Evangelische Kreditgenossenschaft eG	17
17	Hannoversche Volksbank eG	18
18	Bank im Bistum Essen eG	19
19	DKM Darlehnskasse Münster eG	20
20	Dortmunder Volksbank eG	21
21	Bank für Kirche und Caritas eG	22
22	Volksbank Paderborn-Höxter-Detmold eG	23
23	Evangelische Darlehnsgenossenschaft eG	24
24	Sparda-Bank Nürnberg eG	25
25	Bank 1 Saar eG	26
26	Wiesbadener Volksbank eG	28
27	PSD Bank Rhein-Ruhr eG	29
28	Münchner Bank eG	30
29	Sparda-Bank Hamburg eG	31
30	Volksbank eG, Villingen-Schwenningen	32
31	Volksbank Freiburg eG	35
32	Volksbank Pforzheim eG	36
33	Sparda-Bank Münster eG	37
34	Volksbank Bonn Rhein-Sieg eG	38
35	Volksbank Rems eG, Waiblingen	39
36	Volksbank Kur- und Rheinpfalz eG	40
37	Volksbank Oberberg eG	41
38	PSD Bank Nürnberg eG	42
39	Volksbank Ulm-Biberach eG	45
40	Volksbank eG Darmstadt Kreis Bergstraße	46
41	Pax Bank eG	48
42	Volksbank Karlsruhe eG	49
43	Westerwald Bank eG Volks- und Raiffeisenbank	50
44	Volksbank Ludwigsburg eG	51
45	Volksbank Raiffeisenbank Bayern Mitte eG, Ingolstadt	52
46	Volksbank Gütersloh eG	53
47	Vereinigte Volksbank Maingau eG	54
48	Hamburger Volksbank eG	55
49	Volksbank eG Braunschweig Wolfsburg	56
50	Sparda-Bank Regensburg eG	57

No.	Cooperative bank	Rank 2009
51	Volksbank Ruhr Mitte eG	58
52	Volksbank Göppingen eG	59
53	Volksbank Baden-Baden Rastatt eG	60
54	PSD Bank Nord eG	62
55	Volksbank Heilbronn eG	63
56	Volksbank an der Niers eG	64
57	Kasseler Bank eG Volksbank Raiffeisenbank	65
58	VR meine Raiffeisenbank eG, Altötting	67
59	Volksbank RheinAhrEifel eG	69
60	Volksbank Hohenlohe eG, Öhringen	70
61	PSD Bank München eG	71
62	Kölner Bank eG	72
63	Volksbank Kirchheim-Nürtingen eG	73
64	VR-Bank Rhein-Sieg eG	74
65	VR Bank Südpfalz eG	75
66	Volksbank Main-Tauber eG, Tauberbischofsheim	76
67	Volksbank Offenburg eG	77
68	Groß-Gerauer Volksbank eG	79
69	VR Bank HessenLand eG	81
70	Volksbank Gronau-Ahaus eG	83
71	PSD Bank Berlin-Brandenburg eG	84
72	VR Bank Schwäbisch Hall-Crailsheim eG	85
73	Volksbank Neckartal eG, Eberbach	87
74	Volksbank Kurpfalz H + G BANK eG, Heidelberg	88
75	PSD Bank Köln eG	91
76	Volksbank Bad-Oeynhausen-Herford eG	92
77	Volksbank Wiesloch eG	93
78	Volksbank Breisgau Nord eG, Emmendingen	94
79	VR-Bank Rottal-Inn eG, Pfarrkirchen	95
80	Volksbank Raiffeisenbank Dachau eG	96
81	Volksbank Remscheid-Solingen eG	98
82	GLS Gemeinschaftsbank eG	99
83	PSD Bank Karlsruhe-Neustadt eG	101
84	Volksbank eG, Pattensen	102
85	Augusta-Bank eG Raiffeisen-Volksbank, Augsburg	104
86	Volksbank Düsseldorf Neuss eG	105
87	Volksbank Rhein-Ruhr eG	107
88	Sparda-Bank Augsburg eG	109
89	VR-Bank eG, Würselen	111
90	Volksbank Herrenberg-Rottenburg eG	112
91	Volksbank Reutlingen eG	113
92	Volksbank eG, Überlingen	114
93	Volksbank Esslingen eG	118
94	Märkische Bank eG	119
95	Raiffeisenbank Frechen-Hürth eG	120
96	Volksbank Lüneburger Heide eG	121
97	Volksbank Donau-Neckar eG, Tuttlingen	122
98	Raiffeisen-Volksbank Donauwörth eG	123
99	Volksbank Nordheide eG	125
100	Volksbank Plochingen eG	126

Appendix IV.6.2: Top 200 banks, cooperative banks (continued)

No.	Cooperative bank	Rank 2009	No.	Cooperative bank	Rank 2009
101	PSD Bank Hannover eG	127	151	Volksbank Hochrhein eG, Waldshut-Tiengen	192
102	Heidenheimer Volksbank eG	128	152	Volksbank eG Bremerhaven-Cuxland	193
103	Volksbank Rhein-Nahe-Hunsrück eG	129	153	GENO BANK ESSEN eG	194
104	Volksbank Hellweg eG	131	154	Volksbank Mönchengladbach eG	195
105	Volksbank Dreiländereck eG, Lörrach	133	155	VR-Bank Werra-Meißner eG	196
106	Bielefelder Volksbank eG	134	156	Volksbank Kaiserslautern- Nordwestpfalz eG	197
107	Volksbank Sauerland eG	135	157	vr bank Untertaunus eG	198
108	Volksbank Hameln-Stadthagen eG	136	158	Raiffeisenbank im Allgäuer Land eG, Altusried	199
109	Volksbank Hunsrück-Nahe eG	137	159	Volksbank Bruhrain-Kraich-Hardt eG, Oberhausen-Rheinhausen	200
110	Volksbank Nordmünsterland eG	141	160	Volksbank Stade-Cuxhaven eG	201
111	Volksbank Dreieich eG	142	161	Raiffeisenbank eG, Heinsberg	202
112	Ostfriesische Volksbank eG	144	162	Volksbank Ahlen-Sassenberg-Warendorf eG	203
113	Volksbank Metzingen-Bad Urach eG	145	163	VR-Bank Memmingen eG	204
114	Volksbank Siegerland eG	146	164	VR-Bank Passau eG	205
115	Volksbank Raiffeisenbank Nürnberg eG	147	165	Waldecker Bank eG	206
116	VR Bank Kaufbeuren-Ostallgäu eG	149	166	Volksbank Büren und Salzkotten eG	207
117	Volksbank Hamm eG	150	167	Volksbank Bad Saulgau eG	208
118	HEIDELBERGER VOLKSBANK eingetragene Genossenschaft	153	168	Dresdner Volksbank Raiffeisenbank eG	209
119	Volksbank Bühl eG	154	169	Vereinigte Volksbank eG im Regionalverband Saarbrücken	210
120	VR Genossenschaftsbank Fulda eG Volksbank Raiffeisenbank seit 1862	155	170	Raiffeisen-Volksbank Ries eG Nördlingen	211
121	Volksbank Niederrhein eG	156	171	Vereinigte Volksbank Raiffeisenbank eG	212
122	Volksbank Münster eG	157	172	VR Bank Flensburg-Schleswig eG	213
123	Volksbank eG, Osterholz-Scharmbeck	158	173	Aachener Bank eG	214
124	VR Bank Hof eG	159	174	Raiffeisenbank Oberpfalz Süd eG, Donaustauf	215
125	VR Bank Ostholstein Nord - Plön eG	160	175	VR Bank Biedenkopf-Gladenbach eG	216
126	VR-Bank Erlangen-Höchstadt-Herzogenaurach eG	161	176	Volksbank Jever eG	217
127	Volksbank Krefeld eG	162	177	Volksbank Allgäu-West eG, Isny	218
128	Volksbank Straubing eG	164	178	Volksbank Forchheim eG	219
129	VR Bank Pinneberg eG	167	179	Genossenschaftsbank Unterallgäu eG, 87719 Mindelheim	220
130	Volksbank Euskirchen eG	168	180	Raiffeisen-Volksbank Miltenberg eG	221
131	VR-Bank Asperg-Markgröningen eG, Möglingen	169	181	Raiffeisenbank Oberallgäu-Süd eG, Sonthofen	222
132	VR-Bank Rhein-Erft eG	170	182	Volksbank Franken eG, Buchen	223
133	Kieler Volksbank eG	171	183	Raiffeisenbank Neumarkt i.d.OPf. eG	224
134	Raiffeisenbank Aschaffenburg eG	172	184	Untertürkheimer Volksbank eG, Stuttgart	227
135	Emsländische Volksbank eG Meppen	173	185	VR-Bank Uffenheim-Neustadt eG Raiffeisen-Volksbank	228
136	Volksbank Marl-Recklinghausen eG	174	186	Volksbank Mainspitze eG	229
137	Volksbank Raiffeisenbank eG, Neumünster	175	187	VR-Bank Neu-Ulm/Weißenhorn eG	230
138	PSD Bank Westfalen-Lippe eG	176	188	Volksbank Weinheim eG	231
139	Volksbank Rhein-Lahn eG	177	189	Raiffeisenbank Rheinbach Voreifel eG	232
140	Volksbank eG, Konstanz	178	190	VBU Volksbank im Unterland eG, Schwaigern	235
141	RV Bank Rhein-Haardt eG	179	191	VR Bank Westthüringen eG	236
142	Raiffeisenbank Cham-Roding-Furth im Wald eG	180	192	Volksbank Bautzen eG	238
143	Raiffeisenbank Weißenburg-Gunzenhausen eG	182	193	Vereinigte Volksbank eG, Telgte	239
144	Volksbank Bocholt eG	183	194	Freisinger Bank eG Volksbank-Raiffeisenbank	240
145	Volksbank Bochum Witten eG	184	195	Volksbank Erft eG	241
146	Volksbank in Schaumburg eG	185	196	Volksbank Ettlingen eG	242
147	Volksbank Lippstadt eG	186	197	VR-Bank in Mittelbaden eG, Iffezheim	244
148	Volksbank-Raiffeisenbank Bayreuth eG	188	198	Volksbank Saaletal eG	245
149	VR Bank eG, Niebüll	189	199	Volksbank Nagoldtal eG	246
150	Volksbank Breisgau-Süd eG, Heitersheim	190	200	Volksbank Südheide eG	247

Appendix IV.6.2: Top 200 banks, savings banks (continued)

No.	Savings bank	Rank 2009
1	Sparkasse KölnBonn	2
2	Kreissparkasse Köln	3
3	Stadtsparkasse München	5
4	Sparkasse Hannover	6
5	Nassauische Sparkasse	7
6	Ostsächsische Sparkasse Dresden	9
7	Sparkasse Pforzheim Calw	11
8	Kreissparkasse Ludwigsburg	12
9	Sparkasse Aachen	13
10	Sparkasse Nürnberg	14
11	Mittelbrandenburgische Sparkasse in Potsdam	15
12	Stadt- u. Kreissparkasse Leipzig	16
13	Kreissparkasse Esslingen-Nürtingen	17
14	Sparkasse Münsterland Ost	18
15	Sparkasse Essen	19
16	Sparkasse Krefeld	20
17	Kreissparkasse Heilbronn	21
18	Kreissparkasse München Starnberg	23
19	Stadtsparkasse Dortmund	24
20	Kreissparkasse Waiblingen	25
21	Sparkasse Mainfranken-Würzburg	26
22	Kreissparkasse Biberach	27
23	Kreissparkasse Böblingen	28
24	Stadtsparkasse Wuppertal	29
25	Nord-Ostsee Sparkasse	30
26	Sparkasse Saarbrücken	31
27	Sparkasse Heidelberg	32
28	Förde Sparkasse	34
29	Sparkasse Bochum	35
30	Sparkasse Bielefeld	36
31	Stadtsparkasse Duisburg	37
32	Sparkasse Karlsruhe	38
33	Sparkasse Osnabrück	39
34	Sparkasse Südholstein	40
35	Sparkasse Freiburg- Nördlicher Breisgau	41
36	Sparkasse Ulm	42
37	Sparkasse Westmünsterland	44
38	Sparkasse Vest Recklinghausen	45
39	Kreissparkasse Göppingen	46
40	Kreissparkasse Ravensburg	47
41	Sparkasse Rhein Neckar Nord	48
42	Kasseler Sparkasse	49
43	Sparkasse Herford	50
44	Kreissparkasse Tübingen	52
45	Kreissparkasse Ostalb	53
46	Kreissparkasse Reutlingen	54
47	Stadtsparkasse Augsburg	55
48	Sparkasse Bodensee	56
49	Sparkasse Hanau	57
50	Stadtsparkasse Mönchengladbach	58

No.	Savings bank	Rank 2009
51	Sparkasse Hildesheim	59
52	Sparkasse Koblenz	60
53	Stadt und Kreissparkasse Erlangen	61
54	Sparkasse Allgäu	62
55	Sparkasse Offenburg/Ortenau	63
56	Stadt- und Kreissparkasse Darmstadt	64
57	Kreissparkasse Kaiserslautern	65
58	Sparkasse Rosenheim-Bad Aibling	66
59	Taunus Sparkasse	67
60	Sparkasse Langen-Seligenstadt	68
61	Sparkasse Chemnitz	69
62	Sparkasse Memmingen- Lindau-Mindelheim	70
63	Saalesparkasse	71
64	Sparkasse Mittelthüringen	72
65	Sparkasse Aschaffenburg-Alzenau	73
66	Sparkasse Trier	74
67	Kreissparkasse Saarlouis	75
68	Sparkasse Regensburg	76
69	Sparkasse Zollernalb	77
70	Sparkasse Fürstenfeldbruck	78
71	Sparkasse Rhein-Haardt	79
72	Sparkasse Rhein-Nahe	80
73	Sparkasse Fulda	81
74	Sparkasse Harburg-Buxtehude	82
75	Sparkasse Kraichgau	83
76	Sparkasse Siegen	84
77	Sparkasse Landshut	85
78	Sparkasse Hochfranken	87
79	Sparkasse Gelsenkirchen	88
80	Sparkasse Bamberg	89
81	Sparkasse Paderborn	90
82	Sparkasse Marburg-Biedenkopf	91
83	Sparkasse Niederbayern Mitte	92
84	Sparkasse Mittelfranken-Süd	94
85	Sparkasse Leverkusen	95
86	Sparkasse Schwarzwald-Baar	96
87	Sparkasse Vogtland	97
88	Kreissparkasse Tuttlingen	98
89	Sparkasse Ingolstadt	99
90	Sparkasse Tauberfranken	100
91	Kreissparkasse Steinfurt	101
92	Sparkasse Detmold	102
93	Sparkasse Schwäbisch Hall Crailsheim	103
94	Sparkasse am Niederrhein Moers	104
95	Sparkasse Emsland	105
96	Sparkasse Südl.Weinstr. in Landau	106
97	Kreissparkasse Rhein-Pfalz	107
98	OstseeSparkasse Rostock	108
99	Sparkasse Göttingen	109
100	Sparkasse Worms-Alzey-Ried	110

Appendix IV.6.2: Top 200 banks, savings banks (continued)

No.	Savings bank	Rank 2009	No.	Savings bank	Rank 2009
101	Sparkasse Fürth	111	151	Sparkasse Miltenberg-Obernburg	170
102	Kreissparkasse Augsburg	112	152	Sparkasse Baden-Baden Gaggenau	171
103	Sparkasse Westholstein	113	153	Sparkasse Amberg-Sulzbach	173
104	Kreissparkasse Herzogtum Lauenburg	114	154	Sparkasse Burgenlandkreis	175
105	Kreissparkasse Heinsberg	116	155	Sparkasse Neumarkt i.d.Opf.-Parsberg	176
106	Kreissparkasse Groß-Gerau	117	156	Kreissparkasse Schwalm-Eder	177
107	Sparkasse Hochrhein	118	157	Hohenzollerische LandesBank Kreissparkasse Sigmaringen	178
108	Sparkasse Oberlausitz-Niederschlesien	119	158	Sparkasse Mittelsachsen	179
109	Kreissparkasse Syke	120	159	Sparkasse Lüdenscheid	180
110	Sparkasse Spree-Neiße	121	160	Sparkasse Starkenburg	181
111	Sparkasse Gifhorn-Wolfsburg	122	161	Herner Sparkasse	183
112	Sparkasse Zwickau	123	162	Sparkasse im Landkreis Schwandorf	184
113	Sparkasse Singen-Radolfzell	124	163	Sparkasse Gera-Greiz	185
114	Sparkasse Passau	125	164	Sparkasse Bad Hersfeld-Rotenburg	186
115	Sparkasse Lemgo	126	165	Sparkasse Bad Tölz-Wolfratshausen	187
116	Sparkasse Mülheim an der Ruhr	127	166	Kreissparkasse Kusel	189
117	Sparkasse Vorpommern	129	167	Sparkasse Mecklenburg-Schwerin	190
118	Sparkasse Lüneburg	130	168	Kreissparkasse Heidenheim	191
119	Stadtsparkasse Oberhausen	131	169	Sparkasse Rotenburg-Bremervörde	194
120	Sparkasse Dachau	132	170	Sparkasse Stade-Altes Land	195
121	Sparkasse Celle	133	171	Kreis und Stadtsparkasse Erding	196
122	Sparkasse Schaumburg	135	172	Kreissparkasse Traunstein-Trostberg	197
123	Kreissparkasse Verden	136	173	Sparkasse Bensheim	198
124	Salzlandsparkasse	137	174	Rhön-Rennsteig-Sparkasse	199
125	Sparkasse Mittelmosel Eifel Mosel Hunsrück	138	175	Sparkasse Rottal-Inn	200
126	Sparkasse Neckartal-Odenwald	139	176	Sparkasse Werra-Meißner	201
127	Sparkasse Minden-Lübbecke	140	177	Sparkasse Gütersloh	202
128	Sparkasse Hagen	141	178	Sparkasse im Landkreis Neustadt/Aisch-Windshm.	203
129	Sparkasse LeerWittmund	143	179	Kreissparkasse Kelheim	204
130	Sparkasse Dieburg Zweckverbandssparkasse	144	180	Kreissparkasse Saarpfalz	206
131	Sparkasse Markgräflerland	146	181	Sparkasse Rastatt-Gernsbach	207
132	Sparkasse Vorderpfalz Ludwigshafen a.Rh.Schifferstadt	147	182	Vereinigte Sparkassen im Lkr. Weilheim	209
133	Sparkasse Schweinfurt	148	183	Sparkasse Günzburg-Krumbach	211
134	Sparkasse Oder-Spree	149	184	Sparkasse Germersheim-Kandel	212
135	Sparkasse Coburg-Lichtenfels	150	185	Kreissparkasse Mayen	213
136	Sparkasse Meißen	151	186	Sparkasse Jena-Saale-Holzland	214
137	Sparkasse Lörrach-Rheinfelden	153	187	Sparkasse Hamm	217
138	Sparkasse Waldeck-Frankenberg	155	188	Sparkasse Elbe-Elster	218
139	Sparkasse Altötting-Mühldorf	156	189	Sparkasse Weserbergland	219
140	Sparkasse Wetzlar	158	190	Sparkasse der Stadt Iserlohn	220
141	Sparkasse Neuwied	159	191	Stadtsparkasse Remscheid	221
142	Sparkasse Bayreuth	160	192	Kreissparkasse Miesbach-Tegernsee	223
143	Kreissparkasse Wesermünde-Hadeln	161	193	Sparkasse Hohenlohekreis	224
144	Sparkasse Mainz	163	194	Kreissparkasse Limburg	225
145	Sparkasse Neu-Ulm-Illertissen	164	195	Wartburg-Sparkasse	226
146	Sparkasse Gießen	165	196	Sparkasse Deggendorf	227
147	Sparkasse Uelzen Lüchow-Dannenberg	166	197	Sparkasse Landsberg-Dießen	228
148	Sparkasse Südwestpfalz	167	198	Kreissparkasse Westerwald	229
149	Sparkasse Erzgebirge	168	199	Kreis-und Stadtsparkasse Speyer	230
150	Stadtsparkasse Magdeburg	169	200	Kreissparkasse Aue-Schwarzenberg	231

Appendix IV.6.3: Top 150 banks, cooperative banks

No.	Cooperative bank	Rank 2009
1	Deutsche Apotheker- und Ärztebank eG	1
2	Sparda-Bank Baden-Württemberg eG	2
3	Berliner Volksbank eG	3
4	Sparda-Bank Südwest eG	4
5	Sparda-Bank Berlin eG	9
6	Sparda-Bank München eG	11
7	LIGA Bank eG, Regensburg	14
8	Sparda-Bank Hannover eG	16
9	Bank im Bistum Essen eG	19
10	DKM Darlehnskasse Münster eG	20
11	Bank für Kirche und Caritas eG	22
12	Evangelische Darlehnsgenossenschaft eG	24
13	Sparda-Bank Nürnberg eG	25
14	Sparda-Bank Hamburg eG	31
15	Volksbank Pforzheim eG	36
16	Sparda-Bank Münster eG	37
17	Volksbank Bonn Rhein-Sieg eG	38
18	PSD Bank Nürnberg eG	42
19	Pax Bank eG	48
20	Westerwald Bank eG Volks- und Raiffeisenbank	50
21	Volksbank Ludwigsburg eG	51
22	Sparda-Bank Regensburg eG	57
23	Volksbank Baden-Baden*Rastatt eG	60
24	Volksbank Heilbronn eG	63
25	Kasseler Bank eG Volksbank Raiffeisenbank	65
26	PSD Bank München eG	71
27	Kölner Bank eG	72
28	Volksbank Kirchheim-Nürtingen eG	73
29	VR-Bank Rhein-Sieg eG	74
30	Volksbank Offenburg eG	77
31	Groß-Gerauer Volksbank eG	79
32	PSD Bank Berlin-Brandenburg eG	84
33	Volksbank Bad-Oeynhausen-Herford eG	92
34	Volksbank Raiffeisenbank Dachau eG	96
35	Volksbank Remscheid-Solingen eG	98
36	PSD Bank Karlsruhe-Neustadt eG	101
37	Volksbank Düsseldorf Neuss eG	105
38	Volksbank Rhein-Ruhr eG	107
39	Sparda-Bank Augsburg eG	109
40	Volksbank Reutlingen eG	113
41	Volksbank eG, Überlingen	114
42	Volksbank Esslingen eG	118
43	Volksbank Donau-Neckar eG, Tuttlingen	122
44	Volksbank Nordheide eG	125
45	Volksbank Plochingen eG	126
46	PSD Bank Hannover eG	127
47	Volksbank Dreiländereck eG, Lörrach	133
48	Volksbank Nordmünsterland eG	141
49	Volksbank Dreieich eG	142
50	Ostfriesische Volksbank eG	144
51	Volksbank Hamm eG	150
52	HEIDELBERGER VOLKSBANK eingetragene Genossenschaft	153
53	VR Genossenschaftsbank Fulda eG Volksbank Raiffeisenbank seit 1862	155
54	Volksbank Krefeld eG	162
55	Volksbank Straubing eG	164
56	Kieler Volksbank eG	171
57	Volksbank Marl-Recklinghausen eG	174
58	PSD Bank Westfalen-Lippe eG	176
59	Volksbank eG, Konstanz	178
60	Volksbank Bocholt eG	183
61	Volksbank Bochum Witten eG	184
62	Volksbank Lippstadt eG	186
63	Volksbank-Raiffeisenbank Bayreuth eG	188
64	VR Bank eG, Niebüll	189
65	Volksbank Breisgau-Süd eG, Heitersheim	190
66	Volksbank Hochrhein eG, Waldshut-Tiengen	192
67	GENO BANK ESSEN eG	194
68	VR-Bank Werra-Meißner eG	196
69	vr bank Untertaunus eG	198
70	Volksbank Stade-Cuxhaven eG	201
71	Volksbank Ahlen-Sassenberg-Warendorf eG	203
72	VR-Bank Memmingen eG	204
73	Volksbank Büren und Salzkotten eG	207
74	Volksbank Bad Saulgau eG	208
75	Dresdner Volksbank Raiffeisenbank eG	209
76	Vereinigte Volksbank Raiffeisenbank eG	212
77	Aachener Bank eG	214
78	VR Bank Biedenkopf-Gladenbach eG	216
79	Volksbank Jever eG	217
80	Volksbank Allgäu-West eG, Isny	218
81	Genossenschaftsbank Unterallgäu eG, 87719 Mindelheim	220
82	Raiffeisen-Volksbank Miltenberg eG	221
83	Volksbank Franken eG, Buchen	223
84	Untertürkheimer Volksbank eG, Stuttgart	227
85	Volksbank Mainspitze eG	229
86	VR-Bank Neu-Ulm/Weißenhorn eG	230
87	Volksbank Weinheim eG	231
88	Raiffeisenbank Rheinbach Voreifel eG	232
89	VR Bank Westthüringen eG	236
90	Freisinger Bank eG Volksbank-Raiffeisenbank	240
91	Volksbank Erft eG	241
92	Volksbank Ettlingen eG	242
93	Volksbank Nagoldtal eG	246
94	Volksbank Wilferdingen-Keltern eG, Remchingen	248
95	Volksbank Göttingen eG	252
96	Volksbank eG, Waltrop	255
97	Volks- und Raiffeisenbank Neuwied-Linz eG	257
98	Volksbank Rottweil eG	258
99	Volksbank Nordoberpfalz eG	259
100	Volksbank Regensburg eG	262

Appendix IV.6.3: Top 150 banks, savings banks (continued)

No.	Cooperative bank	Rank 2009
101	Rheingauer Volksbank eG	263
102	Volksbank Lingen eG	264
103	Volksbank Region Leonberg eG	265
104	VR-Bank Mainz eG	267
105	Volksbank Wolfenbüttel-Salzgitter eG	271
106	Volksbank eG Minden-Hille-Porta	277
107	Raiffeisenbank München-Süd eG	278
108	Volksbank Helmstedt eG	279
109	Raiffeisenbank Weiden eG	280
110	Bremische Volksbank eG	281
111	Kulmbacher Bank eG Raiffeisen-Volksbank	282
112	VR Bank Kitzingen eG	283
113	Volksbank Filder eG, Neuhausen	285
114	Volksbank Emmerich-Rees eG	286
115	Volksbank Dill eG -Volksbank und Raiffeisenbank	289
116	Volksbank Tettnang eG	294
117	Leutkircher Bank Raiffeisen- und Volksbank eG	295
118	Volksbank Hohenzollern eG, Hechingen	296
119	Rottaler Volksbank-Raiffeisenbank eG, Eggenfelden	297
120	Volksbank Osnabrück eG	298
121	Volksbank Schwäbisch Gmünd eG	302
122	Raiffeisen-Volksbank Varel-Nordenham eG	303
123	PSD Bank Braunschweig eG	304
124	PSD Bank Koblenz eG	308
125	Rüsselsheimer Volksbank eG	311
126	Volksbank Kirchhellen eG	313
127	Volksbank-Raiffeisenbank eG, Husum	314
128	Volksbank Mittweida eG	315
129	VR Bank Südliche Weinstraße eG	316
130	Volksbank Oldenburg eG	320
131	Vereinigte Volksbank eG Limburg	322
132	Volksbank Magdeburg eG	325
133	VR-Bank Ellwangen eG	328
134	Volksbank Eifel Mitte eG	330
135	Ehinger Volksbank eG, Ehingen	331
136	Volksbank Kinzigtal eG, Wolfach	334
137	Volksbank Zuffenhausen eG, Stuttgart	335
138	Volksbank Brüggen-Nettetal eG	336
139	Volksbank Rhein-Wehra eG, Bad Säckingen	338
140	Volksbank Hildesheimer Börde eG	344
141	Raiffeisenbank Rhein-Berg eG	345
142	Volksbank Strohgäu eG, Korntal-Münchingen	348
143	Volksbank Bad Driburg - Brakel - Steinheim eG	349
144	Volksbank Müllheim eG	350
145	Volksbank Möckmühl-Neuenstadt eG	353
146	Raiffeisenbank Kocher-Jagst eG, Ingelfingen	355
147	Rottaler Raiffeisenbank eG, Pocking	356
148	VR-Bank eG, Regen	357
149	Volksbank Brackenheim-Güglingen eG	360
150	Volksbank Balingen eG	361

Appendix IV.6.3: Top 150 banks, savings banks (continued)

No.	Savings bank	Rank 2009
1	Stadtsparkasse München	5
2	Nassauische Sparkasse	7
3	Kreissparkasse Ludwigsburg	12
4	Sparkasse Aachen	13
5	Sparkasse Nürnberg	14
6	Kreissparkasse Esslingen-Nürtingen	17
7	Sparkasse Essen	19
8	Kreissparkasse München Starnberg	23
9	Stadtsparkasse Dortmund	24
10	Kreissparkasse Waiblingen	25
11	Sparkasse Mainfranken-Würzburg	26
12	Kreissparkasse Biberach	27
13	Kreissparkasse Böblingen	28
14	Stadtsparkasse Wuppertal	29
15	Sparkasse Saarbrücken	31
16	Sparkasse Bochum	35
17	Sparkasse Bielefeld	36
18	Sparkasse Osnabrück	39
19	Sparkasse Freiburg- Nördlicher Breisgau	41
20	Sparkasse Ulm	42
21	Kreissparkasse Göppingen	46
22	Kreissparkasse Ravensburg	47
23	Sparkasse Rhein Neckar Nord	48
24	Kasseler Sparkasse	49
25	Sparkasse Herford	50
26	Kreissparkasse Tübingen	52
27	Kreissparkasse Ostalb	53
28	Kreissparkasse Reutlingen	54
29	Stadtsparkasse Augsburg	55
30	Sparkasse Hanau	57
31	Stadtsparkasse Mönchengladbach	58
32	Sparkasse Koblenz	60
33	Stadt und Kreissparkasse Erlangen	61
34	Sparkasse Allgäu	62
35	Sparkasse Offenburg/Ortenau	63
36	Stadt- und Kreissparkasse Darmstadt	64
37	Taunus Sparkasse	67
38	Sparkasse Langen-Seligenstadt	68
39	Sparkasse Chemnitz	69
40	Sparkasse Memmingen- Lindau-Mindelheim	70
41	Sparkasse Aschaffenburg-Alzenau	73
42	Sparkasse Trier	74
43	Kreissparkasse Saarlouis	75
44	Sparkasse Regensburg	76
45	Sparkasse Zollernalb	77
46	Sparkasse Fürstenfeldbruck	78
47	Sparkasse Rhein-Nahe	80
48	Sparkasse Fulda	81
49	Sparkasse Harburg-Buxtehude	82
50	Sparkasse Kraichgau	83

No.	Savings bank	Rank 2009
51	Sparkasse Landshut	85
52	Sparkasse Gelsenkirchen	88
53	Sparkasse Bamberg	89
54	Sparkasse Marburg-Biedenkopf	91
55	Sparkasse Leverkusen	95
56	Sparkasse Vogtland	97
57	Kreissparkasse Tuttlingen	98
58	Sparkasse Ingolstadt	99
59	Sparkasse Schwäbisch Hall Crailsheim	103
60	Sparkasse Emsland	105
61	Sparkasse Südl.Weinstr. in Landau	106
62	Kreissparkasse Rhein-Pfalz	107
63	OstseeSparkasse Rostock	108
64	Sparkasse Göttingen	109
65	Sparkasse Fürth	111
66	Kreissparkasse Augsburg	112
67	Kreissparkasse Herzogtum Lauenburg	114
68	Kreissparkasse Heinsberg	116
69	Kreissparkasse Groß-Gerau	117
70	Sparkasse Hochrhein	118
71	Kreissparkasse Syke	120
72	Sparkasse Spree-Neiße	121
73	Sparkasse Gifhorn-Wolfsburg	122
74	Sparkasse Zwickau	123
75	Sparkasse Singen-Radolfzell	124
76	Sparkasse Passau	125
77	Sparkasse Mülheim an der Ruhr	127
78	Sparkasse Lüneburg	130
79	Stadtsparkasse Oberhausen	131
80	Sparkasse Dachau	132
81	Sparkasse Celle	133
82	Sparkasse Schaumburg	135
83	Kreissparkasse Verden	136
84	Sparkasse Neckartal-Odenwald	139
85	Sparkasse Minden-Lübbecke	140
86	Sparkasse Hagen	141
87	Sparkasse Dieburg Zweckverbandssparkasse	144
88	Sparkasse Markgräflerland	146
89	Sparkasse Lörrach-Rheinfelden	153
90	Sparkasse Waldeck-Frankenberg	155
91	Sparkasse Wetzlar	158
92	Sparkasse Bayreuth	160
93	Kreissparkasse Wesermünde-Hadeln	161
94	Sparkasse Mainz	163
95	Sparkasse Neu-Ulm-Illertissen	164
96	Sparkasse Gießen	165
97	Stadtsparkasse Magdeburg	169
98	Sparkasse Miltenberg-Obernburg	170
99	Sparkasse Amberg-Sulzbach	173
100	Sparkasse Neumarkt i.d.Opf.-Parsberg	176

Appendix IV.6.3: Top 150 banks, savings banks (continued)

No.	Savings bank	Rank 2009
101	Kreissparkasse Schwalm-Eder	177
102	Hohenzollerische LandesBank Kreissparkasse Sigmaringen	178
103	Sparkasse Starkenburg	181
104	Herner Sparkasse	183
105	Sparkasse im Landkreis Schwandorf	184
106	Sparkasse Gera-Greiz	185
107	Sparkasse Bad Hersfeld-Rotenburg	186
108	Sparkasse Bad Tölz-Wolfratshausen	187
109	Kreissparkasse Kusel	189
110	Kreissparkasse Heidenheim	191
111	Sparkasse Rotenburg-Bremervörde	194
112	Sparkasse Stade-Altes Land	195
113	Kreissparkasse Traunstein-Trostberg	197
114	Sparkasse Bensheim	198
115	Rhön-Rennsteig-Sparkasse	199
116	Sparkasse Rottal-Inn	200
117	Sparkasse Werra-Meißner	201
118	Sparkasse Gütersloh	202
119	Sparkasse im Landkreis Neustadt/Aisch-Windshm.	203
120	Kreissparkasse Kelheim	204
121	Kreissparkasse Saarpfalz	206
122	Sparkasse Rastatt-Gernsbach	207
123	Vereinigte Sparkassen im Lkr. Weilheim	209
124	Sparkasse Günzburg-Krumbach	211
125	Sparkasse Germersheim-Kandel	212
126	Kreissparkasse Mayen	213
127	Sparkasse Jena-Saale-Holzland	214
128	Sparkasse Hamm	217
129	Sparkasse Elbe-Elster	218
130	Sparkasse Weserbergland	219
131	Sparkasse der Stadt Iserlohn	220
132	Stadtsparkasse Remscheid	221
133	Kreissparkasse Miesbach-Tegernsee	223
134	Sparkasse Hohenlohekreis	224
135	Kreissparkasse Limburg	225
136	Wartburg-Sparkasse	226
137	Sparkasse Deggendorf	227
138	Sparkasse Landsberg-Dießen	228
139	Kreissparkasse Westerwald	229
140	Kreis-und Stadtsparkasse Speyer	230
141	Kreissparkasse Aue-Schwarzenberg	231
142	Sparkasse Merzig-Wadern	232
143	Sparkasse Odenwaldkreis	233
144	Kreis- u. Stadtsparkasse Unna	235
145	Sparkasse Niederlausitz	236
146	Kreissparkasse Peine	238
147	Sparkasse Höxter	239
148	Städtische Sparkasse Offenbach am Main	240
149	Sparkasse Berchtesgadener Land	241
150	Kreissparkasse Bautzen	242

Appendix IV.6.4: Supervisory board composition, Top 150

Variables		**Mean**	**Std. Dev.**	**Coeff. of Variation**	**Min**	**Max**
Insider (%)	Cooperative banks	2.94	9.19	313.05	0.00	52.94
	Savings banks	24.58	12.16	49.46	0.00	41.67
Outsider (%)	Cooperative banks	97.06	9.19	9.47	47.06	100.00
	Savings banks	75.42	12.16	16.12	58.33	100.00
Employment						
Employed individuals (%)	Cooperative banks	49.61	23.89	48.16	0.00	100.00
	Savings banks	72.50	12.21	16.84	36.36	100.00
Self-employed individuals (%)	Cooperative banks	39.70	25.43	64.05	0.00	90.91
	Savings banks	13.52	9.91	73.32	0.00	47.37
Retired individuals (%)	Cooperative banks	9.74	12.06	123.79	0.00	77.78
	Savings banks	12.64	10.27	81.21	0.00	55.56
Other (%)	Cooperative banks	0.95	2.91	307.03	0.00	16.67
	Savings banks	1.34	2.82	209.61	0.00	12.50
Politicians (officiating)						
Federal politicians (%)	Cooperative banks	0.26	1.52	591.71	0.00	11.11
	Savings banks	0.74	2.37	320.61	0.00	15.38
Federal state politicians (%)	Cooperative banks	0.15	1.18	771.01	0.00	11.11
	Savings banks	2.64	4.36	164.99	0.00	23.08
Regional politicans (%)	Cooperative banks	0.00	0.00	0.00	0.00	0.00
	Savings banks	5.52	4.09	74.14	0.00	20.00
Local politicians (%)	Cooperative banks	1.85	4.44	239.60	0.00	25.00
	Savings banks	15.78	12.86	81.50	0.00	66.67
Officiating and retired politicians (%)	Cooperative banks	3.22	6.31	195.77	0.00	35.29
	Savings banks	28.64	15.39	53.73	0.00	75.00

Appendix IV.6.5: Mean comparison cooperative vs. savings banks, t-test, Top 200

Dependent variables	Group	Mean	Std. error	t	df
z-score	Cooperative banks Savings banks	22.7075 19.4006	0.4285 0.3050	6.2873	2157.6500
NPL ratio	Cooperative banks Savings banks	2.6616 2.1136	0.0573 0.0437	7.6087	2219.4500
ROE	Cooperative banks Savings banks	12.1898 13.5984	0.2183 0.2438	-4.3042	2369.3400
RORWA	Cooperative banks Savings banks	1.2118 1.3301	0.0230 0.0284	-3.2372	2296.5300
Bank level variables					
Financial expertise	Cooperative banks Savings banks	47.7642 64.9789	0.6602 0.4980	-20.8182	2229.7100
Outside financial expertise	Cooperative banks Savings banks	45.2461 53.1539	0.6705 0.6599	-8.4056	2397.3900
Board size	Cooperative banks Savings banks	12.4175 16.8058	0.1282 0.1526	-22.0161	2328.3300
Bank size	Cooperative banks Savings banks	20.9000 21.7833	0.0198 0.0174	-33.4650	2359.7700
Bank size growth	Cooperative banks Savings banks	2.6078 0.2526	0.1380 0.0980	13.9148	2028.4600
Bank efficiency	Cooperative banks Savings banks	66.4850 65.2888	0.2757 0.2112	3.4443	2245.4700
Loan growth	Cooperative banks Savings banks	4.9788 2.8602	0.2228 0.2875	5.8245	2162.4000
Claims on MFI	Cooperative banks Savings banks	11.8889 9.8452	0.1904 0.1892	7.6137	2397.9100
Claims on non-MFI	Cooperative banks Savings banks	58.6740 58.9138	0.3287 0.3464	-0.5022	2391.4400

Confidence level: 95%

Appendix IV.6.6: Summary statistics, Top 150

Dependent variables	Group	Mean	Std. Dev.	Coeff. of Variation	Min	Max
z-score	Cooperative banks	17.69	8.48	47.95	3.95	66.43
	Savings banks	19.16	9.76	50.94	3.02	77.02
NPL ratio (%)	Cooperative banks	2.69	2.10	77.95	0.00	13.47
	Savings banks	2.08	1.46	70.08	0.04	11.56
ROE (%)	Cooperative banks	12.27	8.10	66.03	-21.43	55.21
	Savings banks	14.15	7.61	53.74	-28.36	67.79
RORWA (%)	Cooperative banks	1.20	0.82	68.27	-1.67	6.27
	Savings banks	1.39	0.94	67.68	-2.92	8.34
Bank level variables						
Financial expertise (%)	Cooperative banks	47.53	22.74	47.85	0.00	100.00
	Savings banks	65.46	17.22	26.30	20.00	100.00
Outside financial expertise (%)	Cooperative banks	45.81	23.65	51.63	0.00	100.00
	Savings banks	53.84	22.96	42.64	0.00	100.00
Board size	Cooperative banks	10.81	3.66	33.88	4.00	33.00
	Savings banks	15.89	4.12	25.96	7.00	33.00
Bank size (ln '000 EUR)	Cooperative banks	20.61	0.72	3.50	19.30	24.45
	Savings banks	21.69	0.54	2.47	20.89	23.47
Bank size growth (%)	Cooperative banks	2.52	4.62	183.63	-19.46	30.61
	Savings banks	0.30	3.25	1,074.99	-16.29	14.74
Bank efficiency (%)	Cooperative banks	66.51	9.95	14.96	15.98	112.92
	Savings banks	64.55	7.29	11.29	36.00	90.25
Loan growth (%)	Cooperative banks	4.90	7.18	146.63	-12.36	39.29
	Savings banks	2.76	9.58	347.08	-14.70	104.87
Claims on MFI (%)	Cooperative banks	12.09	6.66	55.07	0.06	37.92
	Savings banks	9.86	6.56	66.55	0.00	44.37
Claims on non-MFI (%)	Cooperative banks	58.57	11.26	19.22	11.17	82.75
	Savings banks	59.79	11.03	18.44	24.21	85.36
Macroeconomic and structural variables						
East/West	Cooperative banks	0.03	0.16	604.49	0.00	1.00
	Savings banks	0.09	0.29	311.85	0.00	1.00
GDP per capita ('000 EUR)	Cooperative banks	28.42	10.13	35.63	14.76	231.16
	Savings banks	27.83	7.70	27.66	14.16	72.20
Population	Cooperative banks	2.49	1.41	56.73	1.00	5.00
	Savings banks	1.56	0.74	47.39	1.00	5.00

Appendix IV.6.7: Mean comparison cooperative vs. savings banks, t-test, Top 150

Dependent variables	**Group**	**Mean**	**Std. error**	**t**	**df**
z-score	Cooperative banks	17.6920	0.2828	-3.4061	1763.7600
	Savings banks	19.1602	0.3253		
NPL ratio	Cooperative banks	2.6882	0.0703	7.0774	1584.4500
	Savings banks	2.0828	0.0488		
ROE	Cooperative banks	12.2717	0.2701	-5.0743	1790.8300
	Savings banks	14.1514	0.2535		
RORWA	Cooperative banks	1.1960	0.0272	-4.5651	1764.7400
	Savings banks	1.3851	0.0312		
Bank level variables					
Financial expertise	Cooperative banks	47.5350	0.7581	-18.8507	1674.5600
	Savings banks	65.4584	0.5738		
Outside financial expertise	Cooperative banks	45.8105	0.7883	-7.3056	1796.4100
	Savings banks	53.8369	0.7652		
Board size	Cooperative banks	10.8133	0.1221	-27.5990	1773.3800
	Savings banks	15.8878	0.1375		
Bank size	Cooperative banks	20.6116	0.0240	-36.1164	1661.5400
	Savings banks	21.6936	0.0179		
Bank size growth	Cooperative banks	2.5163	0.1544	11.7446	1605.1500
	Savings banks	0.3021	0.1082		
Bank efficiency	Cooperative banks	66.5056	0.3316	4.7512	1647.9000
	Savings banks	64.5529	0.2428		
Loan growth	Cooperative banks	4.8971	0.2399	5.3517	1666.8700
	Savings banks	2.7598	0.3193		
Claims on MFI	Cooperative banks	12.0907	0.2219	7.1625	1797.6100
	Savings banks	9.8588	0.2187		
Claims on non-MFI	Cooperative banks	58.5717	0.3752	-2.3106	1797.2300
	Savings banks	59.7853	0.3675		

Confidence level: 95%

Appendix IV.6.8: Cluster analysis, clustered by financial expertise, Top 150

Dependent variables	Group	Cluster 1	Cluster 2	Cluster 3	Delta Cluster 1–3
z-score	Cooperative banks	15.62	17.85	19.61	–3.99
	Savings banks	19.76	18.23	19.49	0.27
NPL ratio (%)	Cooperative banks	3.20	2.58	2.29	0.91
	Savings banks	1.97	2.07	2.21	–0.24
ROE (%)	Cooperative banks	11.59	13.23	11.99	–0.40
	Savings banks	15.85	13.95	12.65	3.21
RORWA (%)	Cooperative banks	1.15	1.25	1.18	–0.03
	Savings banks	1.58	1.36	1.22	0.36
Bank level variables					
Financial expertise (%)	Cooperative banks	71.74	47.16	23.70	48.03
	Savings banks	83.78	65.96	46.64	37.14
Outside financial expertise (%)	Cooperative banks	70.55	44.60	22.28	48.27
	Savings banks	77.32	54.81	29.38	47.95
Board size	Cooperative banks	10.52	10.91	11.02	–0.50
	Savings banks	16.01	16.25	15.41	0.60
Bank size (ln ,000 EUR)	Cooperative banks	20.63	20.69	20.51	0.11
	Savings banks	21.69	21.75	21.64	0.06
Bank size growth (%)	Cooperative banks	1.87	2.97	2.71	–0.84
	Savings banks	0.58	0.18	0.14	0.43
Bank efficiency (%)	Cooperative banks	67.17	65.93	66.42	0.75
	Savings banks	62.34	65.54	65.78	–3.44
Loan growth (%)	Cooperative banks	4.12	5.37	5.21	–1.09
	Savings banks	2.35	2.03	3.89	–1.54
Claims on MFI (%)	Cooperative banks	12.11	12.66	11.50	0.62
	Savings banks	10.63	10.65	8.30	2.33
Claims on non-MFI (%)	Cooperative banks	56.93	58.86	59.92	–2.99
	Savings banks	56.82	59.14	63.39	–6.57

Appendix IV.6.9: Pairwise test of significance between expertise clusters, Top 150

Dependent variables		Cluster 1 vs. 2	Cluster 1 vs. 3	Cluster 2 vs. 3
		t **(*p-value*)**	**t** **(*p-value*)**	**t** **(*p-value*)**
z-score	Cooperative banks	–3.8227***	–5.2972***	–2.5639**
		0.0002	*0.0000*	*0.0108*
	Savings banks	2.1519**	0.2783	–1.5821
		0.0322	*0.7810*	*0.1147*
NPL ratio	Cooperative banks	4.3753***	6.0238***	2.1036**
		0.0000	*0.0000*	*0.0363*
	Savings banks	–1.0372	–2.1583**	–1.2316
		0.3005	*0.0317*	*0.2191*
ROE	Cooperative banks	–2.5850**	–0.6422	2.1633**
		0.0102	*0.5213*	*0.0313*
	Savings banks	3.2540***	6.2159***	2.3510**
		0.0013	*0.0000*	*0.0194*

Dependent variables		Cluster 1 vs. 2	Cluster 1 vs. 3	Cluster 2 vs. 3
		t (*p-value*)	t (*p-value*)	t (*p-value*)
RORWA	Cooperative banks	-1.5285 *0.1275*	-0.4669 *0.6409*	1.1298 *0.2595*
	Savings banks	2.9212*** *0.0038*	5.1308*** *0.0000*	2.0891** *0.0375*
Bank level variables				
Financial expertise	Cooperative banks	42.2232*** *0.0000*	75.5214*** *0.0000*	41.0016*** *0.0000*
	Savings banks	50.1895*** *0.0000*	96.1220*** *0.0000*	44.0866*** *0.0000*
Outside financial expertise	Cooperative banks	32.4137*** *0.0000*	70.3125*** *0.0000*	26.9993*** *0.0000*
	Savings banks	35.2981*** *0.0000*	67.3601*** *0.0000*	29.7499*** *0.0000*
Bank size	Cooperative banks	-1.0340 *0.3020*	2.2612** *0.0245*	2.8167*** *0.0052*
	Savings banks	-1.2410 *0.2156*	1.4256 *0.1550*	2.4038** *0.0168*
Bank efficiency	Cooperative banks	1.5473 *0.1229*	0.9486 *0.3436*	-0.6065 *0.5446*
	Savings banks	-5.1310*** *0.0000*	-5.8860*** *0.0000*	-0.4735 *0.6362*
Bank size growth	Cooperative banks	-2.9847*** *0.0031*	-2.3450** *0.0197*	0.8224 *0.4115*
	Savings banks	1.5352 *0.1258*	1.7050* *0.0892*	0.1416 *0.8875*
Board size	Cooperative banks	-1.6942* *0.0913*	-1.6502* *0.1000*	-0.3398 *0.7342*
	Savings banks	-0.6500 *0.5162*	1.6842* *0.0932*	2.6486*** *0.0085*
Loan growth	Cooperative banks	-3.1168*** *0.0020*	-2.5868** *0.0102*	0.4502 *0.6529*
	Savings banks	0.5969 *0.5510*	-2.3829** *0.0178*	-2.2693** *0.0240*
Claims on MFI	Cooperative banks	-1.0752 *0.2832*	1.1601 *0.2469*	2.3587** *0.0190*
	Savings banks	-0.0377 *0.9700*	4.4976*** *0.0000*	5.0412*** *0.0000*
Claims on non-MFI	Cooperative banks	-2.1078** *0.0359*	-3.5104*** *0.0005*	-1.0176 *0.3097*
	Savings banks	-2.7057*** *0.0072*	-7.0374*** *0.0000*	-5.0723*** *0.0000*

Confidence level: 95%

* indicates significance at the 10% level, ** at the 5% level, and *** at the 1% level, respectively.

Appendix IV.6.10: Correlation matrix, Top 200

	RORWA	ROE	z-score	NPL ratio	FinExp *C	OutFin Exp*C	Bank size*C	Bank effic.*C	Bank size growth*C	Loan growth*C	Claims on MFI*C	Claims on non-MFI*C
RORWA	1.0000											
ROE	0.8827*	1.0000										
z-score	0.0957*	0.0290	1.0000									
NPL ratio	–0.0558*	–0.0725*	–0.0106	1.0000								
FinExp*C	–0.0901*	–0.0996*	0.0366	0.2049*	1.0000							
OutFinExp*C	–0.0829*	–0.0954*	0.0354	0.2346*	0.9855*	1.0000						
Bank size*C	–0.0682	–0.089*	0.1234*	0.1439*	0.8325*	0.8087*	1.0000					
Bank effic.*C	–0.1051*	–0.1310*	0.1212*	0.1725*	0.8228*	0.8075*	0.9772*	1.0000				
Bank size growth*C	–0.0026	–0.0076	0.0004	–0.1406*	0.2637*	0.2438*	0.3789*	0.3476*	1.0000			
Loan growth*C	0.1205*	0.0706*	–0.0052	0.0599*	0.3306*	0.3110*	0.4368*	0.4111*	0.6774*	1.0000		
Claims on MFI*C	–0.0747*	–0.1216*	0.0354	0.1045*	0.6624*	0.6509*	0.7878*	0.7835*	0.3505*	0.3423*	1.0000	
Claims on non-MFI*C	–0.0900*	–0.0956*	0.1850*	0.1899*	0.7978*	0.7801*	0.9609*	0.9497*	0.3229*	0.3780*	0.6929*	1.0000
Board size*C	–0.0662*	–0.0766*	0.1782*	0.1590*	0.7365*	0.7013*	0.8961*	0.8728*	0.3273*	0.3697*	0.6666*	0.8716*
FinExp*S	0.1001*	0.1228*	–0.1380*	–0.1447*	–0.7754*	–0.7577*	–0.9352*	–0.9175	–0.3505*	–0.4032*	–0.7367*	–0.9029*
OutFinExp*S	0.1108*	0.1342*	–0.1137*	–0.1526*	–0.7076*	–0.6916*	–0.8536*	–0.8374*	–0.3194*	–0.3675*	–0.6724*	–0.8240*
Bank size*S	0.0637*	0.0856*	–0.1263*	–0.1561*	–0.8275*	–0.8087*	–0.9982*	–0.9792*	–0.3745*	–0.4309*	–0.7863*	–0.9636*
Bank effic.*S	0.0122	0.0342	–0.1316*	–0.1587*	–0.8180*	–0.7994*	–0.9866*	–0.9679*	–0.3701*	–0.4258*	–0.7772*	–0.9525*
Bank size growth*S	0.0586*	0.0612*	–0.0130	–0.1405*	–0.0439*	–0.0429*	–0.0528*	–0.0518*	–0.0198	–0.0228	–0.0416*	–0.0509*
Loan growth*S	0.1592*	0.1074*	–0.0339	0.1304*	–0.1664*	–0.1624*	–0.2000*	–0.1962*	–0.0750*	–0.0863*	–0.1576*	–0.1930*
Claims on MFI*S	0.0658*	0.0694*	–0.1388*	–0.1654*	–0.6031*	–0.5894*	–0.7274*	–0.7136*	–0.2717*	–0.3126*	–0.5730*	–0.7022*
Claims on non-MFI*S	–0.0179	0.0290	–0.0749*	–0.1238*	–0.7958*	–0.7777*	–0.9599*	–0.9417*	–0.3604*	–0.4146*	–0.7562*	–0.9267*
Board size*S	0.0016	0.0335	–0.1201*	–0.1155*	–0.7567*	–0.7395*	–0.9127*	–0.8954*	–0.3424*	–0.3939*	–0.7190*	–0.8811*
GDP per capita	–0.0808*	–0.0984*	–0.0075	–0.1071*	0.0643*	0.0486*	0.0467*	0.0375	0.0676*	0.0629*	0.1118*	0.0171
Population	–0.0512*	–0.0701*	–0.0518*	–0.1922*	0.3025*	0.2386*	0.3942*	0.3345*	0.2314*	0.2319*	0.3593*	0.3000*
East/West	0.2480*	0.1853*	–0.1749*	–0.0188	–0.1614*	–0.1537*	–0.2108*	–0.1983*	–0.0833*	–0.0936*	–0.1504*	–0.2295*

* indicates significance at the 5% level

Board size*C	FinExp *S	OutFin Exp*S	Bank size*S	Bank effic.*S	Bank size growth*S	Loan growth*S	Claims on MFI*S	Claims on Non-MFI*S	Board size*S	GDP per capita	Population	East/ West
1.0000												
−0.8356*	1.0000											
−0.7626*	0.9709*	1.0000										
−0.8918*	0.9350*	0.8518*	1.0000									
−0.8815*	0.9172*	0.8341*	0.9864*	1.0000								
−0.0475*	0.0752*	0.0972*	0.0526*	0.0389	1.0000							
−0.1799*	0.1712*	0.1237*	0.2016*	0.1882*	0.2411*	1.0000						
−0.6499*	0.7277*	0.6909*	0.7298*	0.7210*	0.1237*	0.1066*	1.0000					
−0.8576*	0.8695*	0.7821*	0.9609*	0.9554*	0.0198	0.1901*	0.6150*	1.0000				
−0.8154*	0.8619*	0.7683*	0.9203*	0.9075*	0.0213	0.1834*	0.6684*	0.8859*	1.0000			
−0.0033	−0.0133	0.0182	−0.0279	−0.0324	0.0547*	−0.0090	0.0075	−0.0149	−0.0335	1.0000		
0.3315*	−0.3515*	−0.3464*	−0.3573*	−0.3668*	−0.0437*	−0.0634*	−0.2596*	−0.3634*	−0.2517	0.256*	1.0000	
−0.1925*	0.2404*	0.2111*	0.2039*	0.1916*	−0.0468*	0.0042	0.2479*	0.0291	0.1432*	−0.2363*	−0.0706*	1.0000

Appendix IV.6.11: Correlation matrix, Top 150

	RORWA	ROE	z-score	NPL ratio	FinExp *C	OutFin Exp*C	Bank size*C	Bank effic.*C	Bank size growth*C	Loan growth*C	Claims on MFI*C	Claims on non-MFI*C
RORWA	1.0000											
ROE	0.8804*	1.0000										
z-score	0.0791*	0.0041	1.0000									
NPL ratio	−0.0884*	−0.1021*	−0.0636*	1.0000								
FinExp*C	−0.1062*	−0.1222*	−0.1213*	0.2421*	1.0000							
OutFinExp*C	−0.1020*	−0.1220*	−0.1163*	0.2682*	0.9879*	1.0000						
Bank size*C	−0.1076*	−0.1181*	−0.0857*	0.1527*	0.8294*	0.8042*	1.0000					
Bank effic.*C	−0.1549*	−0.1731*	−0.0776*	0.1851*	0.8174*	0.8009*	0.9753*	1.0000				
Bank size growth*C	−0.0127	0.0056	−0.0935*	−0.1768*	0.2449*	0.2184*	0.3654*	0.3258*	1.0000			
Loan growth*C	0.0980*	0.0743*	−0.0792*	0.0442	0.3393*	0.3174*	0.4407*	0.4113*	0.6777*	1.0000		
Claims on MFI*C	−0.1172*	−0.1553*	−0.1368*	0.0996*	0.6671*	0.6512*	0.7887*	0.7864*	0.3393*	0.3353*	1.0000	
Claims on non-MFI*C	−0.1301*	−0.1274*	−0.0298	0.2052*	0.7873*	0.7684*	0.9607*	0.9490*	0.3040*	0.3825*	0.7020*	1.0000
Board size*C	−0.1066*	−0.1042*	−0.0154	0.1688*	0.7300*	0.6962*	0.9054*	0.8827*	0.3041*	0.3639*	0.6802*	0.8821*
FinExp*S	0.1377*	0.1475*	0.0699*	−0.1587*	−0.7765*	−0.7572*	−0.9362*	−0.9171*	−0.3373*	−0.4077*	−0.7397*	−0.9046*
OutFinExp*S	0.1387*	0.1521*	0.0800*	−0.1651*	−0.7095*	−0.6919*	−0.8554*	−0.8379*	−0.3081*	−0.3724*	−0.6759*	−0.8265*
Bank size*S	0.1066*	0.1189*	0.0822*	−0.1674*	−0.8279*	−0.8073*	−0.9982*	−0.9778*	−0.3597*	−0.4347*	−0.7886*	−0.9644*
Bank effic.*S	0.0520*	0.0679*	0.0702*	−0.1721*	−0.8180*	−0.7977*	−0.9863*	−0.9662*	−0.3554*	−0.4295*	−0.7793*	−0.9530*
Bank size growth*S	0.0545*	0.0495*	−0.0096	−0.1282*	−0.0544*	−0.0530*	−0.0655*	−0.0642*	−0.0236	−0.0285	−0.0518*	−0.0633*
Loan growth*S	0.1547*	0.1027*	0.0056	0.1171*	−0.1654*	−0.1613*	−0.1993*	−0.1952*	−0.0718*	−0.0868*	−0.1574*	−0.1925*
Claims on MFI*S	0.0896*	0.0957*	−0.0021	−0.1886*	−0.6034*	−0.5884*	−0.7275*	−0.7126*	−0.2620*	−0.3167*	−0.5748*	−0.7029*
Claims on non-MFI*S	0.0266	0.0686*	0.1367*	−0.1347*	−0.8016*	−0.7817*	−0.9665*	−0.9467*	−0.3482*	−0.4209*	−0.7636*	−0.9338*
Board size*S	0.0661*	0.0903*	0.0772*	−0.1365*	−0.7777*	−0.7584*	−0.9377*	−0.9185*	−0.3378*	−0.4083*	−0.7408*	−0.9060*
GDP per capita	−0.0306	−0.0192	−0.0376	−0.0957*	0.0196	0.0108	0.0370	0.0224	0.0722*	0.0618*	0.0945*	0.0228
Population	0.0193	0.0013	−0.1204*	−0.2444*	0.2672*	0.2074*	0.4044*	0.3323*	0.2520*	0.2323*	0.3757*	0.2997*
East/West	0.2743*	0.1872*	−0.1466*	0.0047	−0.1009*	−0.0944*	−0.1425*	−0.1417*	−0.0530*	−0.0671*	−0.1064*	−0.1639*

* indicates significance at the 5% level

Board size*C	FinExp *S	OutFin Exp*S	Bank size*S	Bank effic.*S	Bank size growth*S	Loan growth*S	Claims on MFI*S	Claims on Non-MFI*S	Board size*S	GDP per capita	Population	East/ West
1.0000												
−0.8454*	1.0000											
−0.7725*	0.9721*	1.0000										
−0.9014*	0.9369*	0.8557*	1.0000									
−0.8907*	0.9166*	0.8359*	0.9860*	1.0000								
−0.0592*	0.0789*	0.0937*	0.0663*	0.0534*	1.0000							
−0.1799*	0.1709*	0.1247*	0.2000*	0.1873*	0.2496*	1.0000						
−0.6569*	0.7234*	0.6844*	0.7323*	0.7233*	0.1408*	0.1063*	1.0000					
−0.8728*	0.8821*	0.7976*	0.9672*	0.9614*	0.0398	0.1881*	0.6313*	1.0000				
−0.8467*	0.8907*	0.8059*	0.9422*	0.9284*	0.0464*	0.1889*	0.6984*	0.9104*	1.0000			
0.0077	−0.0133	0.0188	−0.0226	−0.0300	0.0516*	−0.0082	0.0270	−0.0256	−0.0269	1.0000		
0.3392*	−0.3498*	−0.3239*	−0.3699*	−0.3804*	−0.0289	−0.0705*	−0.2514*	−0.3750*	−0.3062*	0.2241*	1.0000	
−0.1397*	0.1542*	0.1258*	0.1348*	0.1211*	−0.0927*	−0.0211	0.1409*	0.0025	0.0907*	−0.1758*	−0.0918*	1.0000

Appendix IV.6.12: Random-effect regressions with dependent variables z-score and NPL ratio, Top 150 banks

Variable		z-score (RE) Financial expertise		z-score (RE) Out. fin. expertise		NPL ratio (RE) Financial expertise		NPL ratio (RE) Out. fin. expertise	
		Coeff.	SE (robust)	Coeff.	SE (robust)	Coeff.	SE (robust)	Coeff.	SE (robust)
Financial expertise	Financial expertise*C	-0.0193	0.0235			0.0125	0.0043***		
	Outside financial expertise*C			-0.0238	0.0232			0.0125	0.0042***
	Financial expertise*S	0.0173	0.0117			0.0046	0.0040		
	Outside financial expertise*S			0.0099	0.0106			0.0010	0.0033
Bank level	Savings	-83.1116	37.1565**	-84.1552	37.4078**	-11.4575	4.2121***	-9.7527	4.3303**
	Bank size*C	-4.4277	1.6046***	-4.4225	1.6222***	-0.5308	0.1501***	-0.4723	0.1537***
	Bank efficiency*C	-0.0138	0.0082*	-0.0135	0.0083	-0.0020	0.0065	-0.0021	0.0065
	Bank size growth*C	-0.0595	0.0168***	-0.0598	0.0168***	-0.1639	0.0161***	-0.1636	0.0161***
	Loan growth*C	0.0052	0.0135	0.0055	0.0135	0.0951	0.0112***	0.0949	0.0112***
	Claims on MFI*C	-0.0320	0.0197	-0.0330	0.0196*	0.0174	0.0123	0.0177	0.0123
	Claims on non-MFI*C	0.0367	0.0282	0.0365	0.0280	0.0362	0.0089***	0.0369	0.0089***
	Board size*C	0.1177	0.1655	0.1114	0.1646	0.0695	0.0301**	0.0716	0.0301**
	Bank size*S	-0.2154	1.2117	-0.1546	1.2045	0.1036	0.1579	0.0977	0.1592
	Bank efficiency*S	-0.0162	0.0180	-0.0163	0.0180	-0.0265	0.0078***	-0.0270	0.0079***
	Bank size growth*S	-0.1143	0.0162***	-0.1144	0.0162***	-0.0911	0.0125***	-0.0911	0.0125***
	Loan growth*S	0.0391	0.0066***	0.0394	0.0067***	0.0475	0.0075***	0.0475	0.0075***
	Claims on MFI*S	0.0166	0.0272	0.0164	0.0271	-0.0179	0.0088**	-0.0178	0.0088**
	Claims on non-MFI*S	0.0216	0.0335	0.0213	0.0333	0.0284	0.0102***	0.0270	0.0101***
	Board size*S	-0.0773	0.0486	-0.0662	0.0513	0.0444	0.0174***	0.0460	0.0173***
Macroeconomic and structural environment	East/West	-6.0046	1.7353***	-5.9156	1.7234***	0.6730	0.3254**	0.6680	0.3269**
	GDP per capita	0.0340	0.0187*	0.0341	0.0189*	-0.0123	0.0045***	-0.0124	0.0045***
	Population	0.9923	0.4704**	0.9648	0.4630**	-0.3270	0.0790***	-0.3223	0.0792***
	constant	104.6185	32.2748***	104.8236	32.6349***	11.1637	3.2571***	9.9083	3.3738***
	Wald Chi^2	317.88	***	311.62	***	448.70	***	450.29	***
	R-sq	0.0548		0.0572		0.3184		0.3184	
	No of observations	1,796		1,796		1,781		1,781	

* indicates significance at the 10% level, ** at the 5% level, and *** at the 1% level, respectively.
Standard errors control for clustering at the bank level.

Appendix IV.6.13: Comparison coefficients with dependent variables z-score and NPL ratio, Top 150 banks

Variable		z-score (RE) Financial expertise		z-score (RE) Out. fin. expertise		NPL ratio (RE) Financial expertise		NPL ratio (RE) Out. fin. expertise	
		chi^2	$P>chi^2$	chi^2	$P>chi^2$	chi^2	$P>chi^2$	chi^2	$P>chi^2$
Financial expertise	Financial expertise: C vs. S	1.9300	0.1649			1.7500	0.1853		
	Outside financial expertise: C vs. S			1.7400	0.1870			4.6200	0.0316**
Bank level	Bank size: C vs. S	5.6500	0.0175**	5.7300	0.0167**	11.6800	0.0006***	9.0200	0.0027***
	Bank efficiency: C vs. S	0.0200	0.9012	0.0200	0.8887	5.8300	0.0157**	5.9400	0.0148**
	Bank size growth: C vs. S	5.6200	0.0177**	5.5700	0.0183**	12.7200	0.0004***	12.5800	0.0004***
	Board size: C vs. S	1.2800	0.2579	1.0600	0.3025	0.5300	0.4674	0.5500	0.4582
	Loan growth: C vs. S	5.1800	0.0228***	5.1600	0.0231**	12.4400	0.0004***	12.3100	0.0005***
	Claims on MFI: C vs. S	2.1100	0.1467	2.1900	0.1389	5.3700	0.0204**	5.3800	0.0203**
	Claims on non-MFI: C vs. S	0.1200	0.7288	0.1200	0.7251	0.3300	0.5641	0.5300	0.4648

* indicates significance at the 10% level, ** at the 5% level, and *** at the 1% level, respectively.

Appendix IV.6.14: Random-effect regressions with dependent variables RORWA and ROE, Top 150 banks

Variable		RORWA (RE) Financial expertise		RORWA (RE) Out. fin. expertise		ROE (RE) Financial expertise		ROE (RE) Out. fin. expertise	
		Coeff.	SE (robust)	Coeff.	SE (robust)	Coeff.	SE (robust)	Coeff.	SE (robust)
Financial expertise	Financial expertise*C	−0.0009	0.0015			−0.0122	0.0166		
	Outside financial expertise*C			−0.0011	0.0014			−0.0144	0.0162
	Financial expertise*S	0.0011	0.0019			0.0218	0.0161		
	Outside financial expertise*S			0.0012	0.0015			0.0229	0.0125*
Bank level	Savings	−1.1028	1.7216	−1.2652	1.7123	−0.1938	17.2103	−2.3867	17.1005
	Bank size*C	−0.2679	0.0603***	−0.2713	0.0583***	−1.7035	0.6555***	−1.7507	0.6324***
	Bank efficiency*C	−0.0286	0.0037***	−0.0286	0.0037***	−0.3032	0.0379***	−0.3029	0.0380***
	Bank size growth*C	−0.0433	0.0078***	−0.0435	0.0078***	−0.2704	0.0732***	−0.2717	0.0732***
	Loan growth*C	0.0413	0.0044***	0.0413	0.0044***	0.2669	0.0398***	0.2674	0.0398***
	Claims on MFI*C	−0.0125	0.0052**	−0.0125	0.0052**	−0.1752	0.0520***	−0.1749	0.0520***
	Claims on non-MFI*C	−0.0135	0.0031***	−0.0136	0.0031***	−0.0601	0.0345*	−0.0610	0.0345*
	Board size*C	0.0083	0.0096	0.0080	0.0097	0.1351	0.1049	0.1308	0.1056
	Bank size*S	−0.0816	0.0674	−0.0788	0.0674	−0.9154	0.6963	−0.8742	0.6957
	Bank efficiency*S	−0.0475	0.0058***	−0.0474	0.0059***	−0.4640	0.0547***	−0.4634	0.0549***
	Bank size growth*S	−0.0121	0.0078	−0.0122	0.0079	−0.0763	0.0648	−0.0782	0.0645
	Loan growth*S	0.0169	0.0029***	0.0170	0.0029***	0.0797	0.0207***	0.0815	0.0209***
	Claims on MFI*S	−0.0140	0.0046***	−0.0141	0.0046***	−0.0924	0.0440**	−0.0941	0.0443**
	Claims onnon-MFI*S	−0.0286	0.0045***	−0.0284	0.0045***	−0.1148	0.0355***	−0.1117	0.0350***
	Board size*S	−0.0206	0.0069***	−0.0202	0.0068***	−0.0726	0.0684	−0.0646	0.0680
Macroeconomic and structural environment	East/West	0.2654	0.1808	0.2724	0.1812	1.9599	1.3122	2.0866	1.3117
	GDP per capita	0.0003	0.0025	0.0002	0.0025	−0.0002	0.0353	−0.0016	0.0361
	Population	0.0645	0.0336*	0.0632	0.0336*	0.3658	0.3418	0.3538	0.3432
	constant	9.2457	1.1455***	9.3397	1.1239***	70.7073	12.7437***	71.9070	12.4292***
	Wald Chi²	405.5	***	403.06	***	414.17	***	415.34	***
	R-sq	0.3371		0.3375		0.2459		0.2472	
	No of observations	1,796		1,796		1,796		1,796	

* indicates significance at the 10% level, ** at the 5% level, and *** at the 1% level, respectively.
Standard errors control for clustering at the bank level.

Appendix IV.6.15: Comparison coefficients with dependent variables RORWA and ROE, Top 150 banks

Variable		**RORWA (RE) Financial expertise**		**RORWA (RE) Out. fin. expertise**		**ROE (RE) Financial expertise**		**ROE (RE) Out. fin. expertise**	
		chi^2	**$P>chi^2$**	**chi^2**	**$P>chi^2$**	**chi^2**	**$P>chi^2$**	**chi^2**	**$P>chi^2$**
Financial expertise	Financial expertise: C vs. S	0.6900	0.4060			2.1100	0.1459		
	Outside financial expertise: C vs. S			1.2700	0.2592			3.2400	0.0719*
Bank level	Bank size: C vs. S	5.6400	0.0176**	6.1700	0.0130**	1.0200	0.3124	1.3000	0.2534
	Bank efficiency: C vs. S	7.4300	0.0064***	7.3700	0.0066***	5.8900	0.0152**	5.8300	0.0158**
	Bank size growth: C vs. S	8.0300	0.0046***	7.9800	0.0047***	3.9700	0.0463**	3.9500	0.0467**
	Board size: C vs. S	5.8100	0.0159**	5.5300	0.0187**	2.7200	0.0992*	2.3900	0.1222
	Loan growth: C vs. S	21.1100	0.0000***	20.9900	0.0000***	17.4300	0.0000***	17.1400	0.0000***
	Claims on MFI: C vs. S	0.0500	0.8282	0.0500	0.8170	1.4500	0.2292	1.3700	0.2410
	Claims on non-MFI: C vs. S	8.5100	0.0035***	8.1500	0.0043***	1.4700	0.2260	1.2800	0.2572

* indicates significance at the 10% level, ** at the 5% level, and *** at the 1% level, respectively.

Appendix IV.6.16: Random-effect regressions with dependent variables z-score and NPL ratio, Top 200 banks, with 1% outlier correction

Variable		z-score (RE) Financial expertise		z-score (RE) Out. fin. expertise		NPL ratio (RE) Financial expertise		NPL ratio (RE) Out. fin. expertise	
		Coeff.	SE (robust)	Coeff.	SE (robust)	Coeff.	SE (robust)	Coeff.	SE (robust)
Financial expertise	Financial expertise*C	−0.0613	0.0450			0.0122	0.0040***		
	Outside financial expertise*C			−0.0836	0.0402**			0.0127	0.0038***
	Financial expertise*S	−0.0148	0.0296			0.0074	0.0037**		
	Outside financial expertise*S			−0.0091	0.0239			0.0028	0.0029
Bank level	Savings	−116.8259	77.6643	−122.1647	78.3245	−9.6770	4.6872**	−7.6533	4.7105
	Bank size*C	−3.2622	3.2207	−3.3643	3.2199	−0.6632	0.1605***	−0.6005	0.1543***
	Bank efficiency*C	−0.0715	0.0285**	−0.0701	0.0286**	−0.0041	0.0063	−0.0041	0.0063
	Bank size growth*C	0.0206	0.0549	0.0187	0.0543	−0.1674	0.0137***	−0.1671	0.0137***
	Loan growth*C	−0.0852	0.0335**	−0.0841	0.0334**	0.1023	0.0098***	0.1019	0.0098***
	Claims on MFI*C	0.0177	0.0721	0.0141	0.0727	0.0335	0.0108***	0.0333	0.0108***
	Claims on non-MFI*C	0.1549	0.1091	0.1501	0.1084	0.0325	0.0082***	0.0333	0.0083***
	Board size*C	−0.1672	0.2326	−0.1863	0.2340	0.0466	0.0194**	0.0491	0.0195**
	Bank size*S	1.9323	2.0587	1.9931	2.0641	−0.1210	0.1793	−0.1320	0.1807
	Bank efficiency*S	0.0235	0.0345	0.0235	0.0347	−0.0237	0.0074***	−0.0242	0.0075***
	Bank size growth*S	−0.1162	0.0249***	−0.1162	0.0249***	−0.1087	0.0119***	−0.1086	0.0120***
	Loan growth*S	0.0449	0.0079***	0.0443	0.0076***	0.0580	0.0053***	0.0581	0.0053***
	Claims on MFI*S	0.0283	0.0416	0.0279	0.0418	−0.0188	0.0084**	−0.0186	0.0084**
	Claims onnon-MFI*S	0.0322	0.0520	0.0331	0.0524	0.0247	0.0096***	0.0233	0.0096**
	Board size*S	−0.0021	0.1028	−0.0053	0.1042	0.0378	0.0121***	0.0400	0.0119***
Macroeconomic and structural environment	East/West	−6.4073	1.9334***	−6.3765	1.9536***	0.4057	0.3040	0.4170	0.3042
	GDP per capita	−0.0151	0.0786	−0.0116	0.0784	−0.0324	0.0077***	−0.1763	0.0667***
	Population	−0.4519	0.9878	−0.5489	0.9811	−0.1833	0.0668***	−0.0321	0.0076***
	constant	93.1832	71.5405	96.7972	71.7857	14.5980	3.4664***	13.1956	3.3843***
	Wald Chi²	182.68	***	183.24	***	682.72	***	680.89	***
	R-sq	0.0875		0.0897		0.2915		0.2931	
	No of observations	2,278		2,278		2,259		2,259	

* indicates significance at the 10% level, ** at the 5% level, and *** at the 1% level, respectively.
Standard errors control for clustering at the bank level.

Appendix IV.6.17: Comparison coefficients with dependent variables z-score and NPL ratio, Top 200 banks, with 1% outlier correction

Variable		**z-score (RE) Financial expertise**		**z-score (RE) Out. Fin. expertise**		**NPL ratio (RE) Financial expertise**		**NPL ratio (RE) Out. fin. expertise**	
		chi^2	**$P>chi^2$**	**chi^2**	**$P>chi^2$**	**chi^2**	**$P>chi^2$**	**chi^2**	**$P>chi^2$**
Financial expertise	Financial expertise: C vs. S	0.7400	0.3893			0.7800	0.3784		
	Outside financial expertise: C vs. S			2.5300	0.1120			4.2900	0.0383**
Bank level	Bank size: C vs. S	2.2900	0.1300	2.4000	0.1213	7.1800	0.0074***	5.4200	0.0199**
	Bank efficiency: C vs. S	4.6200	0.0316**	4.4400	0.0350**	4.1300	0.0421**	4.2800	0.0386**
	Bank size growth: C vs. S	5.2000	0.0226**	5.1400	0.0233**	10.4800	0.0012**	10.3600	0.0013***
	Board size: C vs. S	0.4500	0.5045	0.5300	0.4685	0.1500	0.6959	0.1600	0.6866
	Loan growth: C vs. S	14.1700	0.0002***	14.0200	0.0002***	15.8600	0.0001***	15.4500	0.0001***
	Claims on MFI: C vs. S	0.0200	0.8994	0.0300	0.8694	14.5900	0.0001***	14.4000	0.0001***
	Claims on non-MFI: C vs. S	1.1800	0.2766	1.0900	0.2964	0.3900	0.5308	0.6500	0.4191

* indicates significance at the 10% level, ** at the 5% level, and *** at the 1% level, respectively.

Appendix IV.6.18: Random-effect regressions with dependent variables RORWA and ROE, Top 200 banks, with 1% outlier correction

Variable		RORWA (RE) Financial expertise		RORWA (RE) Out. fin. expertise		ROE (RE) Financial expertise		ROE (RE) Out. fin. expertise	
		Coeff.	**SE (robust)**	**Coeff.**	**SE (robust)**	**Coeff.**	**SE (robust)**	**Coeff.**	**SE (robust)**
Financial expertise	Financial expertise*C	−0.0010	0.0012			−0.0039	0.0131		
	Outside financial expertise*C			−0.0013	0.0012			−0.0064	0.0128
	Financial expertise*S	0.0020	0.0016			0.0374	0.0149**		
	Outside financial expertise*S			0.0022	0.0012*			0.0337	0.0111***
Bank level	Savings	−2.5350	1.5845	−2.7708	1.5757*	−12.0046	16.6273	−13.1084	16.3341
	Bank size*C	−0.2778	0.0582***	−0.2823	0.0561***	−1.9017	0.6549***	−1.9086	0.6268***
	Bank efficiency*C	−0.0250	0.0032***	−0.0250	0.0032***	−0.2618	0.0307***	−0.2612	0.0307***
	Bank size growth*C	−0.0435	0.0072***	−0.0436	0.0072***	−0.2641	0.0694***	−0.2649	0.0694***
	Loan growth*C	0.0452	0.0038***	0.0453	0.0038***	0.2748	0.0340***	0.2752	0.0339***
	Claims on MFI*C	−0.0075	0.0048	−0.0074	0.0048	−0.1196	0.0444***	−0.1189	0.0445***
	Claims on non-MFI*C	−0.0118	0.0027***	−0.0118	0.0027***	−0.0519	0.0289*	−0.0512	0.0288*
	Board size*C	0.0063	0.0064	0.0059	0.0064	0.0876	0.0645	0.0848	0.0650
	Bank size*S	−0.0382	0.0672	−0.0334	0.0675	−0.4193	0.6266	−0.3695	0.6275
	Bank efficiency*S	−0.0458	0.0045***	−0.0456	0.0045***	−0.4727	0.0452***	−0.4720	0.0453***
	Bank size growth*S	−0.0120	0.0074	−0.0123	0.0074*	−0.0378	0.0628	−0.0417	0.0624
	Loan growth*S	0.0220	0.0026***	0.0222	0.0026***	0.1035	0.0206***	0.1066	0.0208***
	Claims on MFI*S	−0.0146	0.0048***	−0.0147	0.0048***	−0.1377	0.0456***	−0.1400	0.0458***
	Claims onnon-MFI*S	−0.0236	0.0033***	−0.0232	0.0033***	−0.1074	0.0301***	−0.1042	0.0299***
	Board size*S	−0.0177	0.0057***	−0.0169	0.0056***	−0.1103	0.0550**	−0.0971	0.0545*
Macroeconomic and structural environment	East/West	0.1155	0.1220	0.1285	0.1215	1.0523	1.0904	1.2370	1.0958
	GDP per capita	−0.0039	0.0028	−0.0041	0.0028	−0.0884	0.0317***	−0.0912	0.0319***
	Population	0.0098	0.0274	0.0097	0.0273	0.0168	0.2365	0.0209	0.2363
	constant	9.3987	1.1262***	9.5061	1.0898***	74.6851	13.2673***	74.9441	12.7012***
	Wald Chi²	613.62	***	616.48	***	536.74	***	534.78	***
	R-sq	0.3263		0.3272		0.2447		0.2458	
	No of observations	2,278		2,278		2,278		2,278	

* indicates significance at the 10% level, ** at the 5% level, and *** at the 1% level, respectively.
Standard errors control for clustering at the bank level.

Appendix IV.6.19: Comparison coefficients with dependent variables RORWA and ROE, Top 200 banks, with 1% outlier correction

Variable		RORWA (RE) Financial expertise		RORWA (RE) Out. fin. expertise		ROE (RE) Financial expertise		ROE (RE) Out. fin. expertise	
		chi^2	$P>chi^2$	chi^2	$P>chi^2$	chi^2	$P>chi^2$	chi^2	$P>chi^2$
Financial expertise	Financial expertise: C vs. S	2.2700	0.1318			4.3000	0.0381**		
	Outside financial expertise: C vs. S			3.9700	0.0462**			5.5800	0.0182**
Bank level	Bank size: C vs. S	10.7500	0.0010***	11.8800	0.0006**	3.8500	0.0498**	4.3600	0.0367**
	Bank efficiency: C vs. S	14.5800	0.0001**	14.3500	0.0002***	15.1000	0.0001***	15.0100	0.0001***
	Bank size growth: C vs. S	9.3500	0.0022***	9.2200	0.0024***	5.8900	0.0152**	5.7700	0.0163**
	Board size: C vs. S	7.7400	0.0054***	7.0800	0.0078***	5.4000	0.0201**	4.5500	0.0329**
	Loan growth: C vs. S	25.1600	0.0000***	24.7800	0.0000***	18.5000	0.0000***	17.8500	0.0000***
	Claims on MFI: C vs. S	1.0900	0.2955	1.1700	0.2797	0.0800	0.7762	0.1100	0.7425
	Claims on non-MFI: C vs. S	9.3000	0.0023***	8.6100	0.0033***	2.1700	0.1403	2.0100	0.1565

* indicates significance at the 10% level, ** at the 5% level, and *** at the 1% level, respectively.

Appendix IV.6.20: Random-effect regressions with dependent variables z-score and NPL ratio, Top 150 banks, with 1% outlier correction

Variable		z-score (RE) Financial expertise		z-score (RE) Out. fin. expertise		NPL ratio (RE) Financial expertise		NPL ratio (RE) Out. fin. expertise	
		Coeff.	SE (robust)	Coeff.	SE (robust)	Coeff.	SE (robust)	Coeff.	SE (robust)
Financial expertise	Financial expertise*C	–0.0160	0.0173			0.0121	0.0044***		
	Outside financial expertise*C			–0.0209	0.0168			0.0122	0.0043***
	Financial expertise*S	0.0147	0.0110			0.0055	0.0040		
	Outside financial expertise*S			0.0089	0.0100			0.0024	0.0031
Bank level	Savings	–68.8123	34.9631**	–69.3353	34.8976**	–14.2733	4.4148***	–12.7481	4.4770***
	Bank size*C	–5.1143	1.5692***	–5.1056	1.5670***	–0.5785	0.1626***	–0.5274	0.1613***
	Bank efficiency*C	–0.0215	0.0095**	–0.0213	0.0095**	–0.0036	0.0071	–0.0037	0.0071
	Bank size growth*C	–0.0770	0.0168***	–0.0774	0.0167***	–0.1703	0.0164***	–0.1700	0.0164***
	Loan growth*C	0.0017	0.0129	0.0019	0.0129	0.0991	0.0111***	0.0990	0.0111***
	Claims on MFI*C	–0.0408	0.0205**	–0.0420	0.0205**	0.0204	0.0122*	0.0206	0.0122*
	Claims on non-MFI*C	0.0279	0.0303	0.0276	0.0299	0.0386	0.0092***	0.0393	0.0092***
	Board size*C	–0.0001	0.1146	–0.0063	0.1133	0.0588	0.0310*	0.0617	0.0312**
	Bank size*S	–1.6599	1.1577	–1.6259	1.1509	0.1855	0.1672	0.1797	0.1687
	Bank efficiency*S	–0.0251	0.0167	–0.0252	0.0168	–0.0230	0.0072***	–0.0234	0.0073***
	Bank size growth*S	–0.1143	0.0162***	–0.1143	0.0162***	–0.1037	0.0129***	–0.1038	0.0129***
	Loan growth*S	0.0481	0.0059***	0.0484	0.0059***	0.0593	0.0063***	0.0594	0.0063***
	Claims on MFI*S	0.0093	0.0238	0.0090	0.0237	–0.0183	0.0092**	–0.0182	0.0092**
	Claims onnon-MFI*S	0.0369	0.0333	0.0368	0.0330	0.0256	0.0096***	0.0246	0.0096***
	Board size*S	–0.0447	0.0472	–0.0346	0.0492	0.0383	0.0175***	0.0404	0.0173**
Macroeconomic and structural environment	East/West	–5.1094	1.6725***	–5.0207	1.6607***	0.5393	0.3378	0.5426	0.3386
	GDP per capita	0.1675	0.0374***	0.1691	0.0375***	–0.0302	0.0081***	–0.0303	0.0081***
	Population	0.9751	0.3582***	0.9568	0.3570***	–0.2775	0.0759***	–0.2708	0.0757***
	constant	117.2101	31.8826***	117.3096	31.8375***	12.5795	3.5411***	11.4590	3.5525**
	Wald Chi²	342.02	***	336.14	***	543.77	***	543.45	***
	R-sq	0.0375		0.0390		0.3179		0.3183	
	No of observations	1,796		1,796		1,781		1,781	

* indicates significance at the 10% level, ** at the 5% level, and *** at the 1% level, respectively.
Standard errors control for clustering at the bank level.

Appendix IV.6.21: Comparison coefficients with dependent variables z-score and NPL ratio, Top 150 banks, with 1% outlier correction

Variable		z-score (RE) Financial expertise		z-score (RE) Out. fin. expertise		NPL ratio (RE) Financial expertise		NPL ratio (RE) Out. fin. expertise	
		chi²	P>chi²	chi²	P>chi²	chi²	P>chi²	chi²	P>chi²
Financial expertise	Financial expertise: C vs. S	2.2700	0.1315			1.2100	0.2704		
	Outside financial expertise: C vs. S			2.3300	0.1267			3.5300	0.0602**
Bank level	Bank size: C vs. S	4.4500	0.0350**	4.5300	0.0333**	15.3000	0.0001***	12.9600	0.0003***
	Bank efficiency: C vs. S	0.0300	0.8561	0.0400	0.8456	3.6800	0.0550*	3.7600	0.0525*
	Bank size growth: C vs. S	2.5300	0.1119*	2.4800	0.1153*	10.1800	0.0014***	10.0300	0.0015**
	Board size: C vs. S	0.1300	0.7166	0.0500	0.8181	0.3400	0.5579	0.3700	0.5436
	Loan growth: C vs. S	10.6300	0.0011***	10.7000	0.0011***	9.7600	0.0018***	9.6300	0.0019***
	Claims on MFI: C vs. S	2.6100	0.1063	2.7100	0.0999	6.2900	0.0121**	6.3300	0.0119**
	Claims on non-MFI: C vs. S	0.0400	0.8406	0.0400	0.8362	0.9500	0.3288	1.2300	0.2665

* indicates significance at the 10% level, ** at the 5% level, and *** at the 1% level, respectively.

Appendix IV.6.22: Random-effect regressions with dependent variables RORWA and ROE, Top 150 banks, with 1% outlier correction

Variable		**RORWA (RE) Financial expertise**		**RORWA (RE) Out. fin. expertise**		**ROE (RE) Financial expertise**		**ROE (RE) Out. fin. expertise**	
		Coeff.	**SE (robust)**	**Coeff.**	**SE (robust)**	**Coeff.**	**SE (robust)**	**Coeff.**	**SE (robust)**
Financial expertise	Financial expertise*C	−0.0009	0.0015			−0.0112	0.0161		
	Outside financial expertise*C			−0.0011	0.0014			−0.0127	0.0158
	Financial expertise*S	0.0018	0.0018			0.0274	0.0156*		
	Outside financial expertise*S			0.0018	0.0014			0.0276	0.0119**
Bank level	Savings	−1.9979	1.7968	−2.1549	1.7755	−10.7607	17.8966	−12.8457	17.6497
	Bank size*C	−0.2915	0.0659***	−0.2943	0.0643***	−1.9041	0.7413***	−1.9370	0.7224***
	Bank efficiency*C	−0.0276	0.0037***	−0.0276	0.0037***	−0.3027	0.0360***	−0.3023	0.0360***
	Bank size growth*C	−0.0438	0.0081***	−0.0440	0.0081***	−0.2678	0.0778***	−0.2688	0.0779***
	Loan growth*C	0.0417	0.0044***	0.0418	0.0044***	0.2662	0.0397***	0.2666	0.0396***
	Claims on MFI*C	−0.0119	0.0052**	−0.0119	0.0052**	−0.1656	0.0511***	−0.1650	0.0511***
	Claims on non-MFI*C	−0.0125	0.0034***	−0.0126	0.0034***	−0.0481	0.0358	−0.0486	0.0358
	Board size*C	0.0088	0.0097	0.0084	0.0098	0.1449	0.1012	0.1400	0.1024
	Bank size*S	−0.0705	0.0651	−0.0667	0.0652	−0.6298	0.6929	−0.5731	0.6934
	Bank efficiency*S	−0.0456	0.0051***	−0.0456	0.0051***	−0.4534	0.0489***	−0.4527	0.0490***
	Bank size growth*S	−0.0135	0.0075*	−0.0137	0.0075*	−0.0747	0.0633	−0.0774	0.0631
	Loan growth*S	0.0214	0.0025***	0.0216	0.0025***	0.0917	0.0212***	0.0942	0.0214***
	Claims on MFI*S	−0.0123	0.0047***	−0.0124	0.0047***	−0.0912	0.0460**	−0.0929	0.0462
	Claims onnon-MFI*S	−0.0264	0.0038***	−0.0262	0.0038***	−0.1059	0.0331***	−0.1030	0.0324***
	Board size*S	−0.0208	0.0068***	−0.0201	0.0067***	−0.0889	0.0688	−0.0789	0.0684
Macroeconomic and structural environment	East/West	0.2090	0.1723	0.2176	0.1720	1.3214	1.3312	1.4572	1.3251
	GDP per capita	−0.0036	0.0033	−0.0038	0.0033	−0.0635	0.0409	−0.0667	0.0413
	Population	0.0720	0.0343**	0.0710	0.0344	0.4667	0.3432	0.4570	0.3450
	constant	9.6835	1.2651***	9.7611	1.2431***	75.3750	14.3722***	76.2650	14.0815***
	Wald Chi^2	513.29	***	512.77	***	483.35	***	485.09	***
	R-sq	0.3425		0.3432		0.2434		0.2449	
	No of observations	1,796		1,796		1,796		1,796	

* indicates significance at the 10% level, ** at the 5% level, and *** at the 1% level, respectively.
Standard errors control for clustering at the bank level.

Appendix IV.6.23: Comparison coefficients with dependent variables RORWA and ROE, Top 150 banks, with 1% outlier correction

Variable		**RORWA (RE) Financial expertise**		**RORWA (RE) Out. fin. expertise**		**ROE (RE) Financial expertise**		**ROE (RE) Out. fin. expertise**	
		chi²	**P>chi²**	**chi²**	**P>chi²**	**chi²**	**P>chi²**	**chi²**	**P>chi²**
Financial expertise	Financial expertise: C vs. S	1.3000	0.2535			2.9400	0.0864*		
	Outside financial expertise: C vs. S			1.9800	0.1596*			4.1200	0.0424**
Bank level	Bank size: C vs. S	7.0900	0.0078***	7.7800	0.0053*	2.4200	0.1201	2.9000	0.0888*
	Bank efficiency: C vs. S	8.3500	0.0039***	8.3200	0.0039***	6.3100	0.0120**	6.2700	0.0123**
	Bank size growth: C vs. S	7.6400	0.0057***	7.5400	0.0060***	3.7300	0.0536*	3.6700	0.0555*
	Board size: C vs. S	6.1100	0.0134**	5.6900	0.0171**	3.5800	0.0583*	3.1000	0.0785*
	Loan growth: C vs. S	15.9800	0.0001***	15.8000	0.0001***	15.0500	0.0001***	14.6600	0.0001***
	Claims on MFI: C vs. S	0.0000	0.9542	0.0100	0.9382	1.1600	0.2821	1.0800	0.2982
	Claims on non-MFI: C vs. S	8.6600	0.0033***	8.4000	0.0038***	1.6800	0.1952	1.5200	0.2171

* indicates significance at the 10% level, ** at the 5% level, and *** at the 1% level, respectively.

Appendix IV.6.24: Random-effect regressions with dependent variables z-score and NPL ratio, Top 200 banks, with 5% outlier correction

Variable		z-score (RE) Financial expertise		z-score (RE) Out. fin. expertise		NPL ratio (RE) Financial expertise		NPL ratio (RE) Out. fin. expertise	
		Coeff.	SE (robust)	Coeff.	SE (robust)	Coeff.	SE (robust)	Coeff.	SE (robust)
Financial expertise	Financial expertise*C	-0.0497	0.0400			0.0124	0.0037***		
	Outside financial expertise*C			-0.0689	0.0368*			0.0129	0.0035***
	Financial expertise*S	-0.0149	0.0228			0.0044	0.0034		
	Outside financial expertise*S			-0.0132	0.0205			0.0007	0.0026
Bank level	Savings	-63.1907	66.8176	-65.7156	67.2402	-9.5436	4.4046**	-7.7266	4.3933*
	Bank size*C	-2.0985	2.8577	-2.1198	2.8643	-0.7135	0.1750***	-0.6586	0.1696***
	Bank efficiency*C	-0.0919	0.0290***	-0.0896	0.0291***	-0.0090	0.0062	-0.0093	0.0062
	Bank size growth*C	-0.0025	0.0500	-0.0050	0.0494	-0.1765	0.0142***	-0.1757	0.0142***
	Loan growth*C	-0.0961	0.0289***	-0.0947	0.0291***	0.1056	0.0101***	0.1050	0.0101***
	Claims on MFI*C	0.0416	0.0604	0.0377	0.0612	0.0300	0.0110***	0.0298	0.0109***
	Claims on non-MFI*C	0.1440	0.0889	0.1404	0.0883	0.0315	0.0089***	0.0323	0.0088***
	Board size*C	-0.0582	0.1741	-0.0742	0.1735	0.0438	0.0206**	0.0466	0.0207**
	Bank size*S	0.6247	1.8421	0.6643	1.8486	-0.1519	0.1496	-0.1649	0.1504
	Bank efficiency*S	0.0154	0.0324	0.0151	0.0323	-0.0296	0.0062***	-0.0299	0.0063***
	Bank size growth*S	-0.1468	0.0250***	-0.1462	0.0248***	-0.1353	0.0110***	-0.1352	0.0110***
	Loan growth*S	0.0676	0.0116***	0.0664	0.0114***	0.0958	0.0059***	0.0960	0.0059***
	Claims on MFI*S	0.0155	0.0302	0.0148	0.0301	-0.0220	0.0080***	-0.0217	0.0080***
	Claims onnon-MFI*S	0.0105	0.0458	0.0099	0.0465	0.0176	0.0083**	0.0163	0.0084*
	Board size*S	0.0494	0.1056	0.0444	0.1061	0.0398	0.0120***	0.0406	0.0119***
Macroeconomic and structural environment	East/West	-5.6937	1.6715***	-5.6803	1.6868***	0.1436	0.2734	0.1427	0.2736
	GDP per capita	0.0378	0.0738	0.0420	0.0732	-0.0417	0.0087***	-0.0414	0.0087***
	Population	-0.7573	0.8120	-0.8379	0.8095	-0.1757	0.0622***	-0.1662	0.0621***
	constant	67.5626	62.3129	69.1274	62.5231	16.2852	3.7900***	15.0631	3.7116***
	Wald Chi²	222.61	***	222.00	***	1031.42	***	1049.92	***
	R-sq	0.1129		0.1153		0.3078		0.3116	
	No of observations	2,278		2,278		2,259		2,259	

* indicates significance at the 10% level, ** at the 5% level, and *** at the 1% level, respectively.
Standard errors control for clustering at the bank level.

Appendix IV.6.25: Comparison coefficients with dependent variables z-score and NPL ratio, Top 200 banks, with 5% outlier correction

Variable		**z-score (RE) Financial expertise**		**z-score (RE) Out. fin. expertise**		**NPL ratio (RE) Financial expertise**		**NPL ratio (RE) Out. fin. expertise**	
		chi²	**P>chi²**	**chi²**	**P>chi²**	**chi²**	**P>chi²**	**chi²**	**P>chi²**
Financial expertise	Financial expertise: C vs. S	0.5700	0.4513			2.5600	0.1093		
	Outside financial expertise: C vs. S			1.7400	0.1868			7.9300	0.0049***
Bank level	Bank size: C vs. S	0.8400	0.3603	0.8600	0.3527	8.6700	0.0032***	6.8600	0.0088***
	Bank efficiency: C vs. S	6.2500	0.0124**	5.9600	0.0146**	5.4800	0.0192**	5.5000	0.0190**
	Bank size growth: C vs. S	6.8200	0.0090***	6.7000	0.0096***	5.2700	0.0217**	5.0900	0.0241**
	Board size: C vs. S	0.3000	0.5857	0.3600	0.5478	0.0300	0.8672	0.0700	0.7967
	Loan growth: C vs. S	28.0000	0.0000***	27.0400	0.0000***	0.7000	0.4023	0.6000	0.4402
	Claims on MFI: C vs. S	0.1500	0.6976	0.1100	0.7352	14.7400	0.0001***	14.5300	0.0001***
	Claims on non-MFI: C vs. S	2.0000	0.1574	1.9200	0.1655	1.2700	0.2596	1.6800	0.1944

* indicates significance at the 10% level, ** at the 5% level, and *** at the 1% level, respectively.

Appendix IV.6.26: Random-effect regressions with dependent variables RORWA and ROE, Top 200 banks, with 5% outlier correction

Variable		RORWA (RE) Financial expertise		RORWA (RE) Out. fin. expertise		ROE (RE) Financial expertise		ROE (RE) Out. fin. expertise	
		Coeff.	SE (robust)	Coeff.	SE (robust)	Coeff.	SE (robust)	Coeff.	SE (robust)
Financial expertise	Financial expertise*C	–0.0006	0.0011			–0.0018	0.0115		
	Outside financial expertise*C			–0.0009	0.0011			–0.0055	0.0107
	Financial expertise*S	0.0023	0.0013*			0.0381	0.0139***		
	Outside financial expertise*S			0.0023	0.0010**			0.0333	0.0100***
Bank level	Savings	–2.1237	1.4824	–2.2516	1.4682	–6.8771	15.2530	–7.3802	15.0451
	Bank size*C	–0.2665	0.0575***	–0.2666	0.0559***	–1.6467	0.5878***	–1.6252	0.5713***
	Bank efficiency*C	–0.0232	0.0030***	–0.0232	0.0030***	–0.2482	0.0289***	–0.2472	0.0289***
	Bank size growth*C	–0.0392	0.0063***	–0.0393	0.0063***	–0.2771	0.0617***	–0.2784	0.0617***
	Loan growth*C	0.0407	0.0032***	0.0407	0.0032***	0.2493	0.0313***	0.2497	0.0313***
	Claims on MFI*C	–0.0074	0.0046	–0.0073	0.0046	–0.1048	0.0436**	–0.1042	0.0437**
	Claims on non-MFI*C	–0.0117	0.0025***	–0.0116	0.0025***	–0.0344	0.0255	–0.0335	0.0255
	Board size*C	0.0044	0.0062	0.0041	0.0062	0.0594	0.0629	0.0563	0.0632
	Bank size*S	–0.0536	0.0602	–0.0487	0.0604	–0.2821	0.5679	–0.2270	0.5677
	Bank efficiency*S	–0.0452	0.0037***	–0.0452	0.0037***	–0.4871	0.0394***	–0.4873	0.0394***
	Bank size growth*S	–0.0219	0.0052***	–0.0221	0.0052***	–0.0747	0.0562	–0.0782	0.0560
	Loan growth*S	0.0301	0.0030***	0.0303	0.0030***	0.1436	0.0280***	0.1471	0.0282***
	Claims on MFI*S	–0.0126	0.0043***	–0.0127	0.0043***	–0.1440	0.0427***	–0.1452	0.0428***
	Claims onnon-MFI*S	–0.0212	0.0027***	–0.0209	0.0027***	–0.1161	0.0285***	–0.1131	0.0283***
	Board size*S	–0.0146	0.0053***	–0.0138	0.0053***	–0.0820	0.0533	–0.0696	0.0533
Macroeconomic and structural environment	East/West	–0.0556	0.0968	–0.0416	0.0968	0.5346	0.9569	0.7249	0.9620
	GDP per capita	–0.0069	0.0034**	–0.0070	0.0034**	–0.1412	0.0347***	–0.1424	0.0348***
	Population	0.0125	0.0228	0.0118	0.0229	–0.0019	0.1975	–0.0072	0.1987
	constant	9.1314	1.1325***	9.1466	1.1028***	69.1807	11.8283***	68.8446	11.5145***
	Wald Chi²	1036.85	***	1,034.31	***	727.27	***	722.93	***
	R-sq	0.3237		0.3249		0.2612		0.2623	
	No of observations	2,278		2,278		2,278		2,278	

* indicates significance at the 10% level, ** at the 5% level, and *** at the 1% level, respectively.
Standard errors control for clustering at the bank level.

Appendix IV.6.27: Comparison coefficients with dependent variables RORWA and ROE, Top 200 banks, with 5% outlier correction

Variable		RORWA (RE) Financial expertise		RORWA (RE) Out. fin. expertise		ROE (RE) Financial expertise		ROE (RE) Out. fin. expertise	
		chi^2	$P>chi^2$	chi^2	$P>chi^2$	chi^2	$P>chi^2$	chi^2	$P>chi^2$
Financial expertise	Financial expertise: C vs. S	2.6500	0.1038			4.8700	0.0273**		
	Outside financial expertise: C vs. S			4.7100	0.0300**			7.0100	0.0081***
Bank level	Bank size: C vs. S	9.3700	0.0022***	10.1000	0.0015**	3.8400	0.0499**	4.2000	0.0405**
	Bank efficiency: C vs. S	21.3700	0.0000***	21.4200	0.0000***	24.2500	0.0000***	24.4800	0.0000***
	Bank size growth: C vs. S	4.5200	0.0335**	4.4400	0.0350**	5.9200	0.0149**	5.8100	0.0160**
	Board size: C vs. S	5.4200	0.0199**	4.7900	0.2860**	2.9400	0.0866*	2.3100	0.1283
	Loan growth: C vs. S	5.7600	0.0164**	5.5400	0.1860**	6.3200	0.0119**	5.9200	0.0149**
	Claims on MFI: C vs. S	0.7000	0.4016	0.7400	0.3883	0.4100	0.5198	0.4500	0.5025
	Claims on non-MFI: C vs. S	8.0300	0.0046***	7.5800	0.0059***	5.4400	0.0196**	5.2300	0.0222**

* indicates significance at the 10% level, ** at the 5% level, and *** at the 1% level, respectively.

Appendix IV.6.28: Random-effect regressions with dependent variables z-score and NPL ratio, Top 150 banks, with 5% outlier correction

Variable		z-score (RE) Financial expertise		z-score (RE) Out. fin. expertise		NPL ratio (RE) Financial expertise		NPL ratio (RE) Out. fin. expertise	
		Coeff.	SE (robust)	Coeff.	SE (robust)	Coeff.	SE (robust)	Coeff.	SE (robust)
Financial expertise	Financial expertise*C	−0.0083	0.0140			0.0126	0.0044***		
	Outside financial expertise*C			−0.0146	0.0131			0.0128	0.0040
	Financial expertise*S	0.0163	0.0099*			0.0044	0.0040		
	Outside financial expertise*S			0.0099	0.0083			0.0011	0.0031
Bank level	Savings	−48.8893	26.9543*	−49.3610	26.6148*	−14.3194	4.3610***	−12.7041	4.4035***
	Bank size*C	−3.4897	0.8135***	−3.4703	0.7943***	−0.6052	0.1561***	−0.5534	0.1551***
	Bank efficiency*C	−0.0315	0.0091***	−0.0310	0.0091***	−0.0085	0.0072	−0.0088	0.0072
	Bank size growth*C	−0.0790	0.0173***	−0.0799	0.0172***	−0.1745	0.0163***	−0.1738	0.0163***
	Loan growth*C	−0.0084	0.0115	−0.0078	0.0115	0.1050	0.0106***	0.1047	0.0106***
	Claims on MFI*C	−0.0426	0.0199**	−0.0439	0.0199**	0.0170	0.0122	0.0172	0.0122
	Claims on non-MFI*C	0.0340	0.0263	0.0332	0.0260	0.0369	0.0100***	0.0377	0.0100***
	Board size*C	0.0185	0.0841	0.0128	0.0832	0.0662	0.0284**	0.0684	0.0284**
	Bank size*S	−1.0985	1.1021	−1.0596	1.0913	0.1652	0.1591	0.1565	0.1601
	Bank efficiency*S	−0.0427	0.0130***	−0.0427	0.0129***	−0.0256	0.0070***	−0.0260	0.0070***
	Bank size growth*S	−0.1256	0.0187***	−0.1259	0.0186***	−0.1272	0.0124***	−0.1273	0.0125***
	Loan growth*S	0.0662	0.0081***	0.0668	0.0081***	0.0898	0.0069***	0.0900	0.0069***
	Claims on MFI*S	0.0229	0.0241	0.0232	0.0241	−0.0170	0.0089*	−0.0167	0.0089*
	Claims onnon-MFI*S	0.0547	0.0327*	0.0548	0.0325*	0.0244	0.0091***	0.0232	0.0091***
	Board size*S	−0.0168	0.0447	−0.0059	0.0466	0.0329	0.0200*	0.0338	0.0198*
Macroeconomic and structural environment	East/West	−4.0013	1.4602***	−3.9041	1.4509***	0.4157	0.3305	0.4097	0.3322
	GDP per capita	0.1345	0.0312***	0.1365	0.0313***	−0.0376	0.0101***	−0.0377	0.0101***
	Population	0.5366	0.2132**	0.5203	0.2151**	−0.2550	0.0682***	−0.2456	0.0676***
	constant	85.4147	16.5889***	85.3585	16.2398***	13.5450	3.4162***	12.4214	3.4173***
	Wald Chi²	317.48	***	314.55	***	809.16	***	819.74	***
	R-sq	0.0572		0.0600		0.3352		0.3379	
	No of observations	1,796		1,796		1,781		1,781	

* indicates significance at the 10% level, ** at the 5% level, and *** at the 1% level, respectively.
Standard errors control for clustering at the bank level.

Appendix IV.6.29: Comparison coefficients with dependent variables z-score and NPL ratio, Top 150 banks, with 5% outlier correction

Variable		**z-score (RE) Financial expertise**		**z-score (RE) Out. fin. expertise**		**NPL ratio (RE) Financial expertise**		**NPL ratio (RE) Out. fin. expertise**	
		chi^2	**$P>chi^2$**	**chi^2**	**$P>chi^2$**	**chi^2**	**$P>chi^2$**	**chi^2**	**$P>chi^2$**
Financial expertise	Financial expertise: C vs. S	2.0800	0.1488			1.9300	0.1648		
	Outside financial expertise: C vs. S			2.5000	0.1135			5.4800	0.0192**
Bank level	Bank size: C vs. S	3.7600	0.0524**	3.9500	0.0470	16.5900	0.0000***	13.9300	0.0002***
	Bank efficiency: C vs. S	0.5100	0.4771	0.5500	0.4567	2.9100	0.0878*	2.9200	0.0873*
	Bank size growth: C vs. S	3.2400	0.0719*	3.2000	0.0738*	5.2700	0.0217**	5.0900	0.0241**
	Board size: C vs. S	0.1400	0.7108	0.0400	0.8444	0.9500	0.3305	1.0300	0.3111
	Loan growth: C vs. S	28.1800	0.0000***	28.1800	0.0000***	1.4600	0.2265	1.3600	0.2444
	Claims on MFI: C vs. S	4.4500	0.0348**	4.6800	0.0305**	5.0700	0.0243**	5.0600	0.0245**
	Claims on non-MFI: C vs. S	0.2400	0.6222	0.2700	0.6034	0.7900	0.3754	1.0700	0.3001

* indicates significance at the 10% level, ** at the 5% level, and *** at the 1% level, respectively.

Appendix IV.6.30: Random-effect regressions with dependent variables RORWA and ROE, Top 150 banks, with 5% outlier correction

Variable		RORWA (RE) Financial expertise		RORWA (RE) Out. fin. expertise		ROE (RE) Financial expertise		ROE (RE) Out. fin. expertise	
		Coeff.	SE (robust)	Coeff.	SE (robust)	Coeff.	SE (robust)	Coeff.	SE (robust)
Financial expertise	Financial expertise*C	−0.0002	0.0013			−0.0057	0.0143		
	Outside financial expertise*C			−0.0007	0.0013			−0.0102	0.0136
	Financial expertise*S	0.0025	0.0015*			0.0320	0.0148**		
	Outside financial expertise*S			0.0024	0.0011**			0.0306	0.0110***
Bank level	Savings	−2.3228	1.5546	−2.4137	1.5246	−12.2695	17.0263	−13.6796	16.7380
	Bank size*C	−0.2747	0.0579***	−0.2735	0.0565***	−1.6353	0.6189***	−1.6337	0.6023***
	Bank efficiency*C	−0.0277	0.0035***	−0.0276	0.0035***	−0.3002	0.0347***	−0.2994	0.0347***
	Bank size growth*C	−0.0371	0.0072***	−0.0373	0.0073***	−0.2302	0.0710***	−0.2324	0.0713***
	Loan growth*C	0.0377	0.0038***	0.0378	0.0038***	0.2267	0.0351***	0.2273	0.0351***
	Claims on MFI*C	−0.0113	0.0049**	−0.0112	0.0049**	−0.1520	0.0496***	−0.1516	0.0497***
	Claims on non-MFI*C	−0.0124	0.0031***	−0.0125	0.0031***	−0.0319	0.0327	−0.0330	0.0328
	Board size*C	0.0082	0.0099	0.0077	0.0099	0.1352	0.0992	0.1297	0.1000
	Bank size*S	−0.0642	0.0567	−0.0598	0.0566	−0.2424	0.6472	−0.1870	0.6457
	Bank efficiency*S	−0.0449	0.0039***	−0.0449	0.0038***	−0.4721	0.0436***	−0.4722	0.0433***
	Bank size growth*S	−0.0220	0.0055***	−0.0222	0.0055***	−0.0906	0.0595	−0.0933	0.0594
	Loan growth*S	0.0272	0.0029***	0.0274	0.0029***	0.1178	0.0278***	0.1207	0.0280***
	Claims on MFI*S	−0.0080	0.0043*	−0.0081	0.0043*	−0.0779	0.0448*	−0.0788	0.0449*
	Claims onnon-MFI*S	−0.0203	0.0032***	−0.0201	0.0031***	−0.0925	0.0320***	−0.0899	0.0313***
	Board size*S	−0.0191	0.0069***	−0.0179	0.0069***	−0.0938	0.0761	−0.0780	0.0760
Macroeconomic and structural environment	East/West	−0.0172	0.1268	−0.0046	0.1264	0.9329	1.2033	1.0943	1.1936
	GDP per capita	−0.0074	0.0041*	−0.0075	0.0041*	−0.1356	0.0431***	−0.1367	0.0433***
	Population	0.0702	0.0276**	0.0682	0.0279**	0.4186	0.2828	0.3947	0.2875
	constant	9.4332	1.0922***	9.4422	1.0718***	70.5962	11.9407***	70.9067	11.6758***
	Wald Chi²	877.31	***	875.11	***	613.13	***	613.08	***
	R-sq	0.3226		0.3239		0.2506		0.2528	
	No of observations	1,796		1,796		1,796		1,796	

* indicates significance at the 10% level, ** at the 5% level, and *** at the 1% level, respectively.
Standard errors control for clustering at the bank level.

Appendix IV.6.31: Comparison coefficients with dependent variables RORWA and ROE, Top 150 banks, with 5% outlier correction

Variable		**RORWA (RE) Financial expertise**		**RORWA (RE) Out. fin. expertise**		**ROE (RE) Financial expertise**		**ROE (RE) Out. fin. expertise**	
		chi^2	**P>chi^2**	**chi^2**	**P>chi^2**	**chi^2**	**P>chi^2**	**chi^2**	**P>chi^2**
Financial expertise	Financial expertise: C vs. S	1.9700	0.1601			3.3800	0.0659*		
	Outside financial expertise: C vs. S			3.4400	0.0636*			5.4800	0.0193**
Bank level	Bank size: C vs. S	8.6300	0.0033***	9.3200	0.0023***	3.2900	0.0698*	3.7100	0.0541*
	Bank efficiency: C vs. S	10.8400	0.0010***	10.9900	0.0009***	9.7100	0.0018***	9.8900	0.0017***
	Bank size growth: C vs. S	2.8200	0.0933*	2.7900	0.0948*	2.2900	0.1302	2.2700	0.1322
	Board size: C vs. S	5.0900	0.0241**	4.4700	0.0346**	3.3400	0.0675*	2.7200	0.0990*
	Loan growth: C vs. S	4.8400	0.0279**	4.6600	0.0310**	5.9400	0.0148**	5.6600	0.0170**
	Claims on MFI: C vs. S	0.2500	0.6155	0.2400	0.6264	1.2100	0.2703	1.1700	0.2801
	Claims on non-MFI: C vs. S	3.7700	0.0523*	3.5900	0.0581*	2.0700	0.1498	1.8800	0.1704

* indicates significance at the 10% level, ** at the 5% level, and *** at the 1% level, respectively.

V CDS and Bank Ownership Structures: Does the Credit Side Show Who Advocates More Risk?

Abstract This paper analyzes the impact of ownership concentration on bank risk-taking, by taking national regulation into account. In particular, we examine the effects of the ownership structure on credit risk, which is estimated by CDS spread measures. Considering 86 global privately held and publicly listed banks from 22 countries in a panel analysis for the years 2005–2008, we document that banks with a more concentrated ownership structure tend to be riskier as they have larger CDS spreads. Furthermore, we observe that bank regulation has a negative impact on banks' credit risk. Larger banks exhibit—in line with the "too big to fail" argument—significantly lower risk than smaller banks.

V.1 Introduction

The financial crisis and subsequent bailouts have proved the systemic importance of an intact banking system for the stability and development of an economy (Huang, Zhou, and Zhu, 2009).

These bailouts have been supported by the argument that a financial institution can be "too big to fail," implying that larger banks exhibit high systemic importance (Zhou, 2010a). To limit systemic risk, the legal systems of most developed economies build on general mechanisms beyond the specific regulation of the financial institution. Many observers attribute the origin of the financial crisis to failures in corporate governance mechanisms, which could not prevent excessive risk-taking (Kirkpatrick, 2009). In 1999 and 2006, the Bank Committee on Banking Supervision emphasized that corporate governance for banking organizations is of great importance to the international financial system (Basel Committee on Banking Supervision, 1999a, 2006b).

Governance-related issues are closely connected to the classical principal agent dilemma, which revolves around the mismatch of interests between managers and owners (Jensen and Meckling, 1976). However, bank governance systems are by far more complex than the systems of non-financial institutions, as a larger number of stakeholders are involved. For example, the bank management has to deal with the interests of depositors, debtholders, and shareholders. Theoretical considerations suggest that shareholders have incentives to shift risk after collecting funds from bondholders and depositors (Galai and Masulis, 1976). Consequently, governance mechanisms aligning only the interests of shareholders and managers are inappropriate for banks' specific capital structure (Mullineux,

2006). Previous research has investigated the relationship between governance issues and risk-taking on the equity side (Iannotta, et al., 2007; Laeven and Levine, 2009; Shehzad, et al., 2010). Despite the fact that debtholders are an important stakeholder group, research has paid little attention to the impact of ownership on credit risk. This is surprising, as a credit risk measure has become undoubtedly popular during the crisis. Credit Default Swaps (CDS) have been demonized as an accelerating factor that severely aggravated the crisis (Stulz, 2009). CDS basically provide a default insurance and are a tradable instrument for credit risk transfer (Norden and Wagner, 2008).[14] On the basis of these recent findings and the scarce knowledge on governance with regard to credit risk, the present study analyzes the impact of ownership concentration on banks' credit risk.

There are two contradicting theories regarding the impact of owner concentration on risk-taking. One viewpoint proposes that controlling shareholders reduces bank risk. First, a high degree of ownership concentration enhances effective management monitoring. In this case, ownership concentration can have a positive effect on the cost of debt and its use (Elyasiani, Jia, and Mao, 2010). Second, it is the atomistic shareholders who advocate more risk. An alternative theoretical approach postulates that, without a large and implicitly strong majority shareholder, a bank lacks efficient and strong management oversight (Shleifer and Vishny, 1986). The argument that effective monitoring of management depends on shareholder power is not new; it has been stated decades ago (Berle and Means, 1933). A high degree of ownership concentration can increase risk (Saunders, Strock, and Travlos, 1990). Shareholders participate in the upside potential from risk-taking, while debtholders only share the downside risk when a bank cannot meet its obligations. Vast empirical research has addressed this question on who drives risk-taking in banks and who advocates more risk. However, previous research has been mainly focused on the equity side of bank risk, but there is still no common point of view, as recent studies only reveal ambiguous results. Knowledge regarding the relationship of ownership structure and credit risk is scarce. It remains unclear whether a concentrated ownership structure is positively related to higher credit risk or vice versa.

Besides shareholders, banks have to fulfill the interest of a variety of stakeholders (depositors, debtholders, and the government, as both regulator and insurer of deposits). In particular, debt plays a paramount role in terms of economic relevance (Mehran, Morrison, and Shapiro, 2011b). The importance of debt at

14 The share of more than 20% of the overall market shows that bank CDS belong to the most important frequently traded underlyings (Norden and Weber, 2010).

banks emerged as an approach to make banks safer. In line with the theory on risk-shifting, which it is based on the thought that shareholders generally push for more risky investments. As shareholders and bondholders have contradicting interests regarding risk-taking, the obligation to issue some portion of subordinated debt would reduce bank risk, as bondholders would counteract by demanding compensation for higher risk. For this reason, in the past, measures related to funding have been taken on the credit side of banks. According to the 1988 Basel Accord, banks are allowed to satisfy capital requirements with supplementary capital such as undisclosed reserves, revaluations reserves, hybrid capital instruments, and subordinated term debt (Basel Committee on Banking Supervision, 1998).

This former regulation postulation follows the corporate finance point of view that both equity and debt are not only financial but also governance instruments (Williamson, 1988). Based on this idea, we hypothesize that capital structure-based risk indicators are sensitive to the ownership structure.

Apart from the discussion on whether debt itself reduces or increases bank risk, the debt side of a bank introduces different risk measures beside equity or other balance sheet-based ratios. The need for a tradable credit risk instrument arose. CDS are a relatively new form of marketable derivatives, and research has hardly any knowledge about its long-term effects on underlying assets. Recent research emphasizes that CDS premia reflect the credit risk of banks perceived by the financial markets and provide subsequently financial supervisory authorities an early warning indicator of financial stability (Annaert, Ceuster, Roy, and Vespro, 2010; Blanco, Brennan, and Marsh, 2005).

The use of CDS information to estimate a bank's credit risk offers some important advantages. CDS market participants anticipate credit rating events in advance and consequently react more rapidly to information regarding the changes in the credit quality of the asset in comparison to the bond market (Hull, Predescu, and White, 2004; Norden and Weber, 2004; Zhu, 2006). Among other reasons, this is owing to the fact that no up-front funding is needed, and consequently, there is no dependence on liquidity. In contrast, bond yield spreads experience distortions in the case of illiquidity (Forte and Peña, 2009). Beyond that, no assumption about appropriate benchmark bonds is needed, as CDS spreads are directly observable (Houweling and Vorst, 2005). Additionally, other factors such as the absence of embedded options or different coupon structures make CDS contracts a very clean measure (Ashcraft and Santos, 2009). Altogether, CDS contributes significantly to the transparency of the price of bank's credit risk, which supports further the high relevance to banks (Annaert, et al., 2010; Norden and Wagner, 2008).

To the best of our knowledge, no studies deal with the influence of the ownership structure on banks' credit risk measured at CDS spreads. Therefore, this paper aims at making a substantial contribution to the banking and finance literature and recent research on CDS as well as on governance, risk-taking, and regulation. We apply a panel analysis for the period 2005–2008 in order to extract potential distortions caused by the financial crisis and leave out the year 2009. Further, sector-level and country-level variables are included in order to take into consideration the different governance infrastructures that vary by jurisdiction. We use CDS spreads as a dependent variable. Our approach follows Demirgüç-Kunt and Huizinga (2010) who consider CDS spreads as a prime indicator of expected losses on bank liabilities. They provide empirical evidence that banks may have become too big to save. Further, their results suggest that during the financial crisis, bank valuation is negatively related to public deficits for systemically large banks, while banks' CDS premia are significantlly related to public deficits and conditions. The papers also confirm the view that systemically large banks are too big to fail.

The present paper is structured as follows: Chapter V.2 summarizes related literature. Previous studies on CDS spreads as a credit risk indicator are outlined. Beyond that, studies that generally dealt with the issue of credit risk and ownership structures are presented. The third chapter introduces the data that is used for the empirical analysis. Additionally, we outline the applied methodology. In Chapter V.4, we present the summary statistics and the regression results. Finally, we list our conclusions in Chapter V.5.

V.2 Related Literature

Several recent studies discuss and examine the link between corporate governance and risk measures from different perspectives. Related literature focuses on the following aspects: impact of ownership concentration on credit risk, impact of ownership concentration on bank risk in terms of equity risk and accounting-based risk measures, and the accuracy as well as the adequacy of CDS spreads as a risk measure.

Our study deals with the impact of ownership concentration on credit risk over time. Very few studies deal with this issue in general (Anderson, Mansi, and Reeb, 2003; Ashbaugh-Skaife, Collins, and LaFond, 2006; Bhojraj and Sengupta, 2003; Boubakri and Ghouma, 2010; Elyasiani, et al., 2010; Wang and Zhang, 2009). These papers focus on ownership and the cost of debt while mostly bond yields are used as credit measure. Boubakri and Ghouma (2010) focus on ownership and credit risk measures using bond yield spreads instead of CDS spreads. The study concludes that ultimate ownership is positively related to bond yield spreads. According to the results of Bhojraj and Sengupta (2003), institutional ownership is related to lower bond yields. Despite covering the same conceptual ground, none of these studies focused on the banking industry. The following studies focus on the impact of ownership concentration on risk-taking, but not on the credit side, and report ambiguous results. Iannotta et al. (2007) show that a high degree of ownership concentration is positively related to less bank risk, which is measured by the z-scores. Laeven and Levine (2009) and Ellul and Yerramilli (2010) find that large shareholders increase the level of bank risk-taking compared to banks with a dispersed ownership structure. In the former study, the z-score is also used for risk measurement; additionally, different country regulations are taken into consideration (Laeven and Levine, 2009). Shehzad et al. (2010) do not confirm these findings by showing that an increase in ownership concentration leads to lower bank risk, which is measured by the non-performing loan ratio and the capital adequacy ratio.

The third cluster of related literature comprises studies on the accuracy and adequacy of CDS as well as the impact of bank size on CDS spreads. Despite the growing popularity, there has been little research on the issue of governance structures and credit risk at banks. This is even more striking as the importance of CDS significantly grew in recent years and became a highly important measure for credit risk transfer (Brunnermeier, 2009; Duffie, 2008; Stulz, 2009). Only some studies focus on the relevance and importance of bank CDS spreads, by analyzing the informational content and the market reaction especially during the financial crisis (Annaert, et al., 2010; Duffie, 2008; Eichengreen, Mody, Nedeljkovic, and Sarno, 2009; King, 2009; Norden and Weber, 2010; Dirk Schiereck and Trutwein, 2011). One recent study examines the potential price distortion of CDS spreads due to bank size and concludes that the "too big to fail" phenomena impacts CDS prices (Völz and Wedow, 2011). As CDS spreads have been relatively constant before the financial crisis, this instrument did not attract high attention.

Recent empirical research has focused on the relation between CDS spreads and bond yields and revealed that CDS spreads are a prime indicator for credit risk offering several advantages against bond yields (Blanco, et al., 2005; Houweling and Vorst, 2005; Hull, et al., 2004; Longstaff, Pan, Pedersen, and Singleton, 2007). Ashcraft and Santos (2009) show that other factors such as the absence of embedded options or different coupon structures make CDS contracts a very clean risk measure. A study on the informational content of stocks, bonds, and CDS concludes that CDS lead bonds in terms of information signaling owing to that fact that since no up-front funding is needed, there is no dependence on liquidity (Blanco, et al., 2005; Forte and Peña, 2009). Recent research underlines these findings by highlighting that CDS are a market indicator of risk-taking by banks. CDS spreads indicate the expected losses on bank liabilities (Beck and Demirgüç-Kunt, 2009; Demirguc-Kunt and Huizinga, 2010). Hart and Zingales (2011) propose that CDS spreads display the risks taken by banks and should trigger the issuance of further equity in case they exceed a given threshold (Hart and Zingales, 2011).

V.3 Data and Methodology

V.3.1 Sample and Data

The sample of the present study is based on 86 banks from 22 countries for the period 2005–2008. Our unbalanced panel contains privately and publicly held banks. Most of the government bailouts have been executed at the end of 2008 and 2009, leading to a significant change in ownership but not materially affecting CDS spreads over the sample period. The initial dataset was retrieved from *Bloomberg* that offered CDS data for 147 banks; after adjusting the sample by data for subordinated debt, the CDS data set included 100 banks. In the second step, our sample included banks for which ownership, balance sheet, as well as profit and loss statement data are available for the period 2005–2008. Our final sample includes 86 banks, resulting in a range of 282 to 344 observations per variable. The limitation of sovereign debt CDS data results in 213 observations. Australia, Germany, and the United States are represented in the sample, with 8 banks each, while some countries such as Denmark, Greece, Norway, and Singapore contribute one bank each to the sample. The average total asset size accounts for USD 545 billion, while the smallest bank in the sample has total assets of USD 5.2 billion, and the largest bank has average total assets of USD 2,419.3 billion.

Financial metrics such as bank size, bank growth, bank efficiency, and bank capitalization come from the Bankscope database. Ownership structure data are from *Thomson ONE Banker*. Further data points were hand-collected from individual financial reports. Rating events for issuer ratings are retrieved from *Reuters Xtra* database. The financial crisis support for each bank was checked manually. Data for the sector-level and country-level control variables are from different sources. The data for the banking sector comes from the financial structure dataset (Beck and Demirgüç-Kunt, 2009). The indices on regulation are based on the regulation surveys of 2003 and 2008 of the World Bank (Barth, Caprio, and Levine, 2003; Barth, et al., 2008). The governance indicators are from the *Aggregate Governance Indicators* (Kaufmann, Kraay, and Mastruzzi, 2009). The economic data such as per capita GDP and stock market development are from the *World Development Indicators* (World Bank, 2010). All the later data are retrieved from the World Bank Web site.

V.3.2 Ownership Concentration

For the ownership analysis, we focus on the concentration ratio of the three largest shareholders (*CR3*)—summing up the percentile ownership rights held by the top three owners—of a bank. The underlying idea is that usually a single shareholder does not drive management decisions; instead, it is assumed that a group of the largest shareholders of a bank make the decisions and subsequently exert much more power than does a single shareholder. We follow La Porta, Lopez-de-Silanes, Shleifer, and Vishny (1998) who also use this concentration measurement. The calculation of the CR3 is straightforward and defined as:

$$CR3_{it} = \sum_{j=1}^{3} os_{jt} \qquad \text{(V.1)}$$

where os is the ownership share of shareholder j in bank i at time t. This allows the consideration of any stake of the largest three shareholders. We use concentration ratio CR3 for ownership concentration with two cut-off points at 20% and 50%. In each case, a value of 1 is assigned if the respective threshold is exceeded, and 0 otherwise.

V.3.3 Measurement of Credit Risk

Our primary risk measure is a bank's 5-year CDS contract on subordinated debt. These contracts show the highest liquidity and account for a large volume of the entire CDS market (Demirguc-Kunt and Huizinga, 2010). Following Demirguc-Kunt and Huizinga (2010), we consider CDS spreads as a prime indicator of expected losses on bank liabilities. The level of CDS spread reflects the extent of a bank's credit risk.

Three different CDS spreads are calculated. First, we use the iTraxx financial index in order to benchmark against peers from the banking industry. Second, we use the iTraxx index of non-financial CDS premia 5-year maturity.[15] Generally, iTraxx indices represent tradable CDS indices related to market-wide or sectoral credit risk consisting of the most liquid CDS contracts. The iTraxx index family is often used as a benchmark index. According to the analysis of Ejsing and Lemke

15 The iTraxx non-financial CDS index comprises the 100 non-financial entities from the iTraxx Europe index, which includes also non-euro area firms. The included firms are divided into five broad sectors: Auto, Consumer, Energy, Industrial and Technology/Media/Telecommunications (TMT). The indices are rebalanced every six months.

(2009), this non-financial iTraxx index displays a common risk factor for individual banks. Third, we calculate the spread between banks' 5-year CDS and the respective country CDS.

CDS spreads are based on weekly observations, which will then be averaged over 12 months. This approach follows Annaert et al. (2010) who investigate the determinants of CDS spreads of banks. The panel is tracked over the years 2005–2008. The sample starts on 1 January, 2005 due to limited availability before this date. It ends in December 2008, since banks' CDS spreads in the subsequent months have deteriorated by the different bailouts whose effects have to be analyzed separately.

V.3.4 Control Variables

We apply control variables for country-level, sector-level, and bank-level characteristics, and use various data sources. The following control variables comprise bank specific issues: bank size, bank growth, bank efficiency, bank capitalizsation, bank rating, and government support measures in the course of the financial crisis. Rating events for issuer ratings comprise the rating agencies Standard & Poor's, Moody's, and Fitch. To the corresponding rating clusters of the three agencies, a metric value was assigned to grade the different rating agency scorecards. Based on the available values, weighted averages were computed in case of rating changes within a year. Aunon-Nerin, Cossin, Hricko, and Huang (2002) show that the rating and the change in rating is the major determinant of CDS spreads. 40% of the corporate CDS spreads can be explained by the rating factor;, the explanatory power even increases to 60% when looking at a sample comprising only sovereign CDS. For financial crisis support, we assign a binary variable value of 1 to banks that received government support, and 0 otherwise.

Sector-level control variables comprise banking sector concentration, ownership limitation regulation and indices on audit and disclosure requirement, authorities power, bank activities regulation, capital requirements, and deposit insurance (for details see Appendix V.1).

The country-level control variables set consists of political stability, rule of law, economic strength, and stock market development.

Table V.1: Definition sources of control variables

Bank-level control variables	**Description**	**Source**
a. Bank size	Log of Total Assets	Bankscope
b. Bank growth	Year to year change in Total Assets	Bankscope
c. Bank efficiency (Cost/ Income Ratio)	Operating Expenses divided by net interest and non-interest income	Bankscope
d. Bank capitalization	Total Equity / Total Assets	Bankscope
e. Rating	Index based on Rating	Reuters Xtra
f. Financial crisis support	Binary variable	Own research
Sector-level control variables		
g. CR3 sector concentration	Share in total assets of largest three banks	Beck and Demirgüç-Kunt (2009)
h. Ownership limitation	Binary variable based on regulation survey	Barth et al. (2003), Barth et al. (2008)
i. Capital regulation	Index based on regulation survey	Barth et al. (2003), Barth et al. (2008)
j. Audit and disclosure regulation	Index based on regulation survey	Barth et al. (2003), Barth et al. (2008)
k. Bank activities regulation	Index based on regulation survey	Barth et al. (2003), Barth et al. (2008)
l. Authorities power regulation	Index based on regulation survey	Barth et al. (2003), Barth et al. (2008)
m. Deposit insurance regulation	Index based on regulation survey	Barth et al. (2003), Barth et al. (2008)
Country-level control variables		
n. Political stability	Index	Kaufmann et al. (2009)
o. Rule of Law	Index	Kaufmann et al. (2009)
p. Economic strength	Per capita GDP in USD at current prices	World Bank (2010)
q. Stock market development	Stock market capitalization divided by GDP	World Bank (2010)

V.3.5 Model

We estimate a random effects model as appropriate to examine the variation between banks based on the panel time horizon of four years. We run our model with an unbalanced panel which has a maximum of 315 observations for the spreads with the two iTraxx indices and a minimum of 213 observations for the country spreads. The applied model has the following form:

$$DV_{it} = \alpha + \beta OC_{it} + \gamma B_{it} + \delta S_{it} + \tau C_{it} + \varepsilon_{it} \qquad \text{(V.2)}$$

where DV_{it} is the dependent variable (CDS spread). B is a vector of bank level variables, S stands for a vector of sector- level control variables, C is a vector of country- level control variables, and ε the error term. B comprises the bank variables such as (a) bank size, (b) bank growth, (c) bank efficiency, (d) bank capitalizsation, (e) rating, and (f) financial crisis support. S includes (g) banking sector concentration ratio CR3, (h) ownership limitation, (i) capital regulation index, (j) audit and disclosure index, (k) bank activities index, (l) authorities power index, and (m) deposit insurance index. C comprises (n) political stability, (o) rule of law, (p) economic strength, and (q) stock market development.

Owing to the relevance of issuer ratings in the explanation of banks' CDS spread, we run the regression analysis three times per indicator. We first run our empirical model, including the rating variable. Second, we exclude the rating from the regression in order to make other effects transparent. Third, we run the regression with interaction effects between ownership and rating to test for direct and indirect effects of ratings and ownership concentration individually and jointly.

V.4 Results

V.4.1 Summary Statistics

Table V.2 provides summary statistics and lists the averages of key variables at the bank, sector, and country level. The CDS spreads show a wide range of values. The mean of the CDS iTraxx non-financial spread is the lowest, which leads to the hypothesis that the credit risk of our sample is close to the credit risk of non-financial institutions. In terms of CDS country spreads, our sample is riskier than the government spread, implying that governments have a lower credit risk compared to financial and non-financial institutions. The standard deviation of the risk measure is quite similar. With regard to bank measures, the panel displays a significant variation, which is a result of the extremely volatility of earnings during the financial crisis in 2007–2008. In terms of ownership concentration, the largest three owners hold, on an average, more than 30%.

Table V.2: Summary statistics

	Observations	Mean	Std. Dev.	Min	Max
CDS country spread	213	66.73	132.68	-148.80	1020.79
CDS iTraxx financial spread	315	30.01	106.24	-82.19	1017.37
CDS iTraxx non financial spread	315	8.93	106.41	-105.08	994.48
Bank level					
CR3 (20% Threshold)	344	0.46	0.50	0	1
CR3 (50% Threshold)	344	0.26	0.44	0	1
CR3 stake	339	33.84	31.98	0.25	100
Bank size	320	8.42	0.62	6.30	9.56
Bank growth	320	18.16	27.08	-89.86	207.71
Bank efficiency	331	65.54	57.09	4.59	500.00
Bank capitalisation	318	5.59	2.63	1.24	16.51
Rating Issuer	282	5.74	2.02	0	9.50
Financial crisis support	344	0.10	0.29	0	1
Sector level					
Activities Index	344	9.21	2.52	4	15
Auditing and disclosure Index	344	9.07	0.73	8	10
Authorities Index	344	4.71	1.80	1	7
Capital Index	344	3.74	1.11	2	6
Deposit insurance Index	344	4.71	1.80	1	7
Ownership limitation	344	0.23	0.42	0	1
Sector CR3	340	60.55	19.24	29.62	100.00
Country level					
Rule of law	344	1.25	0.70	-0.90	2.12
Per capita income (in USD)	344	35,188	14,811	740	94,759
Political stability index	344	0.64	0.49	-0.99	1.65
Stock market development	344	89.65	48.00	17.48	312.14

Appendix V.2 displays the key statistics for each country's banks. Large variations exist in the credit risk of banks over this time period. Row 1 of Table V.3 presents the average CDS spread across all banks in the period 2005–2008. CDS spreads experienced two major steps after being relatively flat: one from 2006 to 2007 and the next one from 2007 to 2008. In 2008, for example, when the average CDS spread of the banks was 179 base points, or 1.8% (1 base point = 0.01%), an investor buying USD 10 million worth of protection from Bank A had to pay the bank USD 0.18 million per year. According to Row 3, financial institutions have been perceived riskier by the market compared to non-financial institutions; this is indicated by the positive CDS iTraxx financial spread in 2007–2008, contrary to a negative spread from 2005–2006. Volatility of the average CDS spreads varies from a low of 24 bps for Norway to a high of 200 bps for Greece. The average CDS spread across all countries accounts for 60 bps.

Ownership structure varies moderately over time. As shown in Table V.3, the average concentration ratio of the largest three shareholders (CR3) of a bank increased from 30% to 38% in the period 2005–2008. Applying a 20% threshold, more than 54% of the banks have a concentration ratio of 20% or more, contrary to 2005, while approximately 37% of the banks exceeded the 20% threshold.

Table V.3: Development over time from 2005–2008

Dependent Variables	**2008**	**2007**	**2006**	**2005**
CDS country spread	143.53	35.55	9.14	12.95
CDS iTraxx financial spread	83.02	18.92	6.41	3.93
CDS iTraxx non financial spread	59.82	5.28	-17.69	-19.95
Bank level				
CR3 (20% Threshold)	0.53	0.51	0.43	0.37
CR3 (50% Threshold)	0.30	0.27	0.24	0.24
CR3 stake	37.81	35.93	31.28	30.14
Bank size	8.51	8.46	8.37	8.31
Bank growth	6.16	23.85	27.53	14.77
Bank efficiency	88.38	61.64	54.56	57.03
Bank capitalisation	5.42	5.67	5.60	5.69
Rating Issuer	5.95	5.94	5.62	5.43
Rating Sub	5.76	5.77	5.40	5.17
Financial crisis support	0.38	0.00	0.00	0.00
Sector level				
Activities Index	9.21	9.21	9.21	9.21
Auditing and disclosure Index	9.07	9.07	9.07	9.07
Authorities Index	4.71	4.71	4.71	4.71
Capital Index	3.74	3.74	3.74	3.74
Deposit insurance Index	2.93	2.93	2.93	2.93
Ownership limitation	0.23	0.23	0.23	0.23
Sector CR3	0.66	0.61	0.58	0.58
Country level				
Rule of law	1.27	1.27	1.24	1.23
Per capita income (in USD)	39,463	36,853	33,047	31,389
Political stability index	0.67	0.64	0.64	0.60
Stock market development	51.69	112.11	107.04	87.77

Table V.4 presents the summary statistic clustered by bank size in terms of total assets. Controlling for size displays an important factor as indicated by previous studies (Demirguc-Kunt and Huizinga, 2010; Völz and Wedow, 2011). Thus, we divided the sample into four equal clusters. Cluster 1 consists of the largest banks (average total asset: USD 1.449 billion), and Cluster 4, of the smallest banks of our panel (Average total asset: USD 69 billion). Larger banks display tremendously lower spreads than smaller banks according to different spread calculation, leading to the hypothesis that larger banks are perceived less risky. This underlines the hypothesis following Völz and Wedow (2011) that CDS spreads might be distorted due to a size effect, which emerges when investors expect a public bailout as a result of the phenomenon "too big to fail." Furthermore, large banks are widely held (CR3 ratio amount to 15%) in contrast to smaller banks, which have a CR3 ratio of 39%. Table V.4 shows that smaller banks experienced higher growth than larger banks. In terms of capitalization, larger banks have a better ratio than smaller banks, although they are less efficient. However, none of these effects is significant according to Table V.5. This Table V.5 exhibits that size is definitely an important factor for determination of CDS premia and supports further previous research hypothesis.

Table V.4: Bank cluster by size

Dependent Variables	**Cluster 1**	**Cluster 2**	**Cluster 3**	**Cluster 4**
CDS country spread	34.14	27.60	32.34	98.67
CDS iTraxx financial spread	7.30	-0.56	12.38	80.24
CDS iTraxx non financial spread	-13.90	-21.93	-8.98	59.30
Bank level				
CR3 (20% Threshold)	0.11	0.56	0.55	0.59
CR3 (50% Threshold)	0.06	0.36	0.30	0.32
CR3 stake	15.02	44.75	35.52	38.66
Bank size	9.13	8.72	8.29	7.69
Bank growth	15.91	14.40	14.42	24.99
Bank efficiency	17.43	4.81	5.94	6.99
Bank capitalization	67.37	78.84	58.06	59.05

Table V.5: Pairwise test of significance between clusters by bank size

Dependent variables	Cluster 1 vs. 2	Cluster 1 vs. 3	Cluster 1 vs. 4	Cluster 2 vs. 3	Cluster 2 vs. 4	Cluster 3 vs. 4
	t (*p-value*)	t (*p-value*)	t (*p-value*)	t (*p-value*)	t (*p-value*)	t (*p-value*)
CDS country spread	−2.1648	−3.1262	−3.5665	−2.3574	−2.947	−0.0885
	0.0441**	0.0056***	0.0018***	0.0249**	0.0058***	0.93
CDS iTraxx financial spread	−0.6221	0.0036	−1.9235	0.9838	−3.2796	−3.6169
	0.5372	0.9971	0.0636*	0.3305	0.002***	0.001***
CDS iTraxx non financial spread	−0.725	−0.0821	−1.9366	0.9994	−3.2082	−3.4948
	0.4725	0.9352	0.062*	0.3229	0.0024***	0.0013***
CR3 (20% Threshold)	2.7676	10.8898	4.2525	4.4002	1.5094	−2.4037
	0.0082***	0***	0.0002***	0.0001***	0.1375	0.0214**
CR3 (50% Threshold)	2.242	2.9638	2.4637	0.9522	0.324	−0.5358
	0.0299**	0.0057***	0.0195**	0.3455	0.7473	0.5953
CR3 stake	2.4427	5.2517	4.3183	2.5277	1.069	−1.4927
	0.0186	0***	0.0001***	0.0147	0.2902	0.1442
Bank size	1.3115	2.8951	5.7171	2.8808	7.8101	5.2506
	0.197	0.007***	0***	0.006***	0***	0***
Bank growth	−0.706	−0.568	−1.2919	0.4616	−0.104	−0.9176
	0.4842	0.5743	0.2073	0.6465	0.9176	0.3655
Bank efficiency	0.3387	−2.5718	0.3899	−2.0127	−0.2479	3.5098
	0.7366	0.0151**	0.6993	0.05**	0.8054	0.0012***
Bank capitalisation	0.7311	2.0014	−2.9063	1.499	−3.2566	−4.6563
	0.4689	0.0545*	0.0072***	0.1405	0.0022***	0.0001***

Beside a cluster by bank size, Table V.6 shows a cluster by regulation indices. As documented by previous studies, regulation is of high relevance for banks (Laeven and Levine, 2009; Saunders, et al., 1990). Based on our regulation indices, we divided the sample into four unbalanced clusters, with 14 banks in Cluster 1, 33 banks in Cluster 2, 20 banks in Cluster 3, and lastly, 19 banks in Cluster 4. Cluster 1 represents banks that are strictly regulated according to the regulation indices, while cluster 4 consists of banks with a relaxed environment within the sample. Banks in a stricter regulatory environment display higher spreads against both banking peers and non-banking peers (CDS iTraxx financial spread: 81 bps vs. 8 bps) which is significant according to Table V.7. The strict regulatory environment might imply that banks tend to take greater risks supported by the regulatory framework. Strictly regulated banks also account for higher asset growth in the period 2005–2008 (24% vs. 16%), however, this difference is not supported by any significance as indicated by Table V.7. Although these banks are better capitalized and more efficient, they are perceived riskier in terms of CDS spread. In terms of size, these banks are smaller than banks having a relaxed environment. With regard to ownership concentration, stricter regulation goes along with a slightly more dispersed shareholder structure. The standard deviation of CDS spreads is higher for banks in countries with a strictly regulated environment.

Table V.6: Banks clustered by regulation

Dependent Variables	Cluster 1	Cluster 2	Cluster 3	Cluster 4
CDS country spread	100.20	51.00	36.94	38.20
CDS iTraxx financial spread	81.03	23.31	17.20	8.22
CDS iTraxx non financial spread	60.29	2.19	-4.33	-13.14
Bank level				
CR3 (20% Threshold)	0.48	0.39	0.49	0.55
CR3 (50% Threshold)	0.23	0.17	0.25	0.46
CR3 stake	31.96	26.50	34.36	46.94
Bank size	8.22	8.23	8.54	8.77
Bank growth	24.24	16.65	17.48	16.20
Bank efficiency	56.96	56.54	57.53	94.60
Bank capitalization	7.71	5.62	5.74	3.73

Table V.7: Pairwise test of significance between clusters by level of regulation

Dependent variables	Cluster 1 vs. 2	Cluster 1 vs. 3	Cluster 1 vs. 4	Cluster 2 vs. 3	Cluster 2 vs. 4	Cluster 3 vs. 4
	t (*p-value*)	t (*p-value*)	t (*p-value*)	t (*p-value*)	t (*p-value*)	t (*p-value*)
CDS country spread	−1.6562	−2.1846	−4.0087	−0.7827	−3.2472	−2.1163
	0.1199	0.0432**	0.0004***	0.4418	0.0026***	0.0409**
CDS iTraxx financial spread	−0.1151	1.034	−1.8074	1.7841	−3.117	−4.8131
	0.909	0.3089	0.0775*	0.0839*	0.0032***	0***
CDS iTraxx non financial spread	−0.1158	0.9045	−1.7738	1.629	−2.9782	−4.6119
	0.9084	0.3725	0.083*	0.1131	0.0047***	0***
CR3 (20% Threshold)	3.559	7.5498	6.5608	2.3333	2.0275	−0.4222
	0.001***	0***	0***	0.025**	0.0487**	0.675
CR3 (50% Threshold)	2.5166	5.3385	2.3956	2.3333	−0.1483	−2.6837
	0.0162**	0***	0.0209**	0.025**	0.8828	0.0102**
CR3 stake	3.1006	6.7719	5.3913	2.4082	0.4498	−2.6802
	0.0036***	0***	0***	0.0211	0.6551	0.0104
Bank size	−0.0507	3.1972	−4.3617	5.1973	5.7997	1.7999
	0.9599	0.0029***	0.0001***	0***	0***	0.0794*
Bank growth	−1.3562	−1.1283	−1.6872	0.0551	0.2029	0.1028
	0.184	0.2667	0.0993*	0.9564	0.8403	0.9187
Bank efficiency	0.7475	−2.2167	−0.2656	−1.6248	−0.9461	2.4546
	0.4595	0.0334**	0.7918	0.1137	0.3494	0.0186**
Bank capitalisation	1.2523	1.4552	−1.0685	−0.1074	−1.9435	−2.2056
	0.219	0.1543	0.2917	0.9151	0.0594*	0.0332**

* indicates significance at the 10% level, ** at the 5% level, and *** at the 1% level, respectively.
Standard errors control for clustering at the bank level.

It can be concluded that regulation and bank size matter for credit risk. A small size or a strict regulatory environment goes along with higher credit risk. Our results confirm recent results and the "too big to fail" idea that large banks may have incentives to take greater risks than smaller institutions, increasing their contribution to systemic risk further. In terms of ownership concentration, larger banks might have a more dispersed ownership structure; stricter regulation shows the same patterns.

V.4.2 Regression Results

Table V.8 summarizes the regression results that suggest that an increase in the ownership concentration is positively related with a rise of banks' credit risk measured in a CDS spread. This result holds for all the three spread calculations. The significance of coefficients depends on the inclusion of banks' rating. The analysis shows that ratings have a significant impact on the regression results. This confirms the findings of Aunon-Nerin et al. (2002), who conclude that the rating is a major factor in explaining the CDS spread. In order to extract the ownership effect, we ran the regression including and excluding the rating variable. Lastly, a regression including interaction effects between rating and ownership was applied. All regression models are significant at 1% significance level as indicated by the Wald chi-square test.

The results remain robust using the CR3 50% cut-off point for the ownership concentration. The impact on the CDS spread even increases with an increasing ownership concentration as the comparison of the coefficients shows. This holds for the regression with and without the rating. However, without the rating, the ownership coefficients are significant at 10% for the CR3 20% threshold and at 1% for the CR3 50% threshold.

These results are confirmed considering the iTraxx non-financial institutions spread. Again, depending on the inclusion of banks' rating as independent variable, the impact of ownership concentration on CDS spread is significant or otherwise. The results based on the iTraxx non-financial also confirm the stronger effect of the CR3 50% threshold than of the CR3 20% threshold.

The third regression analysis uses the traditional CDS country spread for a robustness check. This analysis confirms the results of the first two regressions. Again, the bank rating shows a significant impact on CDS spread at 1% significance level. The regression excluding the rating leads to a significant impact of the ownership concentration on CDS spread.

Table V.8: Regression results with iTraxx financial spread as dependent variable

Variable		iTraxx financial with rating(RE)		iTraxx financial with rating(RE)		iTraxx financial w/o rating(RE)		iTraxx financial w/o rating(RE)	
		Coeff.	SE (robust)	Coeff.	SE (robust)	Coeff.	SE (robust)	Coeff.	SE (robust)
Ownership	CR3 Threshold 20	13.70	14.7854			23.31	13.0618*		
	CR3 Threshold 50			21.15	16.4046			36.00	16.6448***
Bank level	Log Total Assets	25.66	26.1306	25.01	24.3735	−8.05	13.4522	−9.77	12.4534
	Total Assets Growth	−0.53	0.2504**	−0.54	0.2557**	−0.50	0.2564*	−0.51	0.2579**
	CIR	0.06	0.1168	0.04	0.1185***	0.11	0.1130	0.08	0.1136
	TE/TA	7.33	4.1838*	7.40	4.1777*	6.47	3.2146**	6.92	3.2574**
	Issuer Rating	−18.04	5.8001***	−18.44	6.0505***				
	Financial crisis support	13.51	16.0834	14.51	15.4344	7.00	14.5708	9.00	14.3901
Sector level	Activities	−18.91	5.9387***	−18.50	5.7909***	−17.75	6.3752***	−16.82	6.1010***
	Capital	18.20	8.6389**	17.78	8.5691**	12.38	7.4633*	10.85	7.5221
	Audit and Disclosure	−26.35	10.0565***	−27.42	10.1839***	−21.36	11.0643*	−23.56	10.9220**
	Authorities	13.52	4.7904***	14.03	4.7451***	20.51	5.4262***	21.41	5.4416***
	Deposit	12.81	5.2319**	13.33	5.1747***	12.95	5.5760**	13.39	5.3358**
	Ownership	56.05	22.7337**	56.09	22.8094**	34.14	25.5069	33.44	24.9281
Country level	Market Cap / GDP	−0.28	−0.1355**	−0.25	0.1306*	−0.32	0.1176***	−0.28	0.1119**
	Per Capita GDP	0.00	0.0006	0.00	0.0006	0.00	0.0006	0.00	0.0006
	SectorCR3	80.83	35.5846**	92.42	35.8800***	70.69	37.3830*	87.90	33.9152***
	Political Stabiliy	54.15	45.2239	49.70	43.4890	42.78	43.6541	37.74	41.9927
	Rule of Law	−121.40	46.4200***	−117.56	45.0893***	−124.44	49.1374**	−120.65	47.5578**
	Constant	176.64	199.6256	174.45	178.3784	321.06	142.4360**	324.81	126.1656***
	Wald Chi²	51.55	***	50.46	***	53.65	***	53.97	***
	R-sq	0.52		0.52		0.43		0.44	
	No of observations	245		245		289		289	

* indicates significance at the 10% level, ** at the 5% level, and *** at the 1% level, respectively.
Standard errors control for clustering at the bank level.

Table V.9: Regression results with iTraxx non-financial spread as dependent variable

Variable		iTraxx non-financial with rating(RE)		iTraxx non-financial w/o rating(RE)		iTraxx non-financial with rating(RE)		iTraxx non-financial w/o rating(RE)	
		Coeff.	SE (robust)	Coeff.	SE (robust)	Coeff.	SE (robust)	Coeff.	SE (robust)
Ownership	CR3 Threshold 20	16.61	15.3163	26.21	13.4219*				
	CR3 Threshold 50					24.23	17.0067	39.15	17.0890**
Bank level	Log Total Assets	28.62	26.7664	−6.18	13.9690	27.51	24.9836	−8.28	12.9116
	Total Assets Growth	−0.52	0.2524**	−0.49	0.2582*	−0.53	0.2580**	−0.50	0.2598*
	CIR	0.06	0.1171	0.11	0.1133	0.04	0.1186	0.08	0.1138
	TE/TA	7.72	4.3188*	6.74	3.3342**	7.78	4.2975*	7.22	3.3591**
	Issuer Rating	−18.07	5.9480***			−18.53	6.2043***		
	Financial crisis support	10.13	16.2990	3.92	14.6607	11.54	15.6278	6.22	14.4917
Sector level	Activities	−19.08	6.0058***	−17.86	6.4563***	−18.60	5.8552***	−16.84	6.1720***
	Capital	17.23	8.8038**	11.27	7.6033	16.67	8.7277*	9.56	7.6485
	Audit and Disclosure	−25.22	10.1181**	−20.34	11.1754*	−26.57	10.2849***	−22.86	11.0562**
	Authorities	14.01	5.0008***	21.04	5.5252***	14.52	4.9305***	21.98	5.5436***
	Deposit	13.15	5.4066**	13.33	5.7156**	13.82	5.3464***	13.88	5.4780**
	Ownership	56.41	23.0453**	35.13	25.8270	56.74	23.2351***	34.58	25.3361
Country level	Market Cap / GDP	−0.24	0.1370*	−0.28	0.1117**	−0.21	0.1324	−0.23	0.1120**
	Per Capita GDP	0.00	0.0007	0.00	0.0006	0.00	0.0007	0.00	0.0006
	SectorCR3	82.37	37.4999**	72.82	38.7888*	96.58	37.3528***	92.17	35.0594***
	Political Stabiliy	56.23	45.9478	43.41	44.3394	51.07	44.2037	38.05	42.5892
	Rule of Law	−126.84	47.1332***	−129.55	49.8217***	−122.52	45.7951***	−125.44	48.1518***
	constant	113.88	205.5734	266.28	146.0704*	155.51	184.4615	273.62	129.8689**
	Wald Chi^2	45.23	***	46.83	***	44.92	***	48.94	***
	R-sq	0.52		0.43		0.52		0.44	
	No of observations	245		289		245		289	

* indicates significance at the 10% level, ** at the 5% level, and *** at the 1% level, respectively.
Standard errors control for clustering at the bank level.

Table V.10: Regression results with country spread as dependent variable

Variable		Country with rating (RE)		Country w/o rating (RE)		Country with rating (RE)		Country w/o rating (RE)	
		Coeff.	SE (robust)	Coeff.	SE (robust)	Coeff.	SE (robust)	Coeff.	SE (robust)
Ownership	CR3 Threshold 20	17.13	21.3673	41.78	21.9538*				
	CR3 Threshold 50					47.59	26.2969*	60.32	30.3804**
Bank level	Log Total Assets	52.71	46.9305	27.34	36.9226	56.15	44.1067	22.51	34.5407
	Total Assets Growth	−0.73	0.3188**	−0.75	0.3257	−0.71	0.3095**	−0.73	0.3134
	CIR	0.15	0.1139	0.16	0.1114	0.13	0.1158	0.15	0.1110
	TE/TA	14.81	6.9713**	16.14	6.6479	15.04	6.7983**	17.15	6.8013
	Issuer Rating	−27.33	8.6144***			−27.85	8.6375***		
	Financial crisis support	12.40	18.6886	4.35	18.5230	10.12	17.6355	7.04	17.5697
Sector level	Activities	−0.20	8.0617	8.73	12.1630	0.50	7.8719	9.22	12.0043
	Capital	4.44	14.0048	−19.99	20.0193	7.20	13.9136	−19.38	21.4978
	Audit and Disclosure	8.78	14.9680	29.98	29.2801	8.75	15.0064	26.59	27.8106
	Authorities	30.76	9.8834***	51.37	16.1075	31.10	9.5075***	51.95	15.8526
	Deposit	−6.57	9.8417	−8.91	14.1917	−5.26	10.2131	−6.29	14.3009
	Ownership	−69.23	50.7949	−149.67	95.6890	−67.74	49.9043	−146.48	95.7414
Country level	Market Cap / GDP	−0.52	0.1643***	−0.55	0.1616	−0.46	0.1642***	−0.50	0.1546
	Per Capita GDP	0.00	0.0010***	0.00	0.0010	0.00	0.0011***	0.00	0.0011
	SectorCR3	5.24	56.1624	22.25	87.1620	11.92	53.9909	36.38	75.3656
	Political Stabiliy	−17.22	68.8464	−25.96	83.8110	−19.60	65.1396	−28.33	79.8839
	Rule of Law	−43.85	61.5625	−49.66	73.7483	−40.88	57.5226	−41.21	70.3464
	Constant	−516.62	400.4782	−709.39	436.1735	−604.21	378.7536	−688.23	406.6570*
	Wald Chi²	156.74	***	134.84	***	156.13	***	136.17	***
	R-sq	0.51		0.34		0.52		0.35	
	No of observations	168		194		168		194	

* indicates significance at the 10% level, ** at the 5% level, and *** at the 1% level, respectively.
Standard errors control for clustering at the bank level.

The regression with interaction terms between ownership concentration and rating shows that ownership has a significant impact on the spread. A higher ownership concentration is associated with a higher credit risk. The interaction term of ownership and rating indicates that a better rating reduces the spread. The coefficients show that the effect of the ownership concentration is by far stronger than the effect of the rating and the interaction term.

V.5 Concluding Remarks

In this paper, we conduct the first empirical assessment of theoretical considerations with regard to banks' credit risk, their ownership structure, and the national regulative environment examining the effect of bank ownership structures on risk-taking for the timeframe 2005–2008. The analysis is based on an unbalanced panel comprising 86 global privately and publicly held banks, leading to a maximum of 344 observations.

Research suggests that risk-taking of banks considering the same regulatory environment varies enormously and depends on the comparative power of shareholders in the governance structure of each bank (Laeven and Levine, 2009; Saunders, et al., 1990). Apart from appraising theories from corporate finance and the banking business, this analysis is essential from a governance perspective as equity and debt are also considered as governance instruments (Williamson, 1988).

We find that banks with a concentrated ownership structure and consequently more powerful owners tend to have higher credit risk, as is indicated by CDS spreads. These results are in conflict with that obtained by Shehzad et al. (2010), who suggest that ownership concentration significantly affects bank risk in terms of loan quality. However, we can affirm the results suggested by Laeven and Levine (2009) regarding equity that banks with a concentrated ownership and subsequently more powerful owners tend to take greater risks, which are measured by the z-score. Furthermore, we demonstrate that bank regulation has a negative impact on bank's credit risk, while each bank's ownership structure has to be taken into account. Banks in heavily regulated countries display higher CDS spreads. The question on whether regulation achieves its goals is unresolved, at least from a credit risk perspective. Lastly, we can confirm recent research that larger banks tend to take greater risk compared to smaller institutions (Völz and Wedow, 2011). This underlines the previous findings regarding the "too big to fail" phenomenon that CDS prices might be distorted owing to the effects of bank size. This bank size effect leads to a dilemma for bank supervisions that the CDS price might not accurately reflect the intrinsic bank risk and therefore send a wrong signal.

V.6 Appendix

Appendix V.6.1: Regulation Indices

Activities index	Auditing and disclosure index	Authorities index
Securities activities	External audit required	Suspension of dividends by supervisor possible
Insurance activities	Licensed or certified Auditors compulsory	Suspension of bonuses by supervisor possible
Real estate activities	Supervisors informed of the auditor's report	Suspension of management fees by supervisor possible
Ownership of voting shares	Right to meet with external auditors for supervisory agency	Replacement of management by supervisor possible
	Potential legal actions of supervisors against external auditors for negligence	Replacement of directors by supervisor possible
	Consolidated accounts covering all bank and any non-bank financial subsidiaries necessary	Existence of more than one supervisory body
	Disclosure of off-balance sheet items to supervisors	Replacement of head of supervisory body possible
	Disclosure of off-balance sheet items to public	Liability of supervisory body for damages to a bank by its actions
	Disclose of risk management procedures to public	
	Liability of bank directors for erroneous information	
	Credit ratings required for commercial banks	
Capital index	**Deposit insurance index**	
Minimum capital requirement	Explicit deposit insurance protection system	
Accordance with 1988 Basel Accord	Ex-ante collection of premia	
Minimum ratio as function of credit risk	Fees based on some risk assessment	
Minimum ratio as function of market risk	Insurance limit per person	
Subordinated debt allowed as part of regulatory capital	Coverage of interbank deposits	
Revaluation gains allowed as part of capital	Participation compulsory for all banks	
Formal definition of a non-performing loan		

Source: Barth, Caprio, and Levine(2004; 2008)

Appendix V.6.2: Country Summary Statistics (Mean values)

Country	**actual CR3 stake**	**CR3 (20%)**	**CR3 (50%)**	**CDS itraxx financial spread**	**CDS itraxx non financial spread**	**CDS country spread**
Australia	8.11	0.00	0.00	6.51	−14.70	110.02
Austria	73.51	1.00	0.75	23.40	0.61	53.45
Belgium	32.35	0.67	0.08	1.66	−21.12	33.89
China	75.89	0.92	0.58	28.55	7.35	25.05
Denmark	34.92	1.00	0.00	−9.90	−31.10	4.15
France	31.82	0.33	0.33	−9.20	−30.41	21.46
Germany	69.57	0.75	0.75	8.74	−12.27	40.37
Greece	3.56	0.00	0.00	90.42	52.09	82.54
India	35.08	0.50	0.33	113.27	93.26	
Ireland	11.19	0.00	0.00	25.95	4.75	136.52
Italy	33.87	0.46	0.29	−5.73	−27.08	10.88
Japan	17.64	0.25	0.08	23.74	2.86	408.73
Netherlands	4.59	0.00	0.00	−8.95	−30.15	67.44
Norway	50.43	1.00	0.50	−12.55	−33.75	
Portugal	37.05	0.75	0.50	−0.14	−21.34	20.31
Singapore	24.73	1.00	0.00	6.61	−14.59	5.71
South Korea	39.79	0.60	0.40	38.45	17.96	13.18
Spain	46.21	0.50	0.40	24.36	3.16	47.12
Sweden	29.98	1.00	0.00	−9.36	−30.56	21.93
Switzerland	11.32	0.00	0.00	3.39	−17.81	
UK	17.59	0.25	0.08	9.47	−11.73	45.84
USA	15.69	0.25	0.00	36.59	15.93	172.48

Appendix V.6.3: Regression results with interaction terms

Variable		iTraxx financial with rating(RE)		iTraxx financial with rating(RE)		iTraxx non-financial with rating(RE)		iTraxx non-financial with rating(RE)	
		Coeff.	**SE (robust)**	**Coeff.**	**SE (robust)**	**Coeff.**	**SE (robust)**	**Coeff.**	**SE (robust)**
Ownership	CR3 Threshold 20	196.53	63.7377***			204.94	64.2354***		
	CR3 Threshold 50			224.53	81.3880***			230.66	81.8607
Banklevel	Log Total Assets	21.82	22.7067	21.00	20.9425	23.88	22.9174	22.77	21.3508
	Total Assets Growth	−0.42	0.2052**	−0.34	0.1913*	−0.41	0.2035**	−0.33	0.1904
	CIR	0.03	0.1053	0.04	0.1041	0.04	0.1048	0.04	0.1034
	TE/TA	6.20	3.8561	7.36	3.8539*	6.51	4.0240	7.67	3.9642
	Issuer Rating	−7.01	3.8454*	−11.55	4.9296**	−6.56	4.0608	−11.35	5.0749
	CR3 Threshold*Rating	−33.62	10.3504***	−39.13	13.5260***	−34.78	10.4230***	−39.82	13.5761
	Financial crisis support	18.94	15.2998	29.17	14.4121**	16.17	15.3745	26.52	14.4788
Sectorlevel	Activities	−13.16	4.6552***	−12.98	3.8164***	−13.09	4.6862***	−12.96	3.8706
	Capital	15.38	7.8713*	15.19	6.8239**	14.14	7.9721*	13.98	6.9581
	Audit and Disclosure	−27.66	10.2201***	−17.49	7.6325**	−26.69	10.2253***	−16.62	7.7216
	Authorities	10.37	3.8990***	8.65	3.6143**	10.65	4.0585***	8.98	3.7673
	Deposit	9.72	4.8903**	9.42	4.5005**	10.01	5.0466**	9.83	4.6630
	Ownership	43.23	21.5162**	41.24	19.7581**	43.29	21.7563**	41.61	20.2557

Variable		iTraxx financial with rating(RE)		iTraxx financial with rating(RE)		iTraxx non-financial with rating(RE)		iTraxx non-financial with rating(RE)	
		Coeff.	**SE (robust)**	**Coeff.**	**SE (robust)**	**Coeff.**	**SE (robust)**	**Coeff.**	**SE (robust)**
	Market Cap / GDP	−0.31	0.1324**	0.29	0.1203**	−0.27	0.1331**	−0.25	0.1210
	Per Capita GDP	0.00	0.0006	0.00	0.0005	0.00	0.0006	0.01	0.0005
Countrylevel	SectorCR3	109.68	37.5519***	71.79	30.2678**	112.82	38.6463***	75.11	31.5401
	Political Stabiliy	28.96	37.9757	12.57	31.1385	29.92	38.2966	13.17	32.7253
	Rule of Law	−81.03	34.6243**	−62.73	15.8966**	−84.96	34.9720**	−66.36	26.4810
	Constant	98.81	190.6605	53.25	177.1566	35.51	192.4684	−0.05	180.0901
	Wald Chi^2	75.45	***	61.86	***	63.04	***	55.54	
	R-sq	0.5745		0.6016		0.5744		0.6012	
	No of observations	245		245		245		245	

Appendix V.6.4: Correlation matrix

	CDSitraxxf..	CDSitraxxn~d	CDSi~bspread	CDSc~yspread	CDSc~bspread	CR3Thresh~20	CR3Thresh~50	CR3Owner	LogAvgTA	GrowthTota~s	TE_TA	CIR
CDSitraxxf..	1.0000											
CDSitraxxn~d	0.9990*	1.0000										
CDSi~bspread	0.9282*	0.9100*	1.0000									
CDSc~yspread	0.8118*	0.8088*	0.7854*	1.0000								
CDSc~bspread	0.7268*	0.6954*	0.7579*	0.9765*	1.0000							
CR3Thresh~20	0.1902*	0.1934*	−0.0027	0.0678	−0.0455	1.0000						
CR3Thresh~50	0.1704*	0.1721*	0.0225	0.0290	−0.0236	0.6469*	1.0000					
CR3Owner	0.2410*	0.2441*	0.0012	0.0720	−0.0428	0.7785*	0.9032*	1.0000				
LogAvgTA	−0.3812*	−0.3824*	−0.1004	−0.3096*	−0.0269	−0.2804*	−0.2240*	−0.2672*	1.0000			
GrowthTota~s	−0.0617	−0.0539	−0.0377	−0.1310	−0.1274	−0.0582	0.0201	−0.0073	−0.1767*	1.0000		
TE_TA	0.2797*	0.2831*	−0.1467	0.2342*	−0.1799	0.0264	−0.0363	−0.0071	−0.3949*	0.1211*	1.0000	
CIR	−0.0049	−0.0065	0.1321	0.1032	0.1443	0.0821	0.1603*	0.1835*	0.1108*	−0.1780*	−0.2508*	1.0000
Activities	0.1506*	0.1528*	−0.0483	0.1240	−0.0682	0.0896	0.0130	0.0503	−0.3510*	0.0498	0.4551*	−0.1494*
Auditingan~e	−0.0227	−0.0229	0.0679	−0.0400	0.1481	−0.1129*	−0.0032	−0.0761	−0.1773*	0.0138	−0.1559*	−0.0824
Authorities	0.0513	0.0520	0.2035*	0.2617*	0.2953*	−0.2102*	−0.2697*	−0.2851*	−0.2337*	−0.0269	0.0822	−0.1086*
Capital	0.0367	0.0380	−0.0033	0.1007	0.0694	−0.2901*	−0.3302*	−0.3745*	0.0255	0.0985	0.2066*	−0.1886*
Deposit	0.1049	0.1062	−0.1415	0.1021	−0.3860*	0.0742	−0.0248	−0.0082	0.1254*	−0.0441	0.1667*	0.0312
Ownership	0.0026	0.0036	0.0765	−0.0880	0.4552*	−0.0549	−0.0025	−0.0351	−0.2483*	0.0406	0.0943	−0.1250*
MarketCapGDP	−0.2169*	−0.2050*	−0.0751	−0.2328*	−0.3392*	−0.2264*	−0.3256*	−0.3470*	0.1653*	0.1092	0.0674	−0.1299*
PercapitaGDP	−0.2313*	−0.2302*	0.0568	0.0665	0.5026*	−0.1495*	−0.2716*	−0.2753*	0.4262*	−0.1637*	−0.2510*	0.1698*
PoliticalS~y	−0.1416*	−0.1427*	0.1826*	0.1004	0.2877*	−0.0224	−0.1074*	−0.1215*	0.1080	−0.1671*	−0.2816*	0.1636*
RuleofLaw	−0.3360*	−0.3376*	0.1385	−0.0637	0.2940*	−0.1556*	−0.2535*	−0.3031*	0.4304*	−0.2083*	−0.3823*	0.1895*
SectorCR3	0.0049	0.0034	0.0310	−0.0134	0.1688	0.2818*	0.1257*	0.1981*	−0.0069	−0.0719	−0.3465*	0.0727
IssuerRating	−0.5403*	−0.5403*	−0.2277*	−0.4418*	0.0273	−0.2831*	−0.2913*	−0.3743*	0.7642*	−0.1758*	−0.4293*	0.0062
Ratingsub	−0.4445*	−0.4395*	−0.2945*	−0.1681	−0.0507	−0.2913*	−0.1583*	−0.2832*	0.6122*	0.0144	−0.3226*	−0.1679*
FinancialC~t	0.1464*	0.1363*	0.1534	0.2443*	0.4383*	0.0346	0.0061	0.0173	0.2040*	−0.1733*	−0.1594*	0.2881*

Activities	Auditingan~e	Authorities	Capital	Deposit	Ownership	MarketCapGDP	PercapitaGDP	PoliticalS~y	RuleofLaw	SectorCR3	IssuerRating	Ratingsub	FinancialC~t
1.0000													
−0.2044*	1.0000												
0.1007	0.1844*	1.0000											
0.1187*	0.1800*	0.3351*	1.0000										
0.0623	−0.4320*	−0.0765	0.1078*	1.0000									
0.3256*	0.4765*	0.3035*	0.0524	−0.5615*	1.0000								
−0.0355	0.0840	0.3376*	0.5262*	−0.0651	0.1363*	1.0000							
−0.4134*	−0.1687*	−0.0005	0.1676*	0.1597*	−0.3886*	0.1233*	1.0000						
−0.2887*	0.0650	0.1395*	−0.0029	−0.0997	−0.2931*	0.0332	0.6991*	1.0000					
−0.5611*	0.0408	0.2054*	0.1525*	0.0054	−0.2206*	0.2936*	0.8242*	0.7069*	1.0000				
−0.2854*	0.4094*	−0.0381	0.0274	−0.2074*	−0.0982	−0.0954	0.1627*	0.3995*	0.2062*	1.0000			
−0.3736*	−0.0125	−0.1801*	0.2383*	−0.0555	−0.1333*	0.2488*	0.5949*	0.1977*	0.6077*	0.0800	1.0000		
−0.2140*	0.0941	−0.0747	0.2956*	−0.0426	−0.1700*	0.2047*	0.4088*	0.1908*	0.3305*	0.1646*	0.9174*	1.0000	
−0.1367*	−0.1126*	−0.0022	0.0128	0.1402*	−0.1326*	−0.2717*	0.2630*	0.1230*	0.1772*	0.0449	0.1471*	0.0558	1.0000

VI Main Concluding Remarks

The four studies shed light on two highly relevant governance themes which are closely related: composition of supervisory boards and financial expertise as well as ownership structure. The first part of the investigation – consisting of the studies 1 to 3 – concentrates on the composition of supervisory boards and its member's financial expertise, its influence on a banks' risk and performance profile, and its contribution to bank stability - also across different legal ownership compositions. The underlying investigation is a consequence of the recent financial and banking crisis which resulted in a demand for more financial expertise within the banking governance framework (R. Adams, B., 2012; Erkens, et al., 2009). The second part – comprising the fourth study – focuses on the effect of ownership concentration on credit risk analyzing the role of debtholders as stakeholder group within an international context.

The first study highlights that regional banks, comprising savings and cooperative banks, have a significant concentration of financial expertise. Within the regional banks it becomes evident that savings banks have, on average, a much higher fraction of financial expertise compared to cooperative banks (65% vs. 48%). This higher concentration can be partially explained through the prescribed employee representation at savings banks but the values controlled for insiders show that savings banks have still more supervisory board members with financial expertise than cooperative banks (53% vs. 45%). These values are relatively high comparing it to a study of Hau and Thum (2008) who are analysing private and large public banks. The values of their study show that the financial expertise concentration for private banks is between 31% and 40% and between 10% and 30% for large public banks, also taking Landesbanken into consideration.

Despite of the results showing a relative high concentration of financial expertise, a fraction of 35% (savings banks) and of 52% (cooperative banks) of the supervisory board members of regional banks is not represented by financial experts. This results are in line with a recent study which documents that the general qualification of supervisory board members is relatively high; however, the study also reveals that the assumed expertise is derived mainly from employee representatives who have assumed bank expertise (Körner, et al., 2014).

In the light of the recent financial and banking crisis as well as the intensively debated deficiencies of internal bank governance frameworks and structures, the regulative environment should be responsive and oblige banks to increment their fraction of financial experts on supervisory boards. In addition to that, the regulative environment needs to be more stringent with respect to the implementation of concepts for supervisory board members who cannot show financial expertise. The current legal framework do not exhibit any specific requirements or exceptions.

The analysis of the composition of supervisory boards within the second study indicates that with more financial expertise bank performance declines and risk goes up. These results induce concerns that mandating financial expertise on boards is not beneficial for the risk-return profile of regional banks in the form of cooperative banks. It appears that overconfidence of entrepreneurs is a reasonable explanation for this unfavorable development since they represent the largest fraction of professionals within the sample of cooperative banks. These results are a challenge for the regulative banking environment since financial experts on regional banks allow bank managers to reduce the stability and increase the risk.

From a regulator's perspective these outcomes provide evidence that the prescription of universal financial expertise in bank's internal goverance mechanisms does not lead to the desired effect of increasing the stability of the banking system. The results indicate that the new German legislation is not necessarily contributing to an enhancement of banking system stability as it was intended to. Further, owners of the banks should be also concerned since the financial expertise does not automatically lead to the targeted positive performance.

Based on these findings the third study substantiates the detrimental influence of financial expertise on a bank's risk-return profile. This outcome can be demonstrated across different ownership types. In particular political decision makers and regulators shall take these results into account in order to develop improved legislations providing a robust regulative framework. The ask for more expertise in internal bank governance as suggested by articles and consultation papers as well as recommended by international authorities and bodies appears initially perfectly logical but cannot be verified by the present analysis.

This adverse effect of financial expertise can partially explained through behavioural finance theory. Evidence documents that the greater expertise individuals have, the more overconfident they tend to be (e.g. (Daniel, Hirshleifer, and Subrahmanyam, 2001; Manove and Padilla, 1999; Odean, 1998). Further research shows that overconfidence tend to increase with task complexity (Dittrich, et al., 2005). Taking into account these results for the present study and its supervisory board members it shows that alleged expertise results in higher risk-taking and the subsequent underestimatation.

Consequently, the implementation of a legislation prescribing a board composition with assumed 100% financial expertise – without further requirements and details - does not necessarily lead to the reduction of risk and increase of stability. In the light of those findings, it might be more beneficial for the risk-return profile of a bank if the legal requirements ensure that the composition of a supervisory board is based on defined core tasks and responsibilities. It needs to be assured that all core responsibilities are covered by the supervisory board members through the introduction of these requirements by the regulators.

Taking the three present studies as a starting point, there are more options for further analysis at international levels. The professional background of the supervisory board members represents the core element capturing the assessment of assumed financial expertise. This is in line with the majority of similar research. A potential extension of the study could be the reflection of other elements such as education, previous industry experiences, size and location of the enterprise and management experience in order to assess the financial expertise. Another possibility could be the inclusion of banks with a different ownership type and in other countries if the influence of financial expertise within the governance framework can be unambiguously analysed. Given the present analysis focuses on German banks and its particular two-tier board structure, the transposition to institutions with a one-tier structure provides a further avenue of research. As already indicated, the proposed inclusion of legal requirements for core tasks and responsibilities allows an additional area of research. In order to perform such an analysis core tasks and areas need to be determined. On the basis of these definitions, the analysis which expertise and specific areas improve the risk-return profile of banks could provide beneficial information on the implementation of legal requirements for the demand of expertise of supervisory board members for specific areas.

The fourth study examines the effects of the ownership structure on credit risk and documents that banks with a more concentrated ownership structure tend to be riskier as indicated by larger CDS spreads. Furthermore, the analysis exhibits that bank regulation has a negative impact on banks' credit risk. Larger banks exhibit—in line with the "too big to fail" argument—significantly lower risk than smaller banks. From a regulatory perspective these findings are of particular interest given the interrelation of ownership, risk and regulation variables. Firstly, it appears that more powerful owners tend to take greater risks measured by higher credit risk in terms of loan quality. This is not preferable from a regulatory view. Secondly, the study point out that bank regulation has a negative impact on bank's credit risk, while each bank's ownership structure has to be taken into account. Banks in heavily regulated countries display higher CDS spreads. The question on whether regulatory bodies and its legislations achieve its objectives remains open, at least in the context of credit risk. Lastly, the analysis is in line with previous research that larger banks tend to take greater risk compared to smaller institutions (Völz and Wedow, 2011). This underlines previous results regarding the "too big to fail" phenomenon that CDS prices might be distorted owing to the effects of bank size. Therefore, this bank size effect leads to a dilemma for the regulatory environment and supervision that credit risk indicators in the form of CDS price might not accurately reflect the intrinsic bank risk and therefore transmit a misleading and deceptive signal.

References

Acharya, V., Richardson, M., van Nieuwerburgh, S., and White, L. J. (2011). *Guaranteed To Fail: Fannie Mae, Freddie Mac and the Debacle of Mortgage Finance.* Princeton: Princeton University Press.

Acharya, V., and Yorulmazer, T. (2007). Too many to fail - An analysis of time-inconsistency in bank closure policies. *Journal of Financial Intermediation, 16*(1), 1–31.

Adams, R., Almeida, H., and Ferreira, D. (2005). Powerful CEOs and their impact on corporate performance. *Review of Financial Studies, 18*, 1403–1432.

Adams, R., B. (2012). Governance and the Financial Crisis. *International Review of Finance, 12:1*, 7–38.

Adams, R. B., and Mehran, H. (2008). Corporate performance, board structure, and their determinants in the banking industry, *Staff Reports, no. 330*. New York: Federal Reserve Bank of New York.

Aebi, V., Sabato, G., and Schmid, M. (2012). Risk management, corporate governance, and bank performance in the financial crisis. *Journal of Banking & Finance, 36*(12).

Altunbas, Y., Evans, L., and Molyneux, P. (2001). Bank Ownership and Efficiency. *Journal of Money, Credit and Banking, 33*(4), 926–954.

Altunbas, Y., Manganelli, S., and Marques-Ibanez, D. (2011). Bank Risk during the Great Recession: Do business models matter?. *ECB Working Papers Series, 1394.*

Anderson, R. C., Mansi, S. A., and Reeb, D. M. (2003). Founding family ownership and the agency cost of debt. *Journal of Financial Economics, 68*(2), 263–285.

Andres, P. d., and Vallelado, E. (2008). Corporate governance in banking: The role of the board of directors. *Journal of Banking & Finance, 32*(12), 2570–2580.

Annaert, J., Ceuster, M. D., Roy, P. V., and Vespro, C. (2010). What determines euro area bank CDS spreads? *Working Paper Research - National Bank of Belgium, No. 190.*

Ard, L., and Berg, A. (2010). Bank Governance - Lessons from the Financial Crisis, *World Bank, Policy Briefs, Note no. 13*. Washington D.C.: The World Bank.

Ashbaugh-Skaife, H., Collins, D. W., and LaFond, R. (2006). The effects of corporate governance on firms' credit ratings. *Journal of Accounting and Economics, 42*(1–2), 203–243.

Ashcraft, A. B., and Santos, J. A. C. (2009). Has the CDS market lowered the cost of corporate debt? [doi: DOI: 10.1016/j.jmoneco.2009.03.008]. *Journal of Monetary Economics, 56*(4), 514–523.

Ayadi, R., Llewellyn, D. T., Schmidt, R. H., Arbak, E., and Groen, W. P. D. (2010). *Investigating Diversity in the Banking Sector in Europe - Key Developments, Performance and Role of Cooperative Banks*. Brussels: Center for European Policy Studies.

BaFin, and Deutsche Bundesbank. (2010). Merkblatt zur Kontrolle von Mitgliedern von Verwaltungs- und Aufsichtsorganen gemäß KWG und VAG. Retrieved from http://www.bafin.de/cln_152/nn_721290/SharedDocs/Veroeffentlichungen/DE/Service/Merkblaetter/mb__100222__Verwaltungs__und__Aufsichtsorgane.html?__nnn=true

Barberis, N., and Thaler, R. (2003). *A survey of behavioral finance*. Amsterdam: Elsevier.

Barth, J. R., Caprio, G. J., and Levine, R. (2003). *Rethinking Bank Regulation: Till Angels Govern*. New York: Cambridge University Press.

Barth, J. R., Caprio, G. J., and Levine, R. (2004). Bank regulation and supervision: what works best? *Journal of Financial Intermediation, 13*(2), 205–248.

Barth, J. R., Caprio, G. J., and Levine, R. (2008). Bank Regulations Are Changing: For Better or Worse?, *World Bank Policy Research, Working Paper Series, no. 4646*. Washington D.C.: The World Bank.

Basel Committee on Banking Supervision. (1998). International Converver-gence of Capital Measurement and Capital Standards (July 1988, updated to April 1998). Basel Bank of International Settlements.

Basel Committee on Banking Supervision. (1999a). Enhancing Corporate Governance for Banking Organisations: Bank for International Settlements.

Basel Committee on Banking Supervision. (1999b). *Enhancing Corporate Governance for Banking Organisations*. Basel: Bank of International Settlements.

Basel Committee on Banking Supervision. (2006a). *Enhancing Corporate Governance for Banking Organisations*. Basel: Bank of International Settlements.

Basel Committee on Banking Supervision. (2006b). Enhancing corporate governance for banking organisations. Basel: Bank for International Settlements.

Beck, T., and Demirgüç-Kunt, A. (2009). Financial Institutions and Markets Across Countries and over Time: Data and Analysis, *World Bank Policy Research, Working Paper Series, no. 4943*. Washington D.C.: The World Bank.

Beck, T., Hesse, H., Kick, T., and Westernhagen, N. v. (2009). *Bank Ownership and Stability: Evidence from Germany*. Paper presented at the FDIC - Center for Financial Research. Retrieved from http://www.fdic.gov/bank/analytical/cfr/2009/june/CFR_SS_2009_beck.pdf

Beck, T., and Levine, R. (2003). Legal Institutions and Financial Development *NBER Working Paper No. 10126.*

Beck, T., Levine, R., and Loayza, N. (2000). Finance and the sources of growth. *58*(1–2).

Becker, H. P., and Peppmeier, A. (2006). *Bankbetriebslehre* (Vol. 8). Ludwigshafen: Kiehl.

Berger, A. N., Clarke, G. R. G., Cull, R., Klapper, L., and Udell, G. F. (2005). Corporate governance and bank performance: A joint analysis of the static, selection, and dynamic effects of domestic, foreign, and state ownership. *Journal of Banking & Finance, 29*(8–9), 2179–2221.

Berger, A. N., Kick, T., and Schaeck, K. (2012). Executive board composition and bank risk taking, *Discussion Paper Series, Deutsche Bundesbank, No 03/2012.* Frankfurt am Main: Deutsche Bundesbank.

Berger, H., and Nitsch, V. (2011). Too Many Cooks? Committees in Monetary Policy. *Southern Economic Journal, 78*(2), 452–475.

Berle, A. A., and Means, G. C. (1933). *The modern corporation and private property.* New York: MacMillan.

Bermig, A., and Frick, B. (2010). Board Size, Board Composition, and Firm Performance: Empirical Evidence from Germany, *Working Paper.* Paderborn: University of Paderborn.

Bertrand, M., and Schoar, A. (2003). Managing with style: The effect of managers on firm financial policies. *Quarterly Journal of Economics, 118*, 1169–1208.

Bhagat, S., and Black, B. (2000). Board Independence and Long-Term Firm Performance, *Working Paper.* Boulder: University of Colorado.

Bhattacharya, S., Boot, A. W. A., and Thakor, A. V. (1998). The economics of bank regulation. *Journal of Money, Credit, and Banking, 30*(4), 745–770.

Bhojraj, S., and Sengupta, P. (2003). Effect of Corporate Governance on Bond Ratings and Yields: The Role of Institutional Investors and Outside Directors. *Journal of Business, 76*(3), 455–476.

Blanco, R., Brennan, S., and Marsh, I. W. (2005). An Empirical Analysis of the Dynamic Relation between Investment-Grade Bonds and Credit Default Swaps. *The Journal of Finance, 60*(5), 2255–2281.

Böhm-Dries, A., Eggers, H., and Hortmann, S. (2010). Zukunft der Corporate Governance von Sparkassen. *Betriebswirtschaftliche Blätter, 01/2011*, 27–31.

Böhm, C., Froneberg, D., and Schiereck, D. (2012a). Financial Expertise of Supervisory Board Members, Overconfidence, and Bank Risk Taking, *Working Paper.* Darmstadt: University of Technology Darmstadt.

Böhm, C., Froneberg, D., and Schiereck, D. (2012b). Zum offensichtlich erkennbaren bankwirtschaftlichen Sachverstand in den Kontrollorganen deutscher Genossenschaftsbanken und Sparkassen. *Zeitschrift für öffentliche und gemeinwirtschaftliche Unternehmen, Heft 2.*

Börner, C. J., and Büschgen, H. E. (2003). *Bankbetriebslehre* (Vol. 4). Stuttgart: UTB.

Boubakri, N., and Ghouma, H. (2010). Control/ownership structure, creditor rights protection, and the cost of debt financing: International evidence. *Journal of Banking & Finance, 34*(10), 2481–2499.

Boyd, J. H., and Runkle, D. E. (1993). Size and performance of banking firms: Testing the predictions of theory. *Journal of Monetary Economics, 31*(1), 47–67.

Brämer, P., Gischer, H., Pfingsten, A., and Richter, T. (2010). Der öffentliche Auftrag der deutschen Sparkassen aus der Perspektive des Stakeholder-Managements. *Zeitschrift für öffentliche und gemeinwirtschaftliche Unternehmen, 33*(4), 311–332.

Brandao-Marques, L., Correa, R., and Sapriza, H. (2013). International evidence on government support and risk taking in the banking sector. *International Finance Discussion Papers No. 1086 Board of Governors of the Federal Reserve System (U.S.).*

Breuer, W., and Mark, K. (2005). *Perspektiven der Verbundkooperation am Beispiel der Sparkassen-Finanzgruppe*. Berlin: Duncker & Humblot Verlag.

Brown, C. O., and Dinç, I. S. (2011). Too Many to Fail? Evidence of Regulatory Forbearance When the Banking Sector Is Weak. *Review of Financial Studies, 24*(4), 1378–1405.

Brunnermeier, M. K. (2009). Deciphering the Liquidity and Credit Crunch 2007–2008. *Journal of Economic Perspectives, 23*(1), 77–100.

Büschgen, H. E. (1998). *Bankbetriebslehre* (Vol. 5). Wiesbaden: Gabler.

Carcello, J. V., Hollingsworth, C. W., Klein, A., and Neal, T. L. (2008). *Audit Committee Financial Expertise, Competing Corporate Governance Mechanisms, and Earnings Management in a Post-SOX World*. Paper presented at the University of Illinois 18th Symposium on Audit Research. Retrieved from http://www.business.illinois.edu/accountancy/events/symposium/audit/proceedings/proceedings_2008/Papers/Carcello.pdf

Choundhry, M. (2011). Effective bank corporate governance: observations from the market crash and recommendations for policy. *Journal of Applied Finance & Banking, 1*(1), 179–211.

Chuang, W.-I., and Lee, B.-S. (2006). An empirical evaluation of the overconfidence hypothesis. *Journal of Banking & Finance, 30*(9), 2489–2515.

Cihak, M., Demirguc-Kunt, A., Feyen, E., and Levine, R. (2012). Benchmarking financial systems around the world. *World Bank Policy Research, 6175.*

Cihák, M., and Hesse, H. (2007). Cooperative Banks and Financial Stability, *Working Paper Series, WP/07/2.* Washington D.C.: International Monetary Fund.

Claessens, S., and Laeven, L. (2003). What drives bank competition? some international evidence, *World Bank Policy Research, Working Paper Series, no. 3113.* Washington D.C.: The World Bank.

Claussen, C. P. (2003). *Bank- und Börsenrecht* (Vol. 3). München: C.H. Beck.

Coles, J. L., Daniel, N. D., and Naveen, L. (2008). Boards: Does one size fit all. *Journal of Financial Economics, 87*(2), 329–356.

Cooper, A. C., Woo, C. Y., and Dunkelberg, W. C. (1988). Entrepreneurs' perceived chances for success. *Journal of Business Venturing, 3*(2), 97–108.

Cunningham, L. A. (2007). Rediscovering Board Expertise: Legal Implications of the Empirical Literature. *GWU Law School Public Law Research Paper No. 363.*

Daniel, K. D., Hirshleifer, D., and Subrahmanyam, A. (2001). Overconfidence, Arbitrage and Equilibrium Asset Pricing. *The Journal of Finance, LVI*(3).

Davidson, W. N., Xie, B., and Xu, W. (2004). Market reaction to voluntary announcements of audit committee appointments: The effect of financial expertise. *Journal of Accounting and Public Policy, 23*(4), 279–293.

DeFond, M. L., Hann, R. N., and Hu, X. (2005). Does the Market Value Financial Expertise on Audit Committees of Boards of Directors? *Journal of Accounting Research, 43*(2), 153–193.

Dell'Ariccia, G., Detragiache, E., and Rajan, R. (2008). The real effect of banking crises. *Journal of Financial Intermediation, 17*(1), 89–112.

Demirguc-Kunt, A., and Huizinga, H. (2010). *Are Banks Too Big to Fail or Too Big to Save? International Evidence from Equity Prices and CDS Spreads*: SSRN.

Demirgüç-Kunt, A., and Huizinga, H. (2010). Bank activity and funding strategies: The impact on risk and returns. *Journal of Financial Economics, 98*(3), 626–650.

Demirguc-Kunt, A., and Maksimovic, V. (2000). *Funding growth in bank-based and market-based financial systems: evidence from firm level data*: The World Bank.

Dermine, J. (2003). Banking in Europe: Past, present and future. In V. Gaspar, Hartmann, P., Sleijpen, O. (Ed.), *Proceedings of the 2nd ECB Central Banking Conference on the Transformation of the European Financial System.* Frankfurt am Main: ECB.

Deutsche Bundesbank. (2011). Statistik: Zeitreihen. Retrieved 15.02.2011: http://www.bundesbank.de/statistik/statistik_zeitreihen.php.

DeYoung, R., Hunter, W. C., and Udell, G. F. (2004). The Past, Present, and Probable Future for Community Banks. *Journal of Financial Services Research, 25*(2/3), 85.

Dhaliwal, D. S., Naiker, V., and Navissi, F. (2006). Audit Committee Financial Expertise, Corporate Governance and Accruals Quality: An Empirical Analysis, *Working Paper*. Tucson: University of Arizona.

Diamond, D. W. (1991). Monitoring and Reputation: The Choice between Bank Loans and Directly Placed Debt. *Journal of Political Economy, 99*(4), 689–721.

Diamond, D. W., and Rajan, R. G. (2001). Liquidity Risk, Liquidity Creation, and Financial Fragility: A Theory of Banking. *Journal of Political Economy, 109*(2), 287–327.

Dittrich, D. A. V., Güth, W., and Maciejovsky, B. (2005). Overconfidence in investment decisions: An experimental approach. *The European Journal of Finance, 11*(6), 471–491.

Drees, F., Keisers, M., and Schiereck, D. (2006). Zum Erfolg von Sparkassenfusionen - Aktuelle kasuistische Evidenz. *Zeitschrift für öffentliche und gemeinwirtschaftliche Unternehmen, 29*, 24–49.

Duffie, D. (2008). Innovations in credit risk transfer: implications for financial stability. *Working Papers No 255 Bank for International Settlements.*

Eichengreen, B., Mody, A., Nedeljkovic, M., and Sarno, L. (2009). How the Subprime Crisis Went Global: Evidence from Bank Credit Default Swap Spreads. *NBER Working Paper No. 14904.*

Eisenberg, T., Sundgren, S., and Wells, M. T. (1998). Larger board size and decreasing firm value in small firms. *Journal of Financial Economics, 48*(1), 35–54.

Elyasiani, E., Jia, J., and Mao, C. X. (2010). Institutional ownership stability and the cost of debt. *Journal of Financial Markets, 13*(4), 475–500.

Engerer, H., and Schrooten, M. (2004). *Untersuchung der Grundlagen und Entwicklungsperspektiven des Bankensektors in Deutschland (Dreisäulensystem).* Berlin: DIW.

Erkens, D., Hung, M., and Matos, P. (2009). *Corporate Governance in the 2007-2008 Financial Crisis: Evidence from Financial Institutions Worldwide.* Paper presented at the 9th Bank Research Conference. Retrieved from www.fdic.gov/bank/analytical/CFR/bank_research_conference/annual_9th/Matos_P.pdf

Fama, E. F., and Jensen, M. C. (1983). Separation of Ownership and Control. *Journal of Law and Economics, 26*(2), 301–325.

Farhi, E., and Tirole, J. (2012). Collective Moral Hazard, Maturity Mismatch and Systemic Bailouts. *American Economic Review, 102*, 60–93.

Fellner, G., Güth, W., and Maciejovsky, B. (2004). Illusion of expertise in portfolio decisions: an experimental approach. *Journal of Economic Behavior & Organization, 55*(3), 355–376.

Fernandes, N., and Fich, E. M. (2009). Does Financial Experience Help Banks during Credit Crises?, *Mimeo*. Lausanne: IMD.

Fischer, K.-H., and Pfeil, C. (2004). Regulation and Competition in German Banking: An Assessment. In J. P. Krahnen & R. H. Schmidt (Eds.), *The German Financial System* (pp. 291–350). Oxford: Oxford University Press.

Fischhoff, B., Slovic, P., and Lichtenstein, S. (1977). Knowing with certainty: The appropriateness of extreme confidence. *Journal of Experimental Psychology: Human Perception and Performance, 3*(4), 552–564.

Forte, S., and Peña, J. I. (2009). Credit spreads: An empirical analysis on the informational content of stocks, bonds, and CDS. *Journal of Banking & Finance, 33*(11), 2013–2025.

Gabriel, O. W., and Holtmann, E. (2005). *Handbuch Politisches System der Bundesrepublik Deutschland* (Vol. 3). München: Oldenbourg.

Galai, D., and Masulis, R. W. (1976). The option pricing model and the risk factor of stock. *Journal of Financial Economics, 3*(1–2), 53–81.

Geiger, H. (1992). *Die deutsche Sparkassenorganisation* (Vol. 2). Frankfurt am Main: Fritz Knapp Verlag.

Giammarino, R. M., Lewis, T. R., and Sappington, D. E. M. (1993). An Incentive Approach to Banking Regulation. *The Journal of Finance, 48*(4), 1523–1542.

Goddard, J., Molyneux, P., and Wilson, J. O. S. (2004). The Profitability of European Banks: A cross-sectional and dynamic Panel Analysis. *The Manchester School, 72*(3), 363–381.

Goddard, J., Molyneux, P., Wilson, J. O. S., and Tavakoli, M. (2007). European banking: An overview. *Journal of Banking & Finance, 31*(7), 1911–1935.

Güner, A. B., Malmendier, U., and Tate, G. (2008). Financial expertise of directors. *Journal of Financial Economics, 88*(2), 323–354.

Hackethal, A. (2004). German Banks and Banking Structure. In J. P. Krahnen & R. H. Schmidt (Eds.), *The German Financial System* (pp. 71–105). Oxford: Oxford University Press.

Hackethal, A., and Schmidt, R. H. (2005). Structural Change in the German Banking System?, *Working Paper Series, Finance & Accounting No. 147*. Frankfurt am Main: Johann-Wolfgang Goethe University.

Hakenes, H., Hasan, I., Molyneux, P., and Xie, R. (2014). Small Banks and Local Economic Development. *Review of Finance, Published online: February 24, 2014.*

Hakenes, H., Schmidt, R. H., and Xie, R. (2009). Regional Banks and Economic Development: Evidence from German Savings Banks, *Working Paper*. Frankfurt am Main: Johann-Wolfgang Goethe University.

Harris, M., and Raviv, A. (2008). A Theory of Board Control and Size. *The Review of Financial Studies, 21*(4), 1797–1832.

Hart, O., and Zingales, L. (2011). A New Capital Regulation of Large Financial Institutions. *American Law and Economics Review, 13*(2), 453–490.

Hartmann-Wendels, T., Pfingsten, A., and Weber, M. (2007). *Bankbetriebslehre* (Vol. 4). Berlin, Heidelberg: Springer.

Hasan, I., Schmiedel, H., and Song, L. (2012). Returns to Retail Banking and Payments. *Journal of Financial Services Research, 41*(3), 163–195.

Hau, H., and Thum, M. (2008). Wie (in-)kompetent sind die Aufsichtsräte deutscher Banken? *Ifo Schnelldienst, 61*(19), 27–29.

Hau, H., and Thum, M. (2009a). Subprime crisis and board (in-)competence: private versus public banks in Germany. *Economic Policy, 24*(60), 701–752.

Hau, H., and Thum, M. (2009b). Subprime Crisis and Board (In-)Competence: Private vs. Public Banks in Germany. *SSRN eLibrary*.

Hempell, H. S. (2002). Testing for Competition Among German Banks, *Discussion Paper 04/02 Economic Research Centre of the Deutsche Bundesbank*. Frankfurt am Main: Deutsche Bundesbank.

Hermalin, B. E., and Weisbach, M. S. (1991). The Effects of Board Composition and Direct Incentives on Firm Performance. *Financial Management, 20*(4), 101–112.

Hermalin, B. E., and Weisbach, M. S. (2003). Boards of directors as an endogenously determined institution: a survey of the economic literature. *Economic Policy Review*(Apr), 7–26.

Hoggarth, G., Reidhill, J., and Sinclair, P. (2004). On the resolution of banking crises: theory and evidence, *Working Paper no. 229*. London: Bank of England.

Hopt, K. J., and Leyens, P. C. (2004). Board Models in Europe - Recent Developments of Internal Corporate Governance Structures in Germany, the United Kingdom, France, and Italy, *ECGI Working Paper Series in Law, No. 18/2004*. Brussels: European Corporate Governance Institute.

Houweling, P., and Vorst, T. (2005). Pricing default swaps: Empirical evidence. *Journal of International Money and Finance, 24*(8), 1200–1225.

Huang, X., Zhou, H., and Zhu, H. (2009). A framework for assessing the systemic risk of major financial institutions. *Journal of Banking & Finance, 33*(11), 2036–2049.

Hull, J., Predescu, M., and White, A. (2004). The relationship between credit default swap spreads, bond yields, and credit rating announcements. [doi: DOI: 10.1016/j.jbankfin.2004.06.010]. *Journal of Banking & Finance, 28*(11), 2789–2811.

Iannotta, G., Nocera, G., and Sironi, A. (2007). Ownership structure, risk and performance in the European banking industry. *Journal of Banking & Finance, 31*(7), 2127–2149.

International Monetary Fund. (2010). Global financial stability report, April 2010, *World economic and financial surveys.* Washington: International Monetary Fund.

Jensen, M. C. (1993). The Modern Industrial Revolution, Exit, and the Failure of Internal Control Systems. *The Journal of Finance, 48*(3), 831–880.

Jensen, M. C., and Meckling, W. H. (1976). Theory of the firm: Managerial behavior, agency costs and ownership structure. *Journal of Financial Economics, 3*(4), 305–360.

Jensen, M. C., and Ruback, R. S. (1983). The market for corporate control: The scientific evidence. *Journal of Financial Economics, 11*(1–4), 5–50.

Johansen, K., Laser, S., Neuberger, D., and Andreani, E. (2013). Inside or Outside Control of Banks? Evidence from the Composition of Supervisory Boards. *SSRN eLibrary.*

John, K., and Senbet, L. W. (1998). Corporate governance and board effectiveness. *Journal of Banking & Finance, 22*(4), 371–403.

Jungmann, C. (2006). The Effectiveness of Corporate Governance in One-Tier and Two-Tier Board Systems –Evidence from the UK and Germany–. *European Company and Financial Law Review, 3*(4), 426–474.

Kammlott, C., and Schiereck, D. (2000). Wachstum, Förderungsauftrag und Markterfolg von deutschen Kreditgenossenschaften. *Zeitschrift für das gesamte Genossenschaftswesen, 50*, 265–281.

Kaplan, S. N. (1994). Top Executives, Turnover, and Firm Performance in Germany. *Journal of Law, Economics, & Organization, 10*(1), 142–159.

Kaufman, G. G. (2002). Too big to fail in banking: What remains? *The Quarterly Review of Economics and Finance, 42*(3), 423–436.

Kaufmann, D., Kraay, A., and Mastruzzi, M. (2009). Governance Matters VIII: Governance Indicators for 1996–2008 *World Bank Policy Research, Working Paper Series, no. 4978.* Washington D.C.: The World Bank.

King, M. R. (2009). Time to buy or just buying time? The market reaction to bank rescue packages. *BIS Working Papers, No 288.*

Kirkpatrick, G. (2009). The Corporate Governance Lessons from the Financial Crisis, *Financial Market Trends*. Paris: OECD.

Kleff, V., and Weber, M. (2005). Payout Policy and Owners' Interests – Evidence from German Savings Banks, *ZEW Discussion Paper No. 05–59*. Mannheim: ZEW.

Klein, A. (1998). Firm Performance and Board Committee Structure. *Journal of Law and Economics, 41*(1), 275–304.

Koetter, M., Nestmann, T., Stolz, S., and Wedow, M. (2004). Structures and Trends in German Banking, *Working Paper No. 1225*. Kiel: Kiel Institute for the World Economy.

Köhler, M. (2010). Corporate Governance and Current Regulation in the German Banking Sector: An Overview and Assessment, *ZEW Discussion Paper No. 10–002*. Mannheim: ZEW.

Körner, T., Müller, O., Paul, S., and Schmidt, C. M. (2014). Glas halb voll oder halb leer?

Eine Analyse der Qualifikation von Kontrollorganmitgliedern deutscher Banken. *rwi Materialien, Heft 78*.

Kose, M. A., Prasad, E., Rogoff, K., and Wei, S.-J. (2006). Financial Globalization: A Reappraisal. *National Bureau of Economic Research Working Paper Series, 12484*.

Kroszner, R. S., Laeven, L., and Klingebiel, D. (2007). Banking crises, financial dependence, and growth. *Journal of Financial Economics, 84*(1), 187–228.

Laeven, L., and Levine, R. (2009). Bank governance, regulation and risk taking. *Journal of Financial Economics, 93*(2), 259–275.

Lang, G., and Welzel, P. (1996). Efficiency and technical progress in banking Empirical results for a panel of German cooperative banks. *Journal of Banking & Finance, 20*(6), 1003–1023.

Lee, Y. S., Rosenstein, S., and Wyatt, J. G. (1999). The value of financial outside directors on corporate boards. *International Review of Economics & Finance, 8*(4), 421–431.

Levine, R. (1997). Financial Development and Economic Growth: Views and Agenda. *Journal of Economic Literature, 35*(2), 688–726.

Levine, R. (2006). *Finance and Growth: Theory and Evidence*. Amsterdam: Elsevier.

Levine, R., and Zervos, S. (1998). Stock Markets, Banks, and Economic Growth. *The American Economic Review, 88*(3), 537–558.

Lipton, M., and Lorsch, J. W. (1992). Modest Proposal for Improved Corporate Governance. *Business Lawyer, 48*(1), 59–77.

Longstaff, F. A., Pan, J., Pedersen, L. H., and Singleton, K. J. (2007). *How Sovereign is Sovereign Credit Risk?* : National Bureau of Economic Research, Inc.

Luttmer, N. (2010). Bank-Aufsichtsräte müssen nachsitzen. Retrieved from http://www.ftd.de/unternehmen/finanzdienstleister/:machtdemonstration-ba-fin-sortiert-aufsichtsraete-von-banken-aus/50163321.html

Magalhaes, R., Gutiérrez, M., and Tribó, J. A. (2008). *Banks' ownership structure, risk and performance.* Paper presented at the The European Financial Management Association 2008 Meeting. Retrieved from http://www.efmaefm.org/0EFMAMEETINGS/EFMA%20ANNUAL%20MEETINGS/2008-athens/2008.shtml#m

Malmendier, U., and Tate, G. (2005). CEO overconfidence and corporate investment. *Journal of Finance, 60*, 2661–2700.

Manne, H. G. (1965). Mergers and the Market for Corporate Control. *Journal of Political Economy, 73*(2), 110–120.

Manove, M., and Padilla, A. J. (1999). Banking (Conservatively) with Optimists. *RAND Journal of Economics, 30*(2), 324–350.

Mehran, H. (1995). Executive compensation structure, ownership, and firm performance. *Journal of Financial Economics, 38*(2), 163–184.

Mehran, H., Morrison, A., and Shapiro, J. (2011a). Corporate Governance and Banks: What Have We Learned from the Financial Crisis?, *Staff Reports, no. 502.* New York: Federal Reserve Bank of New York.

Mehran, H., Morrison, A., and Shapiro, J. (2011b). Corporate Governance and Banks: What Have We Learned from the Financial Crisis? *Federal Reserve Bank of New York Staff Reports, 502.*

Mercieca, S., Schaeck, K., and Wolfe, S. (2007). Small European banks: Benefits from diversification? *Journal of Banking & Finance, 31*(7), 1975–1998.

Minton, B. A., Taillard, J. P. A., and Williamson, R. (2010). Do Independence and Financial Expertise of the Board Matter for Risk Taking and Performance?, *Fisher College of Business Working Paper Series, 2010-03-014.* Columbus: Ohio State University.

Mishkin, F. S., Stern, G., and Ron, F. (2006). How Big a Problem Is Too Big to Fail? A Review of Gary Stern and Ron Feldman's "Too Big to Fail: The Hazards of Bank Bailouts". *Journal of Economic Literature, 44*(4), 988–1004.

Moore, D. A., and Healy, P. J. (2007). The Trouble with Overconfidence, *Working paper, Carnegie Mellon University, David A. Tepper School of Business and Ohio State University, Department of Economics.* Pittsburgh: Carnegie Mellon University.

Moshirian, F. (2011). The global financial crisis and the evolution of markets, institutions and regulation. *Journal of Banking & Finance, 35*(3), 502–511.

Mullineux, A. (2006). The corporate governance of banks. *Journal of Financial Regulation and Compliance 14*(4), 375–382.

Mullineux, A. (2013). Banking for the public good. *International Review of Financial Analysis, Available online 15 November 2013.*

Myers, S. C., and Majluf, N. S. (1984). Corporate Financing and Investment Decisions.

When Firms have Information that Investors do not have. *Journal of Financial Economics, 13*, 187–211.

Naßmacher, H., and Naßmacher, K.-H. (2007). *Kommunalpolitik in Deutschland* (Vol. 2). Wiesbaden: Verlag für Sozialwissenschaften.

Norden, L., and Wagner, W. (2008). Credit derivatives and loan pricing. *Journal of Banking & Finance, 32*(12), 2560–2569.

Norden, L., and Weber, M. (2004). Informational efficiency of credit default swap and stock markets: The impact of credit rating announcements. *Journal of Banking & Finance, 28*(11), 2813–2843.

Norden, L., and Weber, M. (2010). When Senior meets Junior: Information in Credit Default Swap Spreads of Large Banks. *CEPR Working Paper.*

Odean, T. (1998). Volume, Volatility, Price, and Profit When All Traders Are Above Average. *The Journal of Finance, 53*(6), 1887–1934.

Pang, J., and Wu, H. (2009). Financial markets, financial dependence, and the allocation of capital. *Journal of Banking & Finance, 33*(5), 810–818.

Pathan, S. (2009). Strong Boards, CEO Power and Bank Risk-Taking. *Journal of Banking and Finance, Vol. 33, No. 7, pp. 1340–1350.*

Peni, E., and Vähämaa, S. (2012). Did Good Corporate Governance Improve Bank Performance during the Financial Crisis? . *Journal of Financial Services Research, 41*(1–2), 19–35.

Pfingsten, A. (2010). Stakeholdermanagement bei Sparkassen. In Wissenschaftsförderung der Sparkassen-Finanzgruppe e.V. (Ed.), *Geschäftspolitische Steuerung, Die Sparkassen zwischen Renditeorientierung und Gemeinwohl* (Vol. 1). Bonn: Deutscher Sparkassenverlag.

Rajan, R. (2006). Has Finance Made the World Riskier? *European Financial Management, 12*(4), 499–533.

Rajan, R. G. (1992). Insiders and Outsiders: The Choice between Informed and Arm's-Length Debt. *The Journal of Finance, 47*(4), 1367–1400.

Rajan, R. G., and Zingales, L. (1998). Financial Dependence and Growth. *The American Economic Review, 88*(3), 559–586.

Rosenstein, S., and Wyatt, J. G. (1990). Outside directors, board independence, and shareholder wealth. *Journal of Financial Economics, 26*(2), 175–191.

Roy, A. D. (1952). Safety First and the Holding of Assets. *Econometrica, 20*(3), 431–449.

Santos, J. A. C. (2001). Bank Capital Regulation in Contemporary Banking Theory: A Review of the Literature. *Financial Markets, Institutions & Instruments, 10*(2), 41–84.

Saunders, A., Strock, E., and Travlos, N. G. (1990). Ownership Structure, Deregulation, and Bank Risk Taking. *Journal of Finance, 45*(2), 643–654.

Schiereck, D., and Timmreck, C. (2001). Unternehmenszusammenschlüsse von Kreditgenossenschaften. In Ernst & Young (Ed.), *Mergers & Acquisitions in der Praxis* (pp. 167–188). Frankfurt am Main: FAZ-Institut.

Schiereck, D., and Trutwein, P. (2011). The fast and the furious--Stock returns and CDS of financial institutions under stress. *Journal of International Financial Markets, Institutions and Money, 21*(2), 157–175.

Schmidt, R. H. (2009). The Political Debate about Savings Banks. *Schmalenbach Business Review (sbr), 61*(4), 366–392.

Shehzad, C. T., de Haan, J., and Scholtens, B. (2010). The impact of bank ownership concentration on impaired loans and capital adequacy. *Journal of Banking & Finance, 34*(2), 399–408.

Shleifer, A., and Vishny, R. W. (1986). Large Shareholders and Corporate Control. *Journal of Political Economy, 94*(3), 461–488.

Spong, K. R., and Sullivan, R. J. (2010). Bank Ownership and Risk Taking: Improving Corporate Governance in Banking after the Crisis. *Federal Reserve Bank of Kansas City.*

Stein, J. C. (2002). Information Production and Capital Allocation: Decentralized versus Hierarchical Firms. *The Journal of Finance, 57*(5), 1891–1921.

Stern, G., and Feldman, R. (2004). *Too Big to Fail: The Hazards of Bank Bailouts.* Washington DC: Brookings Institution Press.

Stulz, R. M. (2009). Credit Default Swaps and the Credit Crisis. *NBER and ECGI Finance Working Paper N°. 264/2009.*

Theurl, T. (2002). Shareholder Value und genossenschaftlicher Förderauftrag - Zwei unvereinbare strategische Ausrichtungen? In T. Theurl & R. Greve (Eds.), *Vom Modell zur Umsetzung - Strategische Herausforderungen für Genossenschaften, Münstersche Schriften zur Kooperation* (Vol. 54). Aachen: Shaker.

Vins, O. (2008). How Politics Influence State-owned Banks - the Case of German Savings Banks, *Working Paper Series, Finance & Accounting no. 191.* Frankfurt am Main: Johann-Wofgang Goethe University.

Völz, M., and Wedow, M. (2011). Market discipline and too-big-to-fail in the CDS market: Does banks' size reduce market discipline? *Journal of Empirical Finance, 18*(2), 195–210.

Walker, D. (2009). *A Review of Corporate Governance in UK banks and other Financial Industry Entities: Final Recommendations.* London: The Walker Review Secretariat.

Wallison, P. J. (2008). Cause and Effect: Government Policies and the Financial Crisis. *American Enterprise Institute for Public Policy Research.*

Wang, A. W., and Zhang, G. (2009). Institutional ownership and credit spreads: An information asymmetry perspective. *Journal of Empirical Finance, 16*(4), 597–612.

Westman, H. (2010). Comparison of profitability and risk in commercial, savings and cooperative banks, *Working Paper.* Helsinki: HANKEN School of Economics.

Williamson, O. E. (1988). Corporate Finance and Corporate Governance. *The Journal of Finance, 43*(3), 567–591.

Wintoki, M. B., Linck, J. S., and Netter, J. M. (2012). Endogeneity and the dynamics of internal corporate governance. *Journal of Financial Economics, 105*(3), 581–606.

World Bank. (2010). World Development Indicators (WDI). Retrieved 01.02.2011, from The World Bank: http://data.worldbank.org/indicator

Yermack, D. (1996). Higher market valuation of companies with a small board of directors. *Journal of Financial Economics, 40*(2), 185–211.

Zhou, C. (2010a). Are Banks Too Big to Fail? Measuring Systemic Importance of Financial Institutions. *International Journal of Central Banking, 6*(34), 205–250.

Zhou, C. (2010b). Are Banks Too Big to Fail? Measuring Systemic Importance of Financial Institutions. *International Journal of Central Banking, 34*(6), 205–250.

Zhu, H. (2006). An empirical comparison of credit spreads between the Bond Market and the Credit Default Swap Market *Journal of Financial Services Research, 29*, 211–235.

Corporate Finance and Governance

Herausgegeben von Dirk Schiereck

Band 1 Sebastian Michael Gläsner: Return Patterns of German Open-End Real Estate Funds. An Empirical Explanation of Smooth Fund Returns. 2010.

Band 2 Patrick Ams: Directors' Dealings and Insider Trading in Germany. An Empirical Analysis. 2010.

Band 3 Joachim Vogt: Value Creation within the Construction Industry. A Study of Strategic Takeovers. 2011.

Band 4 Fabian Braemisch: Underpricing, Long-Run Performance, and Valuation of Initial Public Offerings. 2011.

Band 5 Matthäus Markus Sielecki: Creating and Governing an Integrated Market for Retail Banking Services in Europe. A Conceptual-Empirical Study of the Role of Regulation in Promoting a Single Euro Payments Area. 2011.

Band 6 Arne Wilkes: Determinants of Credit Spreads. An Empirical Analysis for the European Corporate Bond Market. 2011.

Band 7 Dirk Schiereck / Martin Setzer (Hrsg.): Bankerfolg und Akquisitionen. Aktuelle Erkenntnisse zur Konsolidierung und Restrukturierung der Finanzindustrie. 2011.

Band 8 Steffen Meinshausen: M&A Activity, Divestitures and Initial Public Offerings in the Fashion Industry. 2012.

Band 9 Malte Helmut Raudszus: Financial Return Risk and the Effect on Shareholder Wealth. 2012.

Band 10 Ramit Mehta: Mergers and Acquisitions in the Global Brewing Industry. A Capital Market Perspective. 2012.

Band 11 Marcel Normann: The Influence of German Top Executives on Corporate Policy and Firm Performance. 2012.

Band 12 Christoph Böhm: Risk-Adjusted Performance and Bank Governance Structures. 2013.

Band 13 Christian Thamm: Minority Shareholder Monitoring and German Corporate Governance. Empirical Evidence and Value Effects. 2013.

Band 14 Robert M. Fraunhoffer: Mergers and Acquisitions in the Energy Sector. The Impact of Synergy Disclosures on Shareholder Wealth and Operating Performance. 2013.

Band 15 Heiko Schön: Pharma M&A versus alliances and its underlying value drivers. Are M&A or alliances the right therapy for an ailing pharmaceutical industry? A capital market perspective. 2015.

Band 16 Sascha Kolaric: Bank mergers and acquisitions in the Asia-Pacific region. An investigation of the shareholder wealth effects of the financial sector consolidation and its impact on the acquirer's cost of debt. 2015.

Band 17 Ulrich Erxleben: Value Creation of Corporate Restructuring. A Market Cycle and Industry View. 2015.

Band 18 Dennis Froneberg: Bank Governance Structures and Risk Taking. 2015.

www.peterlang.de

www.ingramcontent.com/pod-product-compliance
Ingram Content Group UK Ltd.
Pitfield, Milton Keynes, MK11 3LW, UK
UKHW020152290926
15471UKWH00005B/839